HERMENEUTICAL ESSAYS
ON VEDĀNTIC TOPICS

HERMENEUTICAL ESSAYS ON VEDĀNTIC TOPICS

J. G. ARAPURA

MOTILAL BANARSIDASS
Delhi Varanasi Patna Madras

First Edition: Delhi, 1986

MOTILAL BANARSIDASS
Bungalow Road, Jawahar Nagar, Delhi 110 007
Branches
Chowk, Varanasi 221 001
Ashok Rajpath, Patna 800 004
120 Royapettah High Road, Mylapore, Madras 600 004

ISBN: 81–208–0183–0

PRINTED IN INDIA
BY JAINENDRA PRAKASH JAIN AT SHRI JAINENDRA PRESS, A-45 NARAINA INDUSTRIAL AREA, PHASE I, NEW DELHI 110 028 AND PUBLISHED BY NARENDRA PRAKASH JAIN FOR MOTILAL BANARSIDASS, DELHI 110 007

To a Friend and Colleague

PAUL YOUNGER

In Appreciation of My Association
With McMaster University

ACKNOWLEDGEMENTS

I record with appreciation the award of a grant made by McMaster University for the preparation of the manuscript of this book. And I express my deep appreciation of Mrs. Ross (Grace) Gordon for the care she took in typing the manuscript, often transcribing from my long-hand, insertions and corrections and all.

As for permission to reproduce the following published essays/articles of mine, I express thanks to the parties named below:

(1) "*Sat* (Being) in Vedānta", originally entitled, "Some Special Characteristics of *S*at (Being) in Advaita Vedānta", in *The Question of Being*, edited by M. Sprung, 1978, College Park, PA, state University of Pennsylvania Press; to the publisher.

(2) "*Māyā* and the Discourse About *Brahman*". in *The Problem of Two Truths in Buddhism and Vedānta*, edited by M. Sprung, 1973, pp. 109-21, Copyright c 1973 by D. Reidel Publishing Company, Dordrecht, Holland; to the publisher.

(3) "Transcendence and the Transcendent; via the Doctrines of *Brahman* and *Śūnyatā*", originally entitled, "Transcendent *Brahman* or Transcendent Void: Which is Ultimately Real?", in *Transcendence and the Sacred*, edited by A. M. Olson and L. S. Rouner, University of Notre Dame Press, 1981; to the publisher.

(4) "Macro-Micro-Cosmology Approached Through a *Gītā* Text", originally entitled, "The Upside Down Tree of the *Bhagavadgītā*, Ch. XV", in *Numen*, vol. xxii, fasc. 2, pp. 132-44; to E. J. Brill, Leiden, Publisher.

(5) "Time Within Logos and Without: As in Grammar Vedānta and Mādhyamika", originally entitled, "Nāgārjuna and Bhartṛhari on Time", in *The Scottish Journal of Religion*, March 1981 (University of Stirling, Stirling, Scotland); to the Editor, Prof. G. Richards.

(6) "The Question As to the *Jīvan-mukti* Ideal", originally entitled. "The Problem of *Jīva-mukti*", in the Journal, *Studies*

in Religion/Sciences Religieuses, vol. xii, no. 4; to the Editor, Department of Religion, Dalhousie University, Halifax, Nova Scotia, Canada.

In addition, I would like to mention *The Union Seminary Quarterly Review*, New York, vol. xxv, no. 2, (1970), and *The Rajasthan University Studies in Sanskrit and Hindi*, no. 6 (1973-74), inasmuch as from two respective articles in them, i.e. "Language and knowledge" and "Perspectives on Indian Philosophy of Language" (parts i and ii), I have taken substantial parts into my *Appendix: On Language.*

Finally, I extend my thanks to my good friends, the couple, Drs. Jay and Luitgard Soni, of my Department, for their kindness in giving a last, careful going through to the manuscript, in order to ready it for type setting.

And, of course, for any mistakes there still may be lurking I alone am responsible.

CONTENTS

INTRODUCTION

The project that has resulted in this volume began with the selection from my past essays on Vedānta, published and unpublished. The thought to do that came largely at the urging of friends, who persuaded me about its usefulness. However, as I proceeded, I began to completely rewrite several of the essays in ways that reflect my recent, deeper involvement in the topics in question as well as in hermeneutics, with the result that the present volume has turned out to be much like a new work. Besides, in this way I was able to integrate the various pieces into a unified whole in such a way that it might serve as a companion volume to my recent, major work, *GNOSIS AND THE QUESTION OF THOUGHT IN VEDĀNTA,* or at least as an auxiliary.

In these days of increasing enchantment in much of the world with Eastern religions and philosophies, real academic interest in Vedānta has, paradoxically enough, waned. This shift away from the very heart of Indian tradition, visible even among the Indians, may be partly the signs of the times, but is at least partly due to misunderstanding of the nature of the system. That Vedānta is the supreme tradition of India may still be conceded by most scholars, even if they tend not to act upon it. It may be said that of all the Eastern systems it has unequalled philosophical possibilities. These essays here collected have been produced with that awareness. While no great merit can be claimed, or is claimed, for these pieces themselves, it can be affirmed truthfully that they embody an honest effort to take a look inside a tremendously rich realm of the spirit from certain points in its enclosing ramparts. These 'points' give the topics dealt with, and in that sense, it is hoped that they do afford us a view of the inside of the system as a whole.

These essays are mostly written from a comparative perspective, that is, in the currently prevalent sense of the word 'comparative', and that would be considered natural in our present day situation, decisively formed as it is not only by the respective traditions of the East but also by the pervasive influences of Western thought. While the perspective is comparative throughout, either explicitly, or implicitly in a few pieces, there are some specific acts of comparing as well.

It will be noticed that the essays have been described in the title of the volume as hermeneutical rather than comparative. Why this is so is a question that will involve us in the as yet unthought problem of interpenetration of hermeneutics and comparison, or rather the place of the latter in the former. But without going into it deeply, suffice it to say that hermeneutics is to be perceived as that to which comparison itself leads and is its ultimate justification for being undertaken. But it may also be added, reversely, that comparison is an essential dimension of hermeneutics, though that fact has not yet been brought up to conscious recognition either by comparativists or by hermeneutists.

Now, as for hermeneutics, despite its various developments and expressions, it is basically, to borrow a definition from Hans-Georg Gadamer, one of its most eminent exponents, "the theory and practice of understanding and bringing to language, the alien, the strange, and whatever has become alien" ("On the Natural Inclination Toward Philosophy", *Reason in the Age of Science,* trans. F.G. Lawrence, Cambridge, MS, & London, The M.I.T. Press, 1982, p. 149). We might add that "the alien, the strange, and whatever has become alien", is in the hermeneutical situation, a description of something that confronts us —and concerns us—and to some degree claims our attention and wants to be brought to understanding. In this situation comparison initiates itself as a perspective and is perfected, sometimes through specific acts of comparing, as understanding itself is perfected. But reversely, understanding is thwarted by the vicissitudes of comparison—undoubtedly, we have here a two-way street. And then misunderstanding comes in, against which, however, there is no insurance. How do these vicissitudes of comparison come about ? They come about through our imagining that the goal is discovery of similarities, no matter whether correct or incorrect. But hermeneutics as a true intellectual discipline will assist us to guard against it, though not insure against it, and to press on towards understanding, which lies beyond the apprehension of similarities and dissimilarities.

The aim of these hermeneutical essays on various and sundry topics is the understanding of Vedānta, at least as much as in them lies to put it on its way. The topics themselves are nothing out of the way inasmuch as they are but normal foci of customary metaphysical discussions of this kind, i.e., Being, the self, truth, ultimate reality, language, phenomena, knowledge, etc. But they are approached in a rather different way from usual, that is in a manner which shows a leaning towards what the Greeks called *logos*, thus emphasizing an essential character of Vedānta constantly missed both in the mystical and rationalistic interpretations of that system. The position taken in the essays, often explicitly expressed but sometimes remaining only implicit, is that the uniqueness of Vedānta consists in the Indian variant of the logos (*vāk* or *śabda*), upon which it is squarely grounded. But in coming by this position much inspiration had been received from certain crucial ideas of modern European ontology of the phenomenological-existential kind, which take up, no doubt, with a very modern thrust, from where Greek antiquity and, in some cases the philosophical dimensions of the original Christian phenomenon as well, left off. The interest in the parallel, and at the same time very different, development of the Indian logos fully preserved in Vedānta and in its own modern possibilities and also the conviction about Vedānta's phenomenological and existential uses are the motivations behind much of my work in this field, and they will be visible in these essays too.

A word may be said in elucidation of the explicit religious character of all the essays, evident in the prominence given to matters of comparative religion and theology. The Vedāntic logos, that is to say *vāk* or *śabda,* warrants, and is inseparable from, the notion of revealed texts (*śruti*). Accordingly, philosophy in Vedānta is always at the base theology inasmuch as it is the re-expression and development in human terms of an *a priori* seif-disclosure of Ultimate Reality itself. This self-disclosure is not primarily in man's soul, as the mystics would have it, but in pronounceable, ordered, objective texts (Vedas), which have even suggested their own interpretation and also given rise to certain precise disciplines for their grasp and their use. In this manner Vedānta does belong to the family of revealed religions. But on the contrary, it retains a bias towards knowledge of the ground of revelation, of the logos itself, without insistence on faith in the particularity of a particular revelation, and in this it is still equally akin to the Greek tradition. Vedānta in its theology seems to embody a type that stands midway between the highly particularized logos of a religion like Christianity and the unparticularized logos of the Greeks, and yet sharing traits of both. However, none of the essays emphasizes the formal aspects of theology, as such was not the intent. What is really aimed at is the modern phenomenological and existential uses to which the theology or ontology of Vedānta can be put.

In the fourth paragraph of this *Introduction* I referred to the interpenetration between comparison and hermeneutics. The awareness of that has been a dominant background of this work, although written in the manner not so much of a theoretical expression as of concrete exemplification of it. Thus it can be seen that the comparativist-hermeneutical activity sometimes takes place in a framework of contrast within kinship (Vedānta and Buddhism), sometimes showing kinship (or unexpected closeness) within difference (as made possible by the ways of the logos/language), though generally as alternatives between a still lively, unique antiquity (Vedānta) and the dominant world of modern thought grounded in the dialectical coincidence of Greek philosophy and Christianity. These foci are more sharply presented in the *Appendix: On Language,* as ultimately language itself is the bearer of all these issues.

ONE

SAT (BEING) IN VEDĀNTA

The word commonly used in Indian philosophy for 'being' is *sat*. The word itself is the present participle of the root *as*, to be. There is another root, *bhū*, with the same meaning, which also yields a variety of nouns and participles, none of which, however, can be translated "Being" with a capital B, as befits the need of ontology.[1] *Bhūta* at most means *a* being; and *bhāva* means becoming or coming to be, or, even, the way something is.

Let us begin with a look at *sat*, or being, restricted to the ontological realm, and we must take note of the manifold meanings of the word *sat* itself. No doubt, the varieties of meaning the word carries in the religious, ethical, and psycho-metaphysical literature of India must in the last analysis only contribute to a fuller comprehension of ontology itself. The *Bhagavadgītā* tersely condenses this manifoldness stating "Aum, That, Being — this [symbol] is considered to be the threefold recollection device of [i.e., pertaining to] *Brahman*" (17. 23ab). Afterward, it defines *sat* thus : "The word *sat* is employed in the sense of Reality as well as goodness ; [likewise] the word *sat* is used in the sense of praiseworthy action. Steadfastness in sacrifice, austerity, and

1. Caroline Rhys Davids in a treatise, *To Become or Not to Become* (London : Luzac, 1937) examines the problem posed by the two roots *as* and *bhū*. Much of her discussion is very useful, although her main argument seems to be erroneous. In reference to the famous statement of the *Chāndogya Upaniṣad*, *tat tvam asi* (that thou art), she argues that the original verb must have been the dynamic *bhavasi* (from *bhū*), meaning "becomes," and some later editor changed it into *asi*. From there she draws the implausible conclusion that the statement as it originally was in form, in part, or both, "fails to give any support to that sanctity of Being (*Sat*) on which Vedāntist teaching has leaned so heavily" (p. 43).

giving are said to be *sat*, and action aimed at that goal is also called *sat*" (17.26-27).[2]

We may briefly trace the history of the word from its beginnings through the later, sustained, ontological use of it in the sense of being. A movement in the direction of ontology is noticeable within the uses of the word as early as the *Ṛgveda*. The celebrated *Nāsadīya Sūkta* (*Ṛgveda* 10.129) in its opening refers to a 'then' before all time, when neither *sat* (being) nor *asat* (non-being) existed. However, the hymn is too early for the concept of being in its full-fledged, ontological sense. So it is highly likely that *sat* here stood for something midway between the world and pure being, and *asat*, obviously, for the opposite of it.

Both *sat* and *asat* by themselves, as well as in compound formations, appear many times in the major and minor Upaniṣads. However, following the clue of the *Nāsadīya Sūkta*, perhaps the concept of *asat* is mentioned by the Upaniṣads even prior to that of *sat*. The *Taittirīya Upaniṣad* (2.7.1) declares, "In the beginning this was just non-being ; from it being was born. It made itself *ātman*, wherefore it is called well-made."[3] The idea of the priority of being to non-being occurs clearly for the first time in the *Chāndogya Upaniṣad:*

> In the beginning, my dear, this was being itself, one only without a second. Some say that in the beginning this was just non-being, one only without a second; from that non-being being was born. [But] how, indeed, could it be so ? said he, how could being arise from non-being ? [On the contrary], my dear, this was in the beginning being itself, one only without a second (6.2.1-2).

2. Sources of quotations are given in the text. Translations are my own unless otherwise indicated.

3. R.D. Ranade observes : "Commentators on this passage who do not want a privative conception like not-Being to be the 'arche' of all things, rightly understand this passage to signify that at the very beginning of things it was 'as if' nothing existed and not that not-Being was verily the first concrete existent, and that it was from such a semblance of non-existence that Being was created. We could very well conceive how philosophers like Śaṅkarāchārya who believe in an ultimate Being would explain such a passage....." (*A Constructive Survey of Upanishadic Philosophy*, Poona : Oriental Book Agency, 1926, p. 81).

From this we also come to know that the opposite view had already been prevalent in that it is specifically mentioned and refuted.

The Boundaries of the Concept of Sat in the Source Books of Vedānta

What would appear to an unassisted reader as an equivocation between *sat* and *asat* in the Upaniṣads clearly does not remain so in the interpretations given by the systematic originators of Vedānta. They entirely subordinate *asat* to *sat*, and the retionale of their whole approach to the problem will become clear to us only if we perceive that the concept of being is set forth in the Upaniṣads in a manner totally unfamiliar to other philosophies and in a manner that would appear, if approached from another philosophical tradition, to be altogether unexpected. Thus, following the lead of the founding philosophers of Vedānta as a *darśana*, some distinguishing characteristics of the Upaniṣads' presentation of *sat*, may be outlined.

1. The concept of *sat* comes comprehended in *Brahman*, although, no doubt, *sat* is *Brahman* and *Brahman* is *sat*. Accordingly, when we read about *sat*, we are inevitably reading about *Brahman*, but, conversely, when we are reading about *Brahman* we are not always reading about *sat*. This is not to say that the remotest possibility of disequating the two concepts exists and that *sat* is only partially identical with *Brahman*. Nothing of the kind. Such conjectures must be completely avoided.

It is also true that every important concept in the Upaniṣads likewise appears not only in conjunction with but as inseparably identical with *Brahman*, whether language (*vāk*), mind (*manas*), or whatever. But the concept *sat* has a certain priority and uniqueness as the groundwork for all else, as it shares from the start the preeminence of *Brahman*, or *Ātman*, in most places its equivalent, unlike the other concepts which may start from some other phenomenal ground although reaching their ultimate *telos* of identity with *Brahman*.

2. If *sat* came in most places as the conceptual equivalent of *Brahman*, connoting *Brahman*, the case was not one of simple or exceptionless identity. As a wide-ranging concept there re-

mained cases—at least apparently—where *sat* stood for phenomenal reality not covered by the concept *Brahman*, a possibility eventually resisted and overcome not by reason of the connotation of *sat* but by reason of the denotation of *Brahman*. In other words, the concept *sat* was ultimately transvalued and completely comprehended by the implications of Being, universal and exceptionless Being, which *Brahman* was understood to carry. Thus it is *Brahman* which puts its stamp of character upon *sat*, rather than the other way around.

It will help to remember that the word *Brahman* originally indicated a unique power of being, known in the phenomenon of growth, expansion. Śaṅkara defines it thus : "[It is called] *Brahman* because of the property of growing."[4] It is the power whereby things, the world, and the gods themselves are and also are not. The *Kena Upaniṣad* depicts it effectively as the hidden power of Being behind all beings, behind Being itself. The allegory in the *Kena Upaniṣad*, 3, dramatizes it well. It is introduced by the statement that *Brahman* achieved a conquest for the gods and they gloried in it, thinking that the conquest was due to their own power; but when the vainglorious gods *Agni* and *Vāyu* were challenged to perform their accustomed function, like burning and blowing, they found that they could not, as the power behind their deed was an unknown spirit (*yakṣa*), later to be revealed as *Brahman*. Finally, when Indra was asked to find out who this spirit was he hastened toward it, but it vanished. This theme, that *Brahman* is the deity behind all deities is well-established also in all Uttara-mīmāṁsā (Vedānta) interpretations of ritualistic texts of the Veda. But strangely enough, as the boundary of language had been reached, the only means by which to further investigate *Brahman*, the utterly universal Being, was to treat it as if it were a spirit, a god. The *Kena Upaniṣad* had said in a previous passage, "Thither the eye goes not, nor speech, nor mind; we know not, we understand not how we can teach it."[5] Commenting on this, Śaṅkara observes,

4. *bṛhattamatvāt brahma*, Śaṅkara's *Commentary on the Taittirīya Upaniṣad* (2.1), Sanskrit text, ed. V. G. Apte (Poona : Anandasrama, 1929), p. 45.

5. *Kena Upaniṣad* I.3. trans. S. Radhakrishnan, *The Principal Upaniṣads* (London : Allen & Unwin, 1953), p. 582.

"Whatever is perceptible to the senses can be taught to others by the particularities of genus, quality and function. But *Brahman* has none of these."[6]

In the Upaniṣads we notice further a movement, however implicit, from the unquestioned acceptance—for reasons other than conceptual—of *Brahman*'s own Being as the primeval ground of all grounds (*satyasya satyam*) to the idea of *Brahman* as being (*sat*) in the universal and critical sense of the word. This naturally necessitated the rise of the idea of being qua being by reason, essentially, of the juxtaposition and comparison of *Brahman*'s being with the problematic existence of the phenomenal world. In this context the word *sat* is used ambiguously, that is to say, sometimes in the sense of *Brahman*, with or without the totality of phenomenal things, and sometimes in the sense of the world with or without *Brahman*, as its tacit source and center. It is the contention of Vedānta, particularly Advaita, that rigorous rules of exegesis required that *sat* be interpreted under the criteriology of *Brahman* and not at all independently, as the latter would lend itself to dualism. This is the reason for Śaṅkara's vigorous refutation of the Sāṁkhya doctrine of *pradhāna* (original, independent Matter) accounting for the phenomenal world, more especially as carried out in his comments on *Brahma Sūtra*, 1.4.1-14.

The incontestable preeminence of *Brahman*'s own Being compared with the infinitely lower grade—and problematic character—of the being that the world possessed, or seemed to possess, must have contributed to the radical idea that *Brahman* is alone Being, and that in an absolute sense. In other words the deepening and increasing radicalism of the idea of being came about by way of reflection upon the radical, but conceptually elusive, character of *Brahman* (known through scripture), and not the other way around.

3. *Brahman* knowledge is knowledge objectively given, not perfected from an idea originated in the mind by reflection upon the world or human existence. In other words, the Vedānta

6. *yad dhi karaṇagocaraṁ tad anyasmā upadeṣṭuṁ śakyaṁ jātiguṇakriyāviśeṣaṇaiḥ, na tajjātyādiviśeṣaṇavad brahma*, Śaṅkara's *Commentary on the Kena Upaniṣad*, Sanskrit text, ed., V. G. Apte (Poona : Anandasrama, 1934), p. 9.

philosophy of being is the result of drawing the logical conclusions from both the knowledge and the nature of its advent. The idea of being came fundamentally from the objectively given knowledge of *Brahman* which came via the word. (Reflection upon the nature of language is a corollary to this.) In countless places in the source literature this is stated in no uncertain terms. Notable among these is *Brahma Sūtra* 1.1.3, *śāstrayonitvāt*. Śaṅkara, in his comment on it, points out two complementary meanings of the text : *Brahman* is the source of the scripture; and scripture is the source of the knowledge of *Brahman*. In another instance, commenting on the *Kena* passage (I.3) quoted above, which states the total unknowability of *Brahman*, he observes, "*āgamena tu śakyata eva pratyāyayitum* [Only by scripture is it possible to be known]."[7]

This is a central principle not only of Śaṅkara but also of Maṇḍana Miśra, and of all Vedānta writers since their time. Maṇḍana wrote his *Brahmasiddhi* with a view to establishing the authority of the Upaniṣads as the only source of the knowledge of *Brahma*. In the second of the two chapters of this work, entitled *Tarkakāṇḍa*, the point is especially subjected to critical analysis in the light of the different means of knowledge, and it is pointed out that the knowledge of *Brahman* is not something arrived at perceptually or inferentially but by way of direct revelation. This sets an inflexible context for the understanding of the concept of being.

The Problem of Being as It Arose from the Need to Define Brahman

The Upaniṣads present *Brahman* : hence, in the last analysis, *Brahman* is a presentation by the revealing word. The fact that *Brahman* is being (rather than its opposite) and is alone Being (rather than having any other entity with the ability to share such Being) is implicit in that presentation because *Brahman* is indicated to be not only a that (*tat*) but a what (*kim*), implied in the question "what is this spirit ? [*kim idam yakṣam* ?]." The need to interpret *Brahman* comes bound up with the presentation itself; in fact, that it does not come totally

7. Śaṅkara's *Commentary on the Kena Upaniṣad*, p. 9.

uninterpreted is obvious from the body of the Upaniṣads. Concrete examples of correlation, for the purpose of interpretation and communication of *Brahman*, with even the phenomenal (*vyākṛta*) structures of reality, are abundant in these texts. The most obvious paradigmatic instance is the *Māṇḍūkya Upaniṣad* itself, where we find a complex correlation of *Brahman* with levels of language, with the psychic structure of man, and with the structure of the cosmos. *Brahman* is *that*; we can even call it "pure" being only by explicitly correlating it with notional being elicited from the being of the world and beings in the world and by way of a negative conceptual act canceling the latter for methodological purposes. Hence it would seem that denial of being to the world and affirmation of being for *Brahman* go hand in hand, and both are methodological only, occurring in the context where the question as to being is asked. It would even appear that whenever the question is not asked the world is not without being—nor does it possess it except in the most uncritical and conventional way.

The concrete concept of Being is an integrative device of the above-depicted type largely because the opposite of being, nothingness, is a conceptual impossibility and, as Śaṅkara and his followers point out, the notion of nothingness conflicts with our experience every moment. In fact, the trinity of basic principles, *sat* (being), *cit* (consciousness), and *ānanda* (bliss) is likewise forged from the necessity of interpretation. But these principles are considered by no means adventitious but essential signs (*svarūpalakṣaṇa*) of *Brahman*.

The problem of being, however, is really a derivative problem in Vedānta—as is the rest of metaphysics—but the presentation of *Brahman* undoubtedly provokes it. This has required two concurrent procedures : an exegetical integration of texts, and a critical examination of the realms of experience using the canons of human reasoning. The two together respond to the need for interpretation by seeking definitions of *Brahman*. They enable the problem of being to be raised in conformity with the known character of *Brahman*. (This means, of course, that it is not the case that we meet up with the concept of *Brahman* at the conclusion of some presumedly independent investigation of being, but the other way around.)

The ontological inquiry, such as it is, is thus in part acting in compliance with the need for interpretation and definition and in part responding to a demand of the human mind for intelligibility. However, Vedānta as a whole (not only Advaita), along with Pūrva-mīmāṁsā, assumes that intelligibility is also impulsive in character. Knowledge must move persons. While expounding the *samanvayādhikaraṇa* (*Brahma-sūtra*, 1.1.4), Śaṅkara points out the injunctive (or shall we say imperative ?) character of scriptural knowledge pertaining to *Brahman*. It is obviously not given in the form of statements of facts like "the earth has seven islands" and "here goes the king." Mere factual statements do not belong to the Vedānta texts, which are declarations purporting to impel the hearers to a quest, and even an effort *to be* in the spirit of "*brahmavid brahmaiva bhavati* (the knower of *Brahman* becomes *Brahman*)". Also, *sat* has a very definite dynamic character in terms of impelling man toward his supreme end. By making reference to Upaniṣadic sentences like, "the *ātman* should be seen [*ātmā vā are draṣṭavyaḥ*]" (*Bṛhadāraṇyaka Up*., 2.4.5), "he should be investigated, he should be understood [*so 'nveṣṭavyaḥ, so vijijñāsitavyaḥ*]" (*Chāndogya Up.*, 8.7.1), Śaṅkara points out that they undoubtedly contain a certain imperative concerning both our knowing and our *becoming* being. Incidentally, Śaṅkara's principal objective in his exegesis in this place is to discourage the belief that there is a valid realm of action for the purpose of achieving man's ultimate goal apart and aside from the realm of knowledge of *Brahman*. However, dedication to the latter must absorb into itself the essential properties of action as well as the passion inherent in it.

Brahman as Sat-cit-ānanda or Satyaṁ jñānam anantaṁ/ ānandaṁ Brahma

The Taittirīya Upaniṣad 2.1, presents the basic and the oldest formula for defining *Brahman*, that is, as *satyam* (being, truth), *jñānam* (consciousness, knowledge), and *anantam/ānandam* (infinite, bliss). It is the consensus of interpreters that this formula is identical with the later formula *sat-cit-ānanda* (being-consciousness-bliss). The latter as a single formula does not, as is well-known, occur in the major Upaniṣads but appears, as is probably not well-known, in a few of the minor ones, the *Vāsudeva Upaniṣad*, the two *Rāma Upaniṣads*, the two *Nṛsiṁha Upaniṣads*, and the *Muktikā Upaniṣad*. However, tradition has invariably regarded the two formulas as identical.

The formula *sat-cit-ānanda*, as Advaita literature has it, has come to be accepted as the essential definition (*svarūpalakṣaṇa*) of *Brahman*, while another definition, given in terms of the accidental qualities of *Brahman*, like activity and relation to the world, constitute the *taṭasthalakṣaṇa*. This distinction between the two is stated in exactly this manner in the *Vedānta Paribhāṣā* and in its commentary.[8]

Śaṅkara, so far as we know, is the first to write that the formula *sat-cit-ānanda* constitutes the essential definition of *Brahman*. His *Taittirīya Bhāṣya* 2.1.1, expressly puts his stamp of authority on that definition as such, as he declares, "The three words beginning with *satyam*, with qualificatory meanings are the qualifications of *Brahman*."[9] But this effort to define *Brahman* thus must face and forestall a possible misunderstanding, especially in view of the definiens-definiendum (*viśeṣya-viśeṣaṇa*) relation. Advaita should not lend itself to the interpretation such as prevails in realistic systems like Nyāya-Vaiśeṣika, which would accept the formula *sat-cit-ānanda* but only as an adjectival definition of God the Supreme Being, meaning that *sat, cit,* and *ānanda* would be regarded as separate predicates shared, although in a lesser manner, by all beings in their own inherent right. On the grounds of Advaita it can be objected that as defining adjectives are admissible only in order to distinguish an entity from a multitude of other entities of the same nature (*anekāni dravyāṇi ekajātīyāni*), Advaita would contradict itself if it recognized any other entity to exist in its own right besides *Brahman*. Śaṅkara takes full account of this valid objection but argues that there is no scope for such misunderstanding if we understand these words in the defining formula not as actual adjectives but as mere indicators—

8. *svarūpameva lakṣaṇam svarūpalakṣaṇam*. Also, *yāvallakṣyakālam anavasthitatve sati lakṣaṇatvam taṭasthalaksaṇatvamiti*, *The Vedānta Paribhāṣā*, with *Paribhāṣā-Prakāśikā*, ed. Anantakrishna Sastri (Calcutta University Press, 1930), 281. Cf. p. 278.

9. *satyādīni trīṇi viśeṣaṇārthāni padāni viśeṣyasya brahmaṇaḥ*, Śaṅkara's *Commentary on the Taittirīya Upaniṣad*, p. 47.

as that is their meaning—pointing to the invariant entity, *Brahman.*[10] The primary import of *viśeṣaṇāni* (adjectives) must be sought in their function as *lakṣaṇāni* (indicators), not in their qualifying function.[11] The *Vanamālā* on the *Taittirīya Upaniṣad Bhāṣya* of Śaṅkara, in expounding this point, makes it even clearer that the objective of this threefold definition is not to distinguish *Brahman* from any like beings—of which there are none—but to produce grounds for understanding *Brahman's* absoluteness, that is to say, to avoid mistaking *Brahman* for any seeming reality (*kalpitapadārtha*) such as space, time, or the *avyakta* (the Unmanifest) of Sāṁkhya.

In Advaita there is a call for concrete application of this method of distinguishing *Brahman* from seeming entities and to mark it off in this manner. The task is sometimes pursued in the spirit of the *via negativa* (*netivāda*). The most prominent of all concrete instances of this kind of effort is probably in *Brahma Sūtra,* 1.4.15, at least in the light of Śaṅkara's commentary. He explains the non-being (*asat*) principle stated in the *Taittirīya,* 2.7.1, *asadvā idam agra āsīt* ("non-being indeed was this in the beginning"), and in the *Chāndogya,* 3.19.1, *asadeva idam agra āsīt* ("non-being it is that was in the beginning") thus :

> Considering that the word *sat* is generally known to be used in connection with a thing which has been evolved by name and form, it should be understood that *Brahman,* which before creation is of course *sat,* is here spoken of in a secondary sense, as if it were *asat,* with reference to the fact that before creation there was absence of any differentiation by way of names and forms as is to be seen now in the created world.[12]

With respect to this exegesis of Śaṅkara's—and possibly the *Brahma-Sūtra* which provides the context—we can say only this : the thematization of being as against non-being may not belong to the Upaniṣadic texts themselves insofar as there seems to

10. *lakṣaṇārthatvāt viśeṣaṇānām, ibid.,* p. 48
11. *lakṣaṇārthapradhānāni viśeṣaṇāni na viśeṣaṇapradhānāni, loc. cit.*
12. *Brahma-Sūtra Śāṁkara-Bhāṣyam,* trans. V. M. Apte, (Bombay : Popular Book Depot, 1960), p. 253.

prevail there a total rejection of any such possibility as in the *Kena* passage, I.4a, "other indeed is it than the known as well as the unknown," but there is no point in trying to accomplish here a totally independent exegesis. Even Śaṅkara recognizes that either being or non-being can in principle be assigned to *Brahman*, totally depending on with what we first identify being : if it is with the name-form (*nāma-rūpa*) phenomena, then *Brahman* is to be called non-being. But in any case, it is easy to see that the explicit thematization of being as against non-being arises from Śaṅkara himself.

The course Śaṅkara has adopted has been given greater confirmation by similar exegeses of passages of an opposite kind, as in the context of the *Chāndogya* passage, 6.2.1, "being alone, dear one, was this in the beginning, one without a second." Now that Śaṅkara has been forced to make a choice between being and non-being—which to his own mind could not have been, as observed before, the primary intent of the Vedānta texts—insofar as only one of them can be assigned to *Brahman*, he unequivocally makes it in favour of being. He makes the choice because non-being has automatically disqualified itself. Hence being is primarily a category of interpretation-definition; it is also a category of intellectual communication for human beings whose consciousness, phenomenal as it is, is conditioned by the illusion of existence based on awareness of entities that are. In a logical situation of this kind to choose between polar opposites such as being and non-being is inevitable. He obeys the necessity of thematization of the logical opposition between being and non-being and asserts of being as the logical principle by means of which one can intellectually grasp the concept *Brahman*. He explains the words *sad eva* (being itself) of the text in question as *astitāmātram vastu* ("entity which only exists"). The word *mātram* (only) formally expresses the view that a thing cannot both be and not be, and transcendentally expresses the view that because non-being terminates forever the possibility and worthwhileness of meditating upon *Brahman*—the reality which grasps man through the texts and directs him to his goal—such a totally negative concept would do thinking the greatest disservice. Śaṅkara further refers to the notion of pure being which, as a transcendental mental image, responds only to the word *sat* (being).[13]

Śaṅkara further implies another choicc imposed by reason of the individuation of the world as well as of one's own self in human experience. Accordingly, one has to make a choice between what is pointed to as 'this' intentionally, as against every concrete mode of experience as well as of speaking. So we have to add to the general notion of being the notion of 'this' (*idam*). Thus *Brahman* as being also becomes the conceptual object of the word 'this'.[14] In a certain place Śaṅkara even makes the word 'this' in the sentence, "this is *Ātman*" (*ayamātmā*), an object of pointing with a gesture of the hand. "The word 'this', meaning that which appears divided into four quarters, is pointed out as the innermost self with a gesture as in a drama by the statement 'this is *Ātman*.'"[15] However, Śaṅkara does not stop here in the comment referred to above on the *Chāndogya* passage, but goes on, as he must, to explain "one only" (*ekam eva*), and "without a second" (*advitīyam*) so as to disavow any difference in *Brahman* of a homogeneous, heterogeneous, or inherent (*sajātīya*, *vijātīya*, *svagata*) kind. This shows that insofar as *Brahman* is to be grasped intellectually as a response to man's having been first grasped by *Brahman* in the texts, the notion of being as it refers to *Brahman* must be regarded in the sense of "alone Being", without any distinctions within or without.

The foregoing paragraph would lead us to consider the need for the three terms *sat*, *cit* and *ānanda*, used for the essential definition (*svarūpalakṣaṇa*) of *Brahman*. Would not *sat* be enough, for what is more comprehensive than being? It has been suggested that the subject of all definition is one and the same *Brahman*; the concept *sat* is not *per se* the subject of definition, rather it is that by means of which a definition, albeit a necessary and inescapable one, is accomplished. But *sat* also becomes the subject

13. *kevala-sacchabda-buddhi-mātra-gamyam eva iti sad eva idam agra āsīt iti avadhāryate*, Śaṅkara's *Commentary on Chāndogya Upaniṣad* (Poona : Anandasrama, Saka era 1856), p. 323.

14. *sad eva...nāma-rūpa-viśeṣaṇavat idaṁ śabda-buddhi-viṣayam*, *loc. cit.*

15. *abhinayena nirdiśati ayam ātmeti*, Śaṅkara's *Commentary on Māṇḍūkya Upaniṣad* (Poona : Anandasrama, 1963), 13. Cf. The *Māṇḍūkya Upaniṣad*, with Commentary and Gauḍapāda-kārikā, trans. Swami Nikhilananda (Mysore : Sri Ramakrishna Ashram, 1955), P. 12.

of definition derivatively. It may very well be that this derivative character of *sat* as the subject of definition acts as the ground for the *taṭasthalakṣaṇa* kind of definition of *Brahman* which aims at comprehending the structures of the world, time, space, and all possible relativities. The notion of the 'this' is implicit in *Brahman*, but not necessarily implicit in *sat*, which could be interpreted as a vague and general concept of being.

The concept of being needs to be bounded if it is to serve as a definition of *Brahman*—the possibility of all kinds of differences must be removed and oneness asserted. Further it has to be explicity pointed out as 'this'. In order to do that, the further concepts of *cit* and *ānanda* become necessary. Obviously, they are not artificial contrivances, not even the result of any elaborate methodological introspection. So *cit* is just that without which being cannot be present—in fact it is that through which being is always present. The famous dialogue between Yājñavalkya and Janaka (*Bṛhadāraṇyaka Upaniṣad*, 4.3.1-6) enunciates it so powerfully, concluding thus : "When the sun has set, Yājñavalkya and the moon has set and the fire has gone out and speech has stopped, what light does a person here have ? The self, indeed, is his light, said he, for with the self indeed as light, one sits, moves about, does one's work and returns."[16]

And futher, *cit*, Vedānta understands, leads to *ānanda*; *Brahman* is *ānanda*.[17] Again, how *cit* implies *ānanda* must not be misunderstood in the sense that the concept of *cit* formally entails the concept of *ānanda*. Rather, *ānanda* should be understood as a presence in *cit*, but insofar as its presence is not a mere fortuitous occurrence in any localized, fortuitous consciousness it must straightway be called *Brahman*.

The 'this'-ness of *sat* is deepened, in fact made concrete, by means of *cit* and *ānanda*. There have been differences of opinion in the traditional literature as to whether the three words provide three individual and separate definitions or one single definition, although, no doubt, of the same subject(*Brahman*).[18] These

16. *The Bṛhadāraṇyaka Upaniṣad*, 4.3.6. trans. S. Radhakrishnan, *The Principal Upaniṣads*, p. 256.

17. *ānando brahmeti*, *The Tattirīya Upaniṣad*, 3.6.1.

18. Brahmānanda Sarasvatī's gloss on the *Siddhāntabindu* called the *Ratnāvalī* takes the view that the three essentially constitute a single defini-

discussions are somewhat hair-splitting and must not occupy us. There is agreement, as spelled out by Madhusūdana Sarasvatī, that through their *lakṣaṇāśakti* (power of signification) the three words refer to the one object *Brahman*, though through *abhidhā* (analytic presentation of that which qualifies and that which is qualified separately) each denotes a different conceptual entity : reality as marked by the absence of falsity (*sat*), of ignorance (*cit*), of limitation/sorrow (*ānanda*) respectively. Madhusūdana and his predecessor Citsukha have forged this theory under the caption of their comprehensive theory of *akhaṇḍārtha* (indivisible meaning of statements).[19] But these technical elaborations are not apposite here. The important thing is to see how a formula like *satyaṁ jñānam anantaṁ brahma* (or its variant as we more frequently have been using) explicates the implicit 'this'-ness. This formula (like some other sentences) yields an *akhaṇḍārtha*, which must be appropriated by another paradigm formula *tat tvam asi* (that thou art). What is already implicitly present as the meaning of the first formula—the 'this'-ness of being—is made absolutely explicit and concrete by means of the second utterance. 'That' and 'thou' are considered, respectively, to carry the *akhaṇḍārtha* of the two formulas : *satyaṁ jñānam anantaṁ/ ānandaṁ* and *tat tvam asi*. Obviously, the latter is considered a more inclusive one as far as completing the process of pointing out to man that 'that' is 'this', and thereby announcing the presence of Being. According to Madhusūdana at least, the first

tion, as otherwise there is a risk of three reals being implied. The *Vedānta Paribhāṣā* and its commentary do not see such risk but argue that as envisaged in the above gloss and others like it (*pūrvamuktaṁ bindu-ṭīkādi-anusāreṇa*) the risk of three separate [reals] does not arise (*pratyeka-lakṣaṇatvam api na doṣāyeti*), *The Vedānta Paribhāṣā* with Commentary (supra), pp. 278-279.

19. The *akhaṇḍārtha* theory is propounded and elaborately discussed in Citsukha's *Tattvapradīpikā* and Madhusūdana Sarasvatī's *Advaita Siddhi*. There is much stake on the concept of *akhaṇḍa* (impartite) in Advaita. Vidyāraṇya (*Pañcadaśī* 2.20), speaks of three kinds of difference : (1) between the roots, trunk, leaves, and fruits of the self-same tree; (2) between one tree and another; (3) between a tree and a stone. See *Pañcadaśī*, trans. H. P. Sastri (London : Shanti Sadan, 1954). Cf. Nṛsiṁhasarasvatī's definition of *akhaṇḍa*, along the same lines, for which see *The Philosophy of the Vedānta* and the *Vedānta Sāra*, P. Deussen and G. A. Jacob (Calcutta : Susil Gupta), p. 33.

is an elaboration of the word-meaning (*padārtha*), of 'that', while the latter is a sentence-meaning (*vākyārtha*) and, hence, that which completes the former. The pertinent thing to be noted here is that the 'this' of Being has become as concrete and as definite as it can be because it is pointed to as 'thou'.

Some Concluding Observations

A discerning study of Advaita literature will bring home the truth that the pursuit of being was undertaken in the form of two dominant inquiries, centered around, respectively, the problem of the meaning of linguistic expressions and statements and the problem of the real, of being (*satya*) versus the false (*mithyā*). This is even more true of the post-Śaṅkara dialecticians, as they are sometimes called, than of the earlier literature.

As we have seen something of the meaning problem, we must at least cast a quick glance at the even more agonizing problem of reality versus falsity, just in order to see what effect it had on ontology. Here we see a tremendous shift in the burden of the whole problem of being, which we see moving in a particular path. No doubt, it could not have been otherwise for Advaita as we know it. The great preoccupation with this can be guaged only by the varieties of clever dialectical arguments advanced in support of it. Even the question of the real (*satyam*), in a sense, moves into the shadow, and the issue of falsity (*mithyātva*) and how to define it adequately occupies the centre of the philosophical stage. To be sure, this problem was taken up with vigour and passion not for its own sake but indirectly in the interests of the real—being. When the false is negated the real shines by itself.

In fact that which complements the question of being or the real is not the question of non-being. Probably, partly because the word *satya* often serves for both being and the real, any thought of non-being cannot arise as distinct from the unreal. The unreal has been ruled out as mere logical contradiction like "the son of a barren woman".

There has seldom been in Vedānta a problem of non-being as such, as the possibility of non-being having any depth has not been entertained. In truth, *asat* seems to be a mere nullity, and one is not encouraged to waste one's thought on a nullity. The case is clearly different in Buddhism where *śūnya* (nothingness), which comprehends all existences, inevitably has depth.

The formal opposition in Advaita is no longer between *sat* and *asat* but between *satya* and *mithyā*. The care invested in unravelling the character of *mithyā* as that which is neitheir *sat*, nor *asat* through some very skillful definitions is indeed impressive. *Mithyā*, as a third category apart from being and non-being, takes the centre of the philosophical stage for several later Advaitins.

Five definitions of falsity (*mithyātva*) are usually listed:[20]

1. As that which is not the locus of either *sat* or *asat* (*sadasattvānadhikaraṇatvaṁ vā mithyātvam*). Here the false is distinguished from both of them. *Sat* implies non-contradictability or irremovability, which in turn implies non-temporality. *Asat* cannot appear at all. But something (which we call the world) appears, which is also temporal. Hence what appears is neither *sat* nor *asat*. This is the definition of Padmapāda in the *Pañcapādikā*.

2. As that which is eternally negated in the same locus where it is cognized (*pratipannopādhau traikālikaniṣedhapratiyogitvaṁ vā mithyātvam*). For example, when a man mistakes a rope for a snake, he first perceives the snake in the rope, but when he comes closer he perceives the rope for what it is. The false snake appears in the rope temporarily but cannot persist through the three tenses of time. This is given by Prakāśātman in the *Pañcapādikāvivaraṇa*.

3. Another definition is given by Prakāśātman, viz., as that which is dissolved by knowledge (*jñānanivartyatvam*). It means that what appears as the content of illusion-induced cognition and ceases with the cognition of the real content is false.

4. That whose locus is equally the locus of its eternal negation (*svāśrayaniṣṭhātyantābhāvapratiyogitvam*). This, given by Citsukha in the *Tattvapradīpikā*, appears to be the same as Prakāśātman's first definition.

20. The later Vedānta tradition mostly relies on Madhusūdana Sarasvatī's *Advaita Siddhi*, the beginning section, for a comprehensive discussion of the five definitions (*nirūpaṇas*) of *mithyātva*. See *Advaita Siddhi* of Madhusūdana Sarasvatī with Gauḍabrahmānandī and other commentaries edited by Ananta Krishna Sastri, Bombay, Nirnaya-sagar Press, 1937, pp. 47-206.

5. As simply other than *sat* (*sadviviktatvam*). It is given by Ānandabodha in the *Nyāyaratnadīpāvalī*. Obviously, it does not recognize non-being at all.

It may be observed that although the problem of being has been pursued in Advaita in this particular form, sometimes to the exclusion of other possibilities, and although non-being has been literally consigned to itself, that is to say, to the state of a non-problem, there is no doubt that the depth of being (as *saccidānanda*) has continued to be a source of infinite challenge and infinite fascination for Advaita. Here, too, thought is the extension of being, and this guarantees the continued existence of Advaita as a philosophy. It may even be believed, certainly from the Vedānta point of view, that the possibility of philosophy itself rests in the infinite challenge and fascination of being.

This calls for some very general reflections, which, seen in the right perspective will not appear as intrusions. First, it may be observed that despite all the great depth of thought on the question characteristic of Advaita, to the extent that it chose to focus a great part of it on the *mithyātva* problem, it might appear that the general existential condition which initially called forth the particular resolution that *mithyātva* itself is, viz., the collision between being and non-being and the shock it produces, felt as existence, may have been pushed into the shadow. The threat of the impending victory of non-being and the fear that it may prevail, both in terms of personal and universal life, has not a little to do with man's turning his attention to the question of being. The shock-waves produced by this collision and inevitable pervasion of being by non-being and non-being by being, is, it was understood by the ancient thinkers, including Buddha, what constitutes the transitory *saṁsāra*. As *saṁsāra* is, in this way at least, dynamic in that it is the realm generated by the shock-waves from the collision of being and non-being, there is a call for a philosophy of the world different from that which has been registered by the doctrine of *mithyātva*. This suggestion is perhaps not out of place here as it concerns one of the outstanding issues arising from Advaita ontology. On the other side of the ledger, it is certain that, in spite of the inhibition with regard to a philosophy of the world, Advaita, insofar as it dwells on

Brahman as it does, unveils the possibility of standing steadfastly in Being.

The reason for this particular turn—toward *mithyātva* as the central problem governing being, with all that it entails—may be stated briefly as a second general observation. The esoteric-exoteric distinction is an old one in Vedānta, as we know it in the two forms of knowledge, *parāvidyā* and *aparāvidyā*. But that is not what we have in mind when we say that the esoteric as a dimension of thought, particularly pertaining to being, as against the exoteric, seems to have been pushed into the shadow. The debates of philosophy (or dialectics, as some Indian writers nowadays call it), through which not only Advaita but all *darśanas* grew, seem to typify rather the exoteric character of thought in spite of the unmistakable skill and subtlety which pervade it. The esoteric no doubt lives, but more as part of the various *vidyās* of mysticism rather than philosophic thought itself. No doubt the exoteric *tarka* philosophy is well balanced, even in Advaita, with an ample mystical literature. In the ancient times this was true, even in the Upaniṣads, but mystically oriented rituals mediated with thought, even acting as signposts of thought. That, no doubt, we can only try to re-live today by understanding, not by actually duplicating. The question is, having been reduced to thinking of Being—the alternative is not to think of it at all—without the traditional signposts, is it not possible for Advaita to show the way to incorporate the symbols of its mysticism—not as realization techniques (*sādhana*), which is what they are—but as signposts also for thought ? That may be one way of avoiding the typical bifurcation of our striving after Being into the exotericism of *mithyāvāda*, and its attendant *vādas* and the esotericism of ritual mysticism. At this point this is no more than a question, perhaps even an idle question.

Two

MĀYĀ AND THE DISCOURSE ABOUT BRAHMAN

This essay is conceived only as a very restricted kind of inquiry, as the title itself shows. What is maintained here as the prime interest is to discover some of the objectives in the original articulation of the so-called "theory" of *māyā*, or *māyā-vāda*, and then to discuss at some length what may be shown as the principal one among them. The origin and development of the *māyā* concept can be, and has been sometimes, investigated from an historical point of view, which we do not adopt here. There is, again, the approach of the metaphysician who sees himself as a partisan and therefore feels impelled to join issue and to argue for or against this concept, which is one of the most controversial of all Indian philosophical concepts. From the time of Rāmānuja and other critics of *māyā-vāda* and the Śaṅkarite supporters of it, metaphysicians as a rule have had a vested interest in the debate, either for or against. On the contrary, we intend to give an account of this "theory" without becoming partisans for or against.

It is in Śaṅkara that we find the arguments for *māyā* organized into a well laid out theory (*vāda*) although many of them had already been present in Gauḍapāda before him. Śaṅkara, however, combined or even identified the theory with the theory of *avidyā*. History has recognized Śaṅkara as the father of both theories but no one will contend that he was the absolute originator of either the *māyā* or the *avidyā* concepts. As for the two theories, let us say that for all practical purposes they are but one theory. After Śaṅkara the Advaita thinkers developed it further into a general theory of knowledge with the designation *ajñānavāda* (theory of ignorance), not unlike in broad features of dialectics—but quite unlike in metaphysical import—the *vijñānavāda* of Buddhism.

Śaṅkara was in some ways what we could call today a philosophical theologian, whose urgent interest was to explain in the most cogent rational terms the central message of Vedānta. This led him to argue for non-dualism (*advaita*), out of which by sheer force of logical implication arose the subsidiary theory of "illusion" (*māyāvāda, avidyāvāda*). Śaṅkara realized that if duality (in all such ubiquitous forms as subject-object, thinker-thought, thinker-thing, etc.,) is to be avoided while explaining (not explaining away) the world by *māyā*, *avidyā* needs to be recognized as a concomitant condition, for both have the implication of "illusion". Then there is the question, where does *avidyā* actually reside? Śaṅkara himself inclined to the view that it does so in persons who are the subject of illusion. It was felt by later Vedānta writers that a general epistemological theory that distinguished and comprehended *avidyā* and *māyā* was needed, and the result was a vastly more developed and considerably more complex *ajñānavāda*.[1]

Māyā theory has implications for several things, mainly experience, the world and language. The original motivation in articulating the theory was to rationalize these implications by making them cohere with the fundamental metaphysical position of Advaita Vedānta. In this sense it is clear that *māyāvāda* is simply a rational postscript to *advaitavāda*, and is in no way prescriptive of it. But then such a rational postscript has been necessary not only for theoretical considerations but for existential ones as well. It must never be lost sight of that Vedānta, like most other Indian systems, is not only philosophy but also religion. This essential integrity of the two ensconced in the very heart of Indian thinking is a matter of no mean significance for a faithful and objective study of the matter; disregard of this fact would be a violation of the first principles of scientific phenomenology. So then, besides the theoretical purpose of making the

1. The later Vedānta works like *Advaita Siddhi*, *Bhāmatī*, *Vedānta-paribhāṣā*, *Vivaraṇa-prameya-saṁgraha*, *Pañcapādikā*, etc., have been responsible for its elaborate and intricate development. A comprehensive idea of this can be obtained from Ashutosh B. Shastri, *Studies in Post-Śaṅkara Dialectics*, University of Calcutta, Calcutta, 1936; and T. R. V. Murti, "*Ajñāna*—One or Many", Malkani, G. R., Das, R. and Murti, T. R. V., *Ajñāna*, Luzac & Co., London, 1933.

rational implications of this particular metaphysics for experience, the world and language cohere with the fundamental Advaita view of reality, there has been also the existential one of providing a framework and a context for the quest of liberation (*mukti, nirvāṇa*). For this reason, Śaṅkara declares that for Vedānta the thought that there may be no liberation will not arise even in dream,[2] wherein lies, he feels, the incontestable superiority of his position. Actually, the real reason for Śaṅkara's criticism of two among the prevailing systems, viz., the Sāṁkhya dualist realism and Buddhist (Yogācāra) subjective idealism, is their inability to account for liberation. These are singled out precisely because they are diametrically opposite to each other, and because their views, if adhered to, will destroy rational grounds of experience as well as the possibility of a world.

As far as experience is concerned Saṅkara is as realistic as the Sāṁkhyans, only more logically so. Sāṁkya has been hard put to explain experience, its ground and its subject, on the basis of its eternal dualism between *puruṣa* and *prakṛti* (*pradhāna*). By definition, *puruṣa*, which is intelligence, cannot be the principle on which experience springs or in which it resides. But neither can the non-intelligent *pradhāna* be that. Sāṁkhya is really caught in an impossible logical situation, which will undercut the entire meaning of liberation. Logic would reduce Sāṁkhya to the absurd position of having to say that experience (suffering) is itself the experiencer (sufferer).[3] This is where Vedānta comes in with its doctrine of *māyā*, later consolidated with *ajñāna*. "An enquiry obout *ajñāna* is (therefore) an investigation into the *a priori* conditions of experience," writes Prof. T. R. V. Murti, who adds, "such a thesis requires to be elaborated and justified. A general and camprehensive theory has to be formulated."[4] Śaṅkara forces Sāṁkhya to admit that the relation of causes of experience (suffering) with the experiencers (sufferers) is not real but the effect of *avidyā*. At this point Śaṅkara speaks as a meticulous empiricist who will accept the phenomenal experience

2. *aupaniṣadasya...nirmokṣaśaṁkā svapne 'pi na upajāyate*, *Bhāṣya on Brahma Sūtra*, 2.2.10.

3. *na tapter eva taptim abhyupagacchasi*, *ibid.*

4. "*Ajñāna*—One or Many", *op. cit.*, pp. I22-23.

as just what it is and no more or less.[5] Phenomenal reality is its own ground and the true perception of it will reveal the ground of that ground, which is the non-dual Reality.

Against the Buddhist subjective idealists, who denied the existence of the external world, Śaṅkara urges a number of arguments, the first and strongest among which is that we must admit the existence of what we actually perceive. If anyone has any suspicion that Śaṅkara was a subjective idealist himself, let that be laid to rest here. In fact, he almost stoops to sarcasm when he suggests that we should no more pay heed to a man who, while perceiving external things with his senses, denies their existence than believe the report of a man who, while eating and experiencing the feeling of satisfaction, avers that he does not do so.[6] Strange as it may sound, *māyāvāda* implies a very strong affirmation of the reality of the world. In this respect it goes exactly as far as empiricism would want to go. No empiricist ever ascribes absolute reality to the world in any case. Analogical reasoning itself, which is so important in Vedānta philosophy, is based on the reality of the perceived world as it is on the reliability of experience. This is how one prefers the report of perceptions of the waking state to those of the dreaming state as clues to reality. Likewise, the real rope seen as rope rather than as snake, is truer to fact. The genuine philosopher must always respect fact as against the would-be philosopher who denies what he sees.[7]

It is, however, to be acknowledged that a mere assertion that the world exists is of no philosophical value. In fact, even an effort to *prove* the existence of the world is of no value. It does not take a philosopher to do that, as everyday life is lived on such an assumption; neither is there any point in trying to reverse what all life has assumed. The philosopher's task is to explain *the way* the world exists, the knowledge of which will be

5. *vyavahāre tu yatra sathā dṛṣṭay tapyatāpakabhāvaḥ tatra tathaiva sa iti, Bhāṣya on Brahma Sūtra*, 2.2.10.

6. *yathā hi kaścid bhuñjāno bhujisādhyāyāṁ tṛptau svayamanubhūyamānāyām evaṁ brūyānnāhaṁ bhuñje na vā tṛpyāmīti, tadvad indriyasaṁnikarṣeṇa svayamupalabhamāna eva bāhyamarthaṁ nāham upalabhe na ca so 'stīti bruvan katham upādeyavacanaḥ syāt, Ibid.*, 2.2.28.

7. Cf. *ibid.*, 2.2.29.

integral to the search for meaning and the quest for liberation. The Vedānta philosopher is also clear in his mind that the world offers no standpoint from which to speak about the world or to gain knowledge about it. Hence his insistence on *śruti* (revelation). What the world contributes to the knowledge of itself is analogies based on the distinction between fact and non-fact present in its very structure. When that (by definition) transcendentally originated knowledge bodies forth with the aid of analogies provided by the phenomenal world we have a well-ordered and coherent knowledge of the world, giving rise to a system of meaning and a framework for the aspiration towards liberation.

All this leads to the central objective of Vedānta in the advaitic form, which is to explain how speaking about *Brahman*, the Ultimate Reality, is made possible. Vedānta knows that philosophy is about *Brahman*, not about the world or experience. Knowledge about these latter things arises as *modes* of the knowledge of *Brahman*. The inalienable connecting link is discourse itself. Therefore *māyā* must be understood fundamentally as discourse about *Brahman*. This is the line along which we will seek to develop our exposition of *māyāvāda*.

Saṁvṛti and Māyā

We will argue here that one of the main reasons for forging the theory of *māyā* is the quest for making a discourse about *Brahman* (which is indiscoursible) possible. It is a well-known fact that as a dialectical device *māyā* is a variant of the more general theory of *saṁvṛti*, explicitly fashioned by the Mādhyamika dialecticians, headed by Nāgārjuna. It is Gauḍapāda who introduced the Buddhist epistemological method into Vedānta: this too is well-known. The schema adopted by Nāgārjuna necessitated the positing of an absolute reality (*paramārthasatya*) conceived as *śūnya* as against a phenomenal reality (*saṁvṛtisatya*). This division has a parallel in *vijñāvavāda*. However, what appears to be no more than a purely schematic division for the Buddhists was something quite different for Gauḍapāda. The problem at issue is not whether *paramārthasatya* (*śūnya*) in the Mādhyamika language, or *pariniṣpanna* in the *vijñānavāda* language, is ontological reality rather than a mere speculative supposition, that whole matter itself being still controversial, but on what grounds it can bc said to be so if it might be. We should note a very deep divergence here between Gauḍapāda and the Buddhists. Gauḍapāda clearly attests to the fact that the doctrine of *Brahman* and the consequent doctrine of *māyā*—along with that of the identity of the *jīvas* with *Brahman*—are strictly derived from the Upaniṣads and were not taught by the Buddha.[8] Even his celebrated insistence on the primary use of reason as attested, for instance, by his declaration that *śruti* (scripture), while it speeks of creation either from the existent or the non-existent, has to be given up in favour of that which is ascertained by reason, must not lead us to suppose that he used purely rational argumentation in the dialectical form in the free and uninhibited manner of the Buddhists. His essential concern is *Brahman*, but it is only that he goes about demonstrating *Brahman* with the tools that the Buddhists had forged. But the picture becomes much clearer in Śaṅkara's enunciation of Advaita Vedānta from which all ambiguities with respect to the use of the Buddhist method have been removed. Henceforth the difference between a logical method and a purely dialectical method becomes perceptible.

It is possible to see that the *māyā* doctrine of Vedānta has its origin in logical thinking while the *saṁvṛti* doctrine as set forth by all the relevant schools of Buddhism, particularly the Mādhyamika, has its origin in dialectical thinking. 'Logical' here means making it possible for something to be said about Reality (*Brahman* in this context), taking, of course, the original meaning of 'logos'; 'dialectical' likewise means the discovery, through talking, of that about which something may be said. The gist of this may be expressed this way: in the case of the one, there is Reality but it cannot be talked about without some sort of contradiction, and in the case of the other, the possibility of talk is accepted without inquiring, however, into the origin of talk—but there is no knowing what reality or reality-substitute, if any, it will lead to and what significance it will bear.

8. *naitad buddhena bhāṣitam* (this was not spoken by Buddha). *Māṇḍūkya Kārikā*, 4.99. Śaṅkara, commenting on this passage, puts his stamp of approval on it.

Logical Origin of Māyā-vāda

In dealing with this question, first of all the reader must be warned that what is being dealt with here is not the metaphysical theory or theories of language found in Vedānta, about which (in the broader tradition) great classical works like Bhartṛhari's *Vākyapadīya*, not to speak of those that are directly in Uttara-Mīmāṁsā, offer ample instruction. The reason for side-stepping such a momentous issue is not convenience or fear or even want of an opinion but simply the absence of its warrantability in an essay that is conceived as strictly phenomenological in scope. Here then, we are not immersed in thinking about language itself, as ontological or otherwise, but only in specifically formulated *Brahman*-language, which, of course, as Śaṅkara himself believes, is the substance of *śruti*.

There is here an essential—not accidental—definitional schism because *Brahman* is defined as indefinable. If it were a purely dialectical situation the matter could simply rest there as there is nowhere to go; from such a dead-end, however, there may contingently arise different alternate possibilities, only to be instantaneously swallowed up, severally or all together, by some all-consuming frame like the *catuṣkoṭi* (the fourfold frame of the Mādhyamika). As the situation in Vedānta is not purely dialectical but logical, the schism itself has to be given ontic being. The primary reason why it is a logical situation is that *Brahman* is that which reveals itself as the Alone-Being and as the All-Being, needing no other knowledge.[9]

All definitions of *Brahman* must fall outside the intended realm and they involve the character of the subject-matter. The real problem is not what is said about *Brahman* but the saying. Everything that is truly said, on account of the saying of it, is a negation of the intent in the saying, for such is the coherent definition of *Brahman*, the non-dual, the one without a second. *Brahman* is throughout spoken of as attributeless (*nirguṇa*),[10] as

9. This is an ever present theme. Cf. *nityaprakāśasvarūpa iva savitā...na jñānāntaram apekṣate* (eternally self-luminous like the sun...does not depend upon any other knowledge), Śaṅkara's *Bhāṣya on Māṇḍūkya Upaniṣad*, 3.33; Śaṅkara's *Bhāṣya on Brahma Sūtra*, 1.1.5.

10. Cf. Śaṅkara's *Bhāṣya on Chāndogya Upaniṣad*, 8.1.1.

devoid of all differences of space, place and time (*digdeśakālādibhedaśūnya*).[11] The words *śūnya* (devoid of) and *vivarjita* (free from), like many other similar words, added to other predicative terms, form compounds signifying negative attributes of *Brahman*, and there is a prolific use of these in all Advaita Vedānta works. Thus *Brahman* is said to be free from the entire universe (*sarvaprapañcavivarjita*),[12] free from all objects (*sarvaviṣayavivarjita*),[13] free from all phenomenal attributes and determinations (*sarvadharmaviśeṣavivarjita*),[14] etc. Likewise, it transcends all empirical operations (*sarvavyavahāragocarātīta*).[15] Besides, *Brahman* is free from all adjuncts (*nirupādhi*), from all differences (*bhedarahita*), whether homogeneous (*sajātīya*), heterogeneous (*vijātīya*) or inherent (*svagata*). If these and hundreds of other expressions like them are literally true then they are also literally false, for the very fact that they can be formulated militates against their content as well as intent. Statements like *tat tvam asi*, which purport the identity of *Brahman* and the individual self (*jīva*) are especially vulnerable. Śaṅkara, following the lead of Kāśakṛtsna, emphatically advocates such an unqualified identity.[16] *Tat tvam asi* is the most notable *śruti* statement that purports the abolition of the distinction between *Brahman* and the individual self, but by the very fact that it manifests itself as a verbal entity both distinctionlessness and distinction are confirmed together, the one directly and by intent and the other indirectly and without intent.

Avidyā the Existential Starting Point

In order to abolish distinction, however, its real nature and the principle on which it is founded have to be recognized. It is of the nature of *avidyā* (*avidyātmaka*) and made of (by) *avidyā* (*avidyākṛta*).[17] This is an abiding theme for Śaṅkara and his followers. Rendered into the language of phenomenology, *avidyā*

11. *Ibid.*
12. Cf. Śaṅkara's *Bhāṣya on Praśna Upaniṣād*, 5. 7.
13. Cf. Śaṅkara's *Bhāṣya on Māṇḍūkya Upaniṣad*, 1. 37.
14. Cf.Śaṅkara's *Bhāṣya on Praśna Upaniṣad*, 5. 2.
15. Śaṅkara's *Bhāṣya on Kaṭha Upaniṣad*, 1.2.14.
16. Cf. *Bhāṣya on Brahma Sūtra*, 1.4.22.
17. *Ibid.*, 1.1.4.

may be described as the existential fact of consciousness as it confronts itself. *Tat tvam asi* means, then, that the transcendent essence of consciousness is *Ātman* but whenever this truth is verbally expressed there will be a logical contravention of the existential fact of consciousness confronting itself, although the facticity of the fact cannot be intentionally purported. Distinction will not have to be presupposed if the truth remains strictly implicit. Undoubtedly, implicit truth is what is intended in *śruti* statements, but stated truth presupposes extension and therefore distinction. But is there a way in which implicit truth can remain implicit ? There seems to be no direct way whatsoever. Nevertheless, the irony of having to make implicit truth explicit may sometimes be dramatically expressed in silence. Such dramatic expression is what is witnessed in the rather rhetorical silence observed by Bādhva before Bāṣkali, in answer to the question about *Brahman*, followed by the words "silent is this *Ātman*" (*upaśānto 'yam ātma*).[18] From the context where this episode is narrated it is clear that what Śaṅkara has in mind is the irony of having to say what cannot be said, fully knowing that silence itself is excluded from speech only so that the actuality of *Brahman* may be indicated by such dramatic enactment.[19] Silence by itself is no more capable of expressing *Brahman* than speech. The purpose in resorting to the device of irony seems to come clearly to light when we notice that Śaṅkara invokes three well-known passages of the Upaniṣads, viz., "Not this, not this",[20] "It is different from the known, it is also different from the unknown",[21] "Whence words, along with the mind, return, not attaining it."[22] The difference between speech

18. *Ibid.*, 3.2.17.

19. Note : One must detect a faint similarity with Socratic irony here as expressed in dialogues concerning Virtue for example. Kierkegaard says eloquently, "if one must war against irony as a seducer, one must also praise it as a guide." *The Concept of Irony* (transl. by L. M. Chapel), Harper & Row, New York, 1965, p. 339. His interpretation of irony as 'a mastered moment' teaching us to 'actualize actuality' (rather than idealize it) seems to fit this context very well.

20. *neti, neti. Bṛhadāraṇyaka* II.3.6; etc.

21. *anyad eva tad viditād atho aviditād adhi, Kena,* 1.3.

22. *yato vaco nivartante aprāpya manasā saha, Taittirīya,* 2.9.1.

and silence is the analogical measure of the difference between *Brahman* with distinction and *Brahman* without distinction. The difference measured thus is *māyā*: here is the significance of the etymology of the word, from *mā*, to measure. It thus becomes very instructive to note that Śaṅkara himself concludes his narration of the episode with an explanatory quotation from *smṛti*. "The cause, O Nārada, of perceiving me as possessing the qualities of all beings is the *māyā* produced by me; (but) thou shouldst not know (think of) me as such."[23]

Avidyā seems to be the fundamental phenomenological starting point from which *māyā* emerges as an explanatory principle, in some ways supported by perception and inference. *Avidyā* then seems to be a fact of consciousness, while *māyā* appears to be a postulate, drawing its substance from *avidyā* and its raison d'être from the paradoxically expressed aspect of ontological Reality, *Brahnan*. Śaṅkara himself, in the quest for an experiential description of *māyā*, has recourse to *avidyā*. *Avidyā* is that which informs *māyā*.[24] Śaṅkara, therefore, treats both terms synonymously.

The ways in which *avidyā* and *māyā* have been distinguished by later Vedānta dialecticians reflect the particular metaphysical path that an original and genuine phenomenological problem has been obliged to travel. They are distinguished as two forms of *ajñāna*. In treating both *avidyā* and *māyā* as postulates these dialecticians have been forced to regard them as coordinated parts of the same general theory; they have also tended to examine them as some kind of infra-ontological or quasi-ontological entities. If this is the case they have been looking at the matter in a somewhat different way than Śaṅkara himself, who, it seems, on the one hand, thought of *māyā* as the structure of discourse about *Brahman*, keeping in view the character of *Brahman*, revealed in *śruti*, and therefore as the *logos* of the world,[25] and, on the other, thought of *avidyā* as that which

23. *māyā hi eṣā mayā sṛṣṭā yanmāṁ paśyasi nārada. Sarvabhūtaguṇair yuktaṁ naiva māṁ jñātumarhasi. Bhāṣya on Brahma Sūtra*, 3.2.17.

24. *avidyālakṣaṇā anādirmāyā*. Śaṅkara's *Bhāṣya on Māṇḍūkya Kārikā*, 3.36.

25. Note : This aspect of Śaṅkara's thought is often neglected by scholars, but we will become impressed with its great importance when we

informs *māyā*. The idea of distinguishing the two even in a methodological manner clearly found no place in his thinking.

What distinguishes the method of Śaṅkara from that of the later dialecticians is mainly the much higher degree of scholastic speculation prevailing in the latter. The scholastic speculation is principally manifested in the almost literal factuality that is associated with cosmological and psychological explanations, which have always had an important place in Indian philosophy. *As a result, an explanatory account of the genesis and composition of any given condition tends to become a substitute for the immanent or non-immanent, existential meanings of that condition.* But in Śaṅkara the insightful simplicity typical of his utter genius forestalled any domination by that line of scholastic thinking. Having understood the mythic character of all cosmology and psychology, he could wave them away at any time for the sake of the existential. What is significant about the post-Śaṅkarites is not any philosophical gain or loss—there is not much of either—but the interesting speculative results brought about by their formidable analytical skills, comparable to those of the Buddhist dialecticians themselves, who in their own way added little to the paradigmatic insights of Buddha. As an instance of their speculation, there is a fairly universal concern in them to relate *ajñāna* to the *guṇas*, *sattva*, *rajas*, and *tamas*. Likewise, we meet with a great interest in classifying *ajñāna* into types such as, for example, *mūlājñāna* (primordial ignorance) and *tūlājñāna* (diverse, empirical offshoots of *ajñāna*), put forward by Vācaspati Miśra. Again, we notice that *ajñāna* as the causal principle of the universe occupies much attention. One of the truly typical solutions to this problem consists in the proposal, shared by several, that *ajñāna* be seen as two-fold power (*śakti*), namely of veiling (*āvaraṇa*) and projecting (*vikṣepa*).[26] Incidentally, it is not unimportant to note that these speculative efforts are paralleled in the Purāṇas, which are contemporaneous.

---

realize that *Īśvara*, described as *mahāmāyin* (*Bhāṣya on Brahma Sūtra* 2.1.37, etc.) is no negliglible category for him.

26. *asya ajñānasya āvaraṇavikṣepanāmakam asti śaktidvayam, Vedāntasāra*, 52.

In a sense, to study the development of the theory of *ajñāna* is to study the whole history of Advaita Vedānta since Śaṅkara, but then, most of the discussions found there are mainly of historical interest. So we must revert to the phenomenological exposition of *avidyā*; it is possible, however, to remain with it even if we meander through the various scholastic speculations of the post-Śaṅkarites.

Avidyā must be regarded as an existential phenomenon, nevertheless a very special one, as it is essentially consciousness confronting itself under the conditions of the assumption of absolute knowledge, without which it cannot be what it is. Understood that way, it appears to be positive privation, or absence, in fact, the reverse side of absolute knowledge. Its effort to understand itself is the negative aspect of the effort to possess absolute knowledge. This theme receives a particularly cogent examination in Vidyāraṇya's *Vivaraṇaprameyasaṁgraha* and Madhusūdana Sarasvatī's *Advaitasiddhi*. The positive character of *avidyā*, Madhusūdana Sarasvatī argues, is revealed by the intuitive knowledge of *sākṣin* (the witness self), which is described as pure consciousness reflected on the *vṛtti* (mode) of *avidyā*.[27] He is careful to point out that *avidyā* has for its object something that is known *a priori*; it refers to a known unknown, based on a knowledge that is transcendentally originated (through *śruti*), which then becomes the absolute condition of all ignorance. The unknown is *Brahman* itself. Therefore, the statements 'I am ignorant', 'there is no knowledge in me' express existential awareness which has for its object the witness self as it apprehends the known unknown, *Brahman*. We must concede, however, that the existential insight well recognizable in this is often concealed in an archaic cosmology and an equally archaic psychology of sleep, dream and waking, which scholasticism analyzes as literal fact rather than in terms of its deeper mythic significance.

Avidyā must not be understood as talk about the conditions and charactar of human experience independent of *śruti*. It is really nothing but the individual (*sākṣī*) modality of the talk

27. *kiṁ ca kevala cinmātraṁ na sākṣi kiṁ tu avidyāvṛttyupahitam, Advaitasiddhi*, p. 545.

about *Brahman* which in its universal modality is denoted by *māyā*. Some of the modern meanings of the word 'myth' adequately convey the meaning of the word *māyā*. *Māyā* is to be understood as the utmost universalization of mythic being, as the unbounded frame and structure of all individual myths, unified into a single interpretive system. If rhetoric is permitted, it can be described as the fathomless, boundless ocean from which all things come and into which all things disappear. It may be objected that this is the kind of talk that one makes about *Brahman*. Yes, that is precisely the point. *Brahman* talk also turns out to be *māyā* talk. Clearly the subject of discourse, that is *māyā*, is not itself but *Brahman*, and as such the paradox of self-invalidation implied in the statement 'the world is illusory', it being part of that illusory world, resolves itself.[28] If *māyā* is the logical structure of the discourse about *Brahman* then discourse about *māyā* is simply its obverse side, existing only tenuously. It is in that sense that one must speak of it, as has been spoken of by Advaitins, as neither real nor unreal but indefinable (*anirvacanīya*).

The Difference between Māyā of Vedānta and Saṁvṛti of Buddhism

The predominance of the logical in the one and the dialectical in the other has already been noted. However, it is correct to say that Buddhism really got into a bind when Vedānta did not. There is something a bit nonsensical about beginning a talk by denying everything that may serve as the subject of talk, and this could involve a kind of self-contradiction (different from the Vedāntic self-contradiction of discoursing about that which is not discoursible) as it amounts to cutting off the ground of talk. The method of pure dialectical negation, with no ontology involved, means that we make statements aimed at other statements rather than at any state of affairs, and when all state-

28. Professor T. R. V. Murti deals with this problem in "Some Thoughts on the Indian Philosophy of Language", being the presidential address at the 37th session of Indian Philosophical Congress (Chandigarh), 1963, pp. xxi ff. He suggests a possible solution in taking "recourse to a hierarchy of languages" or "at least two levels of languages".

ments demolish one another the entire structure will collapse through the power of dialectics and then we have *Śūnyatā*. Strictly within the procedure of negative dialectics, can *Śūnyatā* be regarded as a state of affairs ? That is the question. As statements have no reference point other than one another they can only nullify one another. In contradistinction, it is clear that in Vedānta each statement nullifies itself in the light of the character of *Brahman* which is implicitly (not explicitly) present in *Brahman* statements, that is to say, as it is there through intent. In other words, each statement collapses by itself, meaning that each is rendered false by being true. Further, as their truthfulness is their undoing they are also redeemed *māyā*-wise through the same truthfulness. The relativism involved in the Mādhyamika position issues in the absolutism of *Śūnyatā*, which strictly from the standpoint of dialectics alone seems to be a negative one; the possibility of an ontology of *Śūnya*, arising from *Śūnyatā* will have to depend upon factors above and beyond sheer dialectics.

In the Buddhist idealist schools, then, in order to make talk significant some limitation needs to be imposed on the process of dialectics. In the Vedāntic idealism the significance of talk is no problem; it is the non-contradictory possibility of it that is at issue. The question is whether *Śūnyatā* or *Śūnya* provides such limitation and thereby significance. It would seem that such cannot be the case although *śūnya* is *paramārthasatya* (Absolute Reality). In the absence of a real ontological limitor to the process of mutual, dialectical demolition of stated points of view, it is *saṁvṛti* itself that performs this role. It is in this context that a distinction between *lokasaṁvṛti* (*saṁvṛti* founded on the empirical world) and *alokasaṁvṛti* (*saṁvṛti* not founded on the empirical world) had to be invented in order to contain the potentiality towards infinite regress and therefore meaninglessness resident in the very concept in question. In Vedānta, on the contrary, limitation exists even before discourse begins; in fact it is the starting point as well as the goal. The limitor is *Brahman* itself, not *saṁvṛti* or *māyā*. Hence the importance of *vastutantra* and *śrutipramāṇa*. *Brahman* is speech (*vāgvai Brahmati*).[29]

29. *Bṛhadāraṇyaka Upaniṣad*, 4.1.2.

Māyāvāda did not develop in Advaita Vedānta as an instrument for limitation of discourse as is quite definitely the case with *saṁvṛtivāda* in dialectical Buddhism. This, then has been an effort on our part to answer the question as to what motivated the articulation of the theory of *māyā*.

A Misunderstanding Dispelled

Simply in the interest of accurate exposition, not partisan defense, a very wide-spread misunderstanding needs to be dispelled. *Māyā* does not mean denial of the world. The ultimate non-being of the world does not have to be stated as a theory, as it is strictly implied in the very definition of *Brahman* itself. As a theory it only seeks to translate the implicit into the explicit, thereby necessitating the complete phenomenological tracing, or retracing, of the paths through which the world-appearance has come into being. *Māyā*, therefore, is a provisional recovery of the world so that its ultimate non-being, along with *Brahman*'s being, may be spoken. Explicit speaking of its non-existence is indirect recognition of its phenomenal existence. Here, again, it is unquestionable that phenomenal reality comes into being through speech. *Māyā* will last as long as *Brahman* can be spoken and the world will last as long as *māyā* will last. The world has the same power of endurance and the same degree of reality that empiricists are willing to ascribe to it. Accordingly, and to this extent, *māyāvāda* is even consistent with an empiricist view of the world. It is possible for Advāita Vedānta to accept the reality *of* the world although not reality *as* the world; this is a crucial difference from empiricism. *Brahman* stands over against the world, and *māyā* is the ground of the provisional distinction between the world and *Brahman*, all distinctions being provisional. Out of the distinctions surely arises *Brahman* as the real though it is not the ground of distinction but of non-distinction.

To treat *māyā* as illusion is to misunderstand it. Truly speaking, it is the cosmic condition of which illusion is the model. All descriptions of *māyā* are given through analogy of human illusory experiences but to identify the terms of analogy is to mistake its purpose. Śaṅkara is very emphatic about the factual reality of the things that are mistaken for something else. The rope that is seen as snake is the objective foundation of the illusion.[30] Likewise, to reverse it, the water that we see in a mirage is unreal but the water that we use is real.[31]

No word of explanation is necessary for omitting some of the more well known aspects of *māyāvāda*, for example that pertaining to name and form (*nāma-rūpa*), as the project undertaken here is not meant to be an exhaustive treatment. The purpose has been simply to bring out some points not often recognized.

30. *rajjur api sarvavikalpasyāspadabhūtā*, Śaṅkara's *Bhāṣya on Māṇḍūkya Kārikā*, 2.32; 3.29.

31. *sacca paramārthodakādi, asacca marīcyudakādi*, Śaṅkara's *Bhāṣya on Praśna Upaniṣad*, 4.5.

THREE

TRANSCENDENCE AND THE TRANSCENDENT : VIA THE DOCTRINES OF BRAHMAN AND ŚŪNYATĀ

The two concepts, *transcendence* and the *transcendent*, though formed terminologically from the same verb—one as abstract noun and the other as adjectival, concrete noun—are quite apart in their application in the present day. The first has become more widely acceptable than the second. The *transcendent* has been the repository of one dominant meaning, namely the *beyond*, standing for a higher reality than the visible world, and as such is very much under question today. This meaning has been inherited from traditional metaphysics of both rational and empirical varieties, and is now under assault along with it.

Traditionally, the concept of the transcendent has stood for the problematic of the higher, or ultimate, reality, which by definition is concealed from—and veiled by—the reality to which our ordinary consciousness has access, and the concept of transcendence has had no separate vogue. In modern thought, however, the situation has become different. One of our objectives in this essay is to find out what kind of light could be cast on the matter by examining it from an Indian perspective.

As is well-known, in Sanskrit the adjective *para* expresses the connotations of the beyond, the ultimate, and the other. Its superlative degree *parama* in combination with two nouns, *artha* (essence, meaning) and *satya* (reality, truth)—or even with the first alone—provides the technical expression for ultimate reality, i.e., *paramārtha* or *paramārtha-satya*. Interestingly enough, however, as we shall soon see in detail, the Sanskrit verb *tarati*, which is the equivalent of the verb 'to transcend', while it gives rise to an abstract noun *taraṇam* meaning transcendence, does not furnish an equivalent adjectival concrete noun corresponding to the *transcendent*. And yet the goal of transcendence in Indian tradition is to reach thc transcendent. We do see an indissoluble association despite the different origins of the respective terms.

In the modern West, while the *transcendent* is under eclipse as a result of the rejection of traditional metaphysics, *transcendence* continues to enjoy some importance because it has become part of some new ontologies of both existentialist and other kinds, and is even tolerated by analytical philosophy. The different situation in the Indian tradition, as exemplified by both the Vedāntic, *Brahman* doctrine and the Buddhist, *Śūnyatā* doctrine, will be shown in this essay. The existential path of *transcendence* (*taraṇam*) is pursued with a sense of complete concord with what the West has largely rejected in the older metaphysics of the *transcendent*.

However, under this framework, the objective of pursuing the problematic of ultimate reality for which the *transcendent* stands will be pursued further via comparison of (or rather contrast between) the Vedāntic doctrine of *Brahman* and the Buddhist doctrine of *Śūnyatā*, not inaccurately translated as the Void, each of which is described as ultimate reality, or *paramārtha-satya*, within the respective persuasions—and a great deal of confusion has prevailed on this matter. In deciding the matter the question ofthe logos will certainly be an issue for us.

The Eclipse of the Transcendent in Modern Thought

The transcendent as an object of philosophic question has gone under eclipse in modern thought. In spite of that, it can still be reasonably maintained that inasmuch as it is the problematic of ultimate reality, it will remain—and in the long run the human mind cannot escape the question of ultimate reality.

Modern thought's disinterest in the transcendent has, no doubt, stemmed from several causes. In philosophy itself its sources are to be found in many and sundry places, but we must make special note of an epoch-making departure made by one of the mordern age's greatest thinkers, Immanuel Kant, who in dealing with the problematic underlying the thought about reality, left a double-barrelled legacy with regard to the question of the transcendent. Indeed Kant wrestled with that question as a genuine problematic the way no one has done in modern times, but also sought to resolve it through the critical philosophy. It is well-known that he rejected through criticism the claimed capacity of pure reason to obtain knowledge of the real as such. It is also well-known that in doing so his hope was to pave the way for that which is ultimately real, i.e. the eternal, to be held as the unconditional reference for moral life, on the one hand, and as the object of faith on the other. So the critical philosophy itself was designed to be a genuine means of achieving moral perfection as well as true reverence and faith. This was Kant's higher objective. On the other hand, insofar as what we can theoretically know was felt to be limited to mere appearances,[1] critical philosophy and the future metaphysics for which it sought to lay the foundation were to serve the goals that were in harmony with the positive sciences.

Kant had no doubt that this method alone would "sever the roots of materialism, fatalism, atheism, free-thinking, fanaticism, and superstition."[2] He argued that appearance and reality must be held apart through critical reason because unlike it, speculative reason, to the contrary, cherishing "pretensions to transcendent insights", transgressed the boundary between appearance and reality, thus actually getting in the way of critical reason being developed in regard to God, freedom and immortality.[3]

These are the ways in which Kant approached the problematic of reality, which led him "to deny knowledge in order to make room for faith."[4] By faith he certainly meant faith in the eternal. That this represents a central part of Kant's philosophical legacy cannot be denied and here he reveals himself as an ultimately concerned protestant thinker. The way this new legacy worked in subsequent European religious thought, especially through the existentialism of Kierkegaard is too huge a matter to be considered here.

By rejecting "transcendent insights" as a possibility of reason Kant closed the high road of metaphysics to the problematic

1. Cf. *Critique of Pure Reason*, translated by Norman Kemp Smith, New York, St. Martin's Press, 1965, p. 29.

2. *Ibid.*, p. 32

3. *Ibid.*, p. 29.

4. *Loc. cit.*

underlying thought about ultimate reality. That high road was henceforth to be used only for other investigations, namely those which participate in science, while an alternative route, that of faith (and so to say of ultimate concern), which linked the human being with the eternal, was opened, nonetheless in continued deference to metaphysics, to be pursued as "religion within the bounds of reason alone." It was not long before "religion" was replaced by immanentist structures of *human* ends and means within the same "bounds of reason". Such became the character of new metaphysics. The transcendent came to be no longer the problematic of ultimate reality because no difference remained even between appearance and reality so as to justify any such thing. No doubt, even within what may have been, under traditional metaphysics, called "immanentist" structures of today, there has still remained some scope for considering what was likewise called "transcendent" reality through the new, moral and existential channels. In the profoundest expressions of immanentism transcendence, although not *the* transcendent, became acceptable, mainly as the deepest dimension to which these essentially, immanently conceived problems can be pushed. Further, notions like the Being of being and the essence of time seem even to revolutionize the concept of transcendence and with it the concept of immanence too.

But side by side with that we find today, partly as the result of the spill-over of some of today's metaphysics into the general fields of intellectual life and partly due to other causes, a certain understandable scepticism in common thinking as well towards things transcendent. At the same time we find a less understandable willingness to substitute in their place certain make-believe structures of ends and means, mixing up some real problems with many more artificial ones, and mixing up solutions too in like fashion. Strangely enough, these structures are also sustained through speculation. Finite cognitive and value judgements keep on making their appearances, putting forth decisive claims to certainty. Freedom in the form of particular kinds of liberation takes its place along with all kinds of temporal and historical immediacies which are zealously and sometimes even fanatically sought after.

The Concepts of Transcendence and the Transcendent, and the Structural Orientation of Consciousness

The transcendent has been described above as the word that expresses the problematic of reality. The term 'transcend' (*trans*-cend) means to pass beyond, to go across, to cross over, to overcome. Its Sanskrit equivalent is *tarati* (he, she, it passes beyond, etc.), from which is formed the noun *taraṇam*. Pursuing the word will be instructive, and so let us look at the original context in which it occurred.

For this purpose let us adopt a variation of the method called "critical phenomenology", which Paul Tillich has hinted at, although did not seem to have developed. We can agree with Tillich that it "is the method best fitted to supply normative descriptions of spiritual (and also Spiritual) meanings."[5] Tillich's preference for it over against "pure" phenomenology is also acceptable because unlike the latter it unites what he calls "an intuitive-descriptive element with an existential-critical element".

The realm in which we apply this method is consciousness (as befits all phenomenology). The application promises to deliver us the truth *that transcendence is the essential structural orientation of consciousness*. But we will use the word 'consciousness' in the double sense which its Sanskrit equivalent, *cit*, warrants, that is to say, as understood in the everyday, empirical parlance as well as extraordinarily in a mystical sense. [Tillich's application of the method, however, in line with phenomenologies of mysticism, seems to omit ordinary consciousness.][6] Accordingly, when we stipulate in advance that transcendence is the essential structural orientation of consciousness, the analysis will have to be both vertical and horizontal, although the two are at least in the primary literatures from which we seek to draw, utterly inseparable.

Consciousness, that is, ordinary, everyday consciousness, can be shown both intuitively-descriptively and existentially-critically as what by its intrinsic nature seeks completion of itself by the grasp of reality as a whole, like water seeking its own level, and

5. Paul Tillich, *Systematic Theology*, Vol. I, Chicago, University of Chicago Press, 1951, pp. 196-8.

6. Cf. *Ibid.*, pp. 108 ff.

yet shrinks from it. Thus consciousness (*cit*) leads to thinking and thoughtfulness (*cintā*). This is where at least the phenomenal origin of the idea of transcendence lies. *Through critical phenomenology it can be found in consciousness just as truly today as it can be discovered in the earliest of our religio-philosophical literatures.*

In consciousness's movement towards reality, self-centredly no doubt, although existentially too, it comes up against a barrier to be crossed, which it also finds it cannot cross. It wants to come to terms with life as given and with death itself and with the mystery of the whole and wants to make sense of existence. It soon finds that it cannot do these things because there is a barrier set between itself and whatever it is that is *ultimately* real. What it seeks to grasp is engulfed in an abyss. This encounter is the presupposition of transcendence (*taraṇam*). Perhaps the encounter with the barrier merely awakens the idea of transcendence from its somnolence. But they clearly function together as they are but two sides of what is but one and the same.

Where ordinary consciousness cannot speak for itself great texts of our primary literature take over the speaking. The great texts can do so because they *are* the language of discovered "mystery" (Sanskrit, *guhyam*, hidden in a cave, or *rahasyam*, secret). These texts awaken in us the sense of the great mystery that consciousness hides in itself, veiled over by everyday activities. It is thus revealed to us that transcendence is the essential structural orientation of consciousness.

Ordinarily, empirical consciousness carries the idea lightly, not giving much thought to it nor being thoughtfully occupied with it. But as expressed through the primary texts of our literatures we see the idea in action. There we see consciousness engaged in heaving itself across the abyss. In that act the abyss too becomes more vividly manifest than ordinarily. In trying to cross over, we learn better what it is we have to cross over, and consciousness is stretched with it. There the tremendum (Sanskrit, *bhayam*, *mahad bhayam*, meaning dread, great dread) of the abyss is unfolded to consciousness. What is it *to* which consciousness heaves itself over the abyss ? That is the "far shore" or "the beyond", which we call *the transcendent*. The "far shore" is, certainly from consciousness's own side, to be primarily understood as a ground or a dimension, or as the Indian tradition calls it the "highest dimension" (*paramaṁ padam*).[7] So, then, the transcendent is to be understood as the dimension to which consciousness is structurally oriented, and in understanding this with clarity the uniting of "the intuitive-descriptive and existential-critical elements" is absolutely indispensable. Reciprocally, it is the method which this understanding spontaneously generates. There is no other, because the understanding is indistinguishable from that which is understood even as, in the words of the *Maitrī Upaniṣad*, "water cannot be distinguished in water, fire in fire, space in space."[8]

Now, let us assume that following this rule, one may become convinced that the transcendent is that to which consciousness is structurally oriented. But we also need clues to its character, in order to know what it is. Otherwise, it will remain merely an appendage or just a supplementary to the idea of transcendence and may be nothing in itself. Actually, this interpretation is totally acceptable to many who will agree that the transcendent is a valid idea, as they find nothing that is different from the abyss which can supply a clue. To them the transcendent always remains eternally undefined and elusive, as it can be taken in no other way than as the abyss itself turned into an absolute, and hence the Void.

Nevertheless, the view that the transcendent is the Void itself, is not taken lightly or facilely by those who take it, for if properly grasped it can be the object of ultimate spiritual concern and hence the saving truth as powerfully demonstrated by Buddhism, to cite but the most conspicuous example. The Buddhists see all things, including consciousness itself as being of the nature of flux (*saṁtāna*). And there is no place other than the whirling flux to survey it from.

Others, however, chiefly the Vedāntists, find substantial clues to the nature of the transcendent, which itself is understood as substantial. According to Vedānta, consciousness's orientation

7. *Maitrī Upaniṣad*, 6. 34; *Dhammapada*, 385; etc., etc.

8. *āpam āpo 'gnir agnau vā vyomni vyoma na lakṣayet*, *Maitrī Upaniṣad*, 6.34.10

to the transcendent itself reveals the transcendent as an eternal and unchanging entity. Consciousness is oriented as it is because its essence is the self (*ātman*) that struggles to free itself from the bondage of phenomena. Therefore, in the very orientation of consciousness the self serves as its own bridge leading to the "far shore" or the ground beyond the abyss. In fact, the far shore, consciousness, the bridge (i.e., the self) and the abyss itself all get welded into one homogeneous and self-identical reality. The *Chāndogya Upaniṣad* has a striking simile to express this truth. It says, "Now this self (*ātman*) is the bridge (*setuḥ*), which is also the barrier (*vidhṛtiḥ*), that keeps these worlds apart. Over that bridge day and night do not cross (*na tarataḥ*), nor old age, nor sorrow, nor good and evil deed. All evils turn back from it for the world of *Brahman* is free from evil."[9] Commentators clearly show that the terms 'day and night', 'death', 'sorrow' and 'evil' stand for temporality, flux and phenomenality (*saṁsāra*). According to Vedānta, although in the way of our studying the path of consciousness's structural orientation, the idea of the transcendent emerges in the context of grasping the nature of the orientation, that is to say, the idea of *transcendence*, in reality it is earlier and is not predicated on consciousness at all. The transcendent is held to be the ground which accounts for the particular behaviour of consciousness, which is not self-accounting nor explicable in terms of the abyss it encounters.

In Buddhism, on the contrary, transcendence that is the structural orientation of consciousness, has no ground other than what it seeks to cross over, on which is predicated the notion of what is crossed over *to*, although, nevertheless, as an existential, religious system it does have an infinite spiritual interest in the latter. In the eyes of Vedānta it is this interest that makes Buddhism self-contradictory ontologically—and it is not the case, as often supposed, that Buddhism has no ontology at all. However, a system which is ontologically self-contradictory need by no means be so spiritually. Had it not been for this self-contradiction the antinomies of reason which Buddhism also faced in its own way, would have remained purely at the formal

9. *Chāndogya Upaniṣad*, 8.4.1.

level. On the contrary, these antinomies of reason became existential "unresolvables" (*avyākṛtavastūni*), rather than remain at the formal level. Thus for instance, the contradiction in the nature of time was seen as the existential contradiction arising from the attempt to resolve the problem of eternity in time, unsteady and constructed of fleeting moments as it is, not having, as in Vedānta, an ontology of eternity in which to solve the problem of time. The same is true of immortality. The same is true of the soul.

But such a fate does not mean that thought must turn away from its forward course or abandon the route of consciousness's orientation to the transcendent. For, Buddhism as an existential system has demonstrated that, far from returning with a feeling of defeat to consciousness's empirical ground thenceforth to forget all about the onward journey, thought can stretch itself to the dimensions of an impossible task, namely, to make the abyss 'devoid of determinate characteristics' (*niḥsvabhāva*) itself serve the cause of transcendence, thus to be held under its inescapable power and spell. Where it is understood clearly and deeply, as done by the Buddhist thinkers, that the urge to transcend does not come from a deliberate choice on man's part, it is self-evident that the impossible alone must be attempted. This course no doubt marks the greatest courage, not lesser than the courage to be.

These preliminary remarks must bring us to a point from where we must undertake a more sustained investigation of transcendent *Brahman* and transcendent *Śūnyatā*, the Void. But fittingly, we shall turn to *Brahman* first.

Transcendent Brahman

In considering the transcendent Vedānta rejects the literal meaning of the verb 'to transcend'. Therefore the philology of the word 'transcendent' is held as irrelevant to grapsing *the transcendent :* the emphasis here is that what is grasped is already at hand and is a definite and concrete ground. This problem is treated in a passage in Śaṅkara's celebrated *Commentary on the Brahma Sūtra.*[10] That very simile of the bridge in

10. Śaṅkara, *Commentary on the Brahma-Sūtra*, 3.2.31-37.

the *Chāndogya Upaniṣad* is cited there. The question is raised as to what is to be understood by 'the transcendent' (here the word used is *para*). Śaṅkara pits a revolutionized meaning over against the conventional, philological one. The hypothetical objectors to whom he replies had assumed that "in view of the accepted meaning of the word 'transcend' " (*taratiśabdaprayogāt*), there can be no bridge that connects with the transcendent but that it must always lie unattainably far beyond in the literal sense.[11] Śaṅkara shows that even in ordinary usage, in some cases 'to transcend' does not mean 'to go beyond indefinitely', but 'to reach'.[12] 'To reach' means to 'grasp entirely' just as when we speak of a student having completely learnt grammar (*yathā vyākaraṇam tīrṇa iti prāpta ityucyate*). Here transcendence does not mean going even further beyond (*na atikrāntaḥ*). The confusion due to literalist philology is now ended. 'To transcend' (*tarati*) is the same as 'to reach', 'to attain', (*āpnoti, or prāpnoti*). The term *āpnoti*, with or without the prefix *pra*, is a verb used with a very strong sense, conveying the meaning of total identity of the attainer and the attained (or the grasper and the grasped). The gulf between them is obliterated.

This understanding revolutionizes the definition of the transcendent as that to which consciousness is structurally oriented. The transcendent comes first and it is its pull that accounts for consciousness's orientation, which is no longer predicated on the barrier it encounters nor on the way consciousness inherently and by itself is.

The beyond does not remain for ever elusive and indefinite but is grasped as the ground close at hand, that upon which we stand. Standing upon it we can ponder the great gulf that has separated it from the consciousness that still seeks to overcome it. From the ground thus grasped the gulf too can be grasped and reduced to zero distance. The gulf so measured is called *māyā*, from the root *mā*, meaning 'to measure'. [The concept permits this interpretation.] How is the measuring done ? It is done by using the one scale namely

11. *setum tīrtvā iti ca taratiśabdaprayogāt. yathā laukikaṁ setuṁ tīrtvā jāṅgalam asetuṁ prāpnoti, evam ātmānaṁ setuṁ tīrtvā anātmānam asetuṁ prāpnoti iti gamyate, op. cit.*, 3.2.31.

12. *tarater atikramāsambhavāt prāpnoti artha eva vartate, op. cit.*, 3.2.32.

the self (*ātman*), which alone is adequate to span a seemingly infinite distance. The absconding of the self from itself through non-knowledge, or *avidyā*, is the mother phenomenon of all infinite distances. Yet this is a metaphor and upon this metaphor are based all notions of temporal and spatial infinity and all antinomies of reason. And how easily our thought gets bogged down on these and all related unresolvables and how it labours and is heavily laden under their yoke !

The transcendent is the ground which is also close at hand. It alone furnishes the certainty by which it can be spoken. If it is not already known, then it must not be spoken. The pharse 'already known' is most important. That in itself answers a whole lot of questions raised about so-called 'transcendent insights'. 'Already known' stresses the fact that the knowledge is that which has come the way it has come and no other way, and that, incidentally, should be part of the proper definition of 'the holy' insofar as it has reference to knowledge.

If, on the contrary, we were to declare some other kind of knowledge of that which is beyond, following in Kant's words, "the common fate of human reason to complete its speculative structures as speedily as may be and only afterwards to inquire whether the foundations are reliable",[13] then we will be guilty of gross dogmatism. This is the temptation to which those who adopt the literal meaning of the word 'transcend' (*tarati*) fall. According to them, "the beyond" must always remain far off and yet they declare that "transcendent insights" are relevant to it. This is the kind of thinking that gave speculation a bad name. Śaṅkara criticizes it as 'groundless speculation' (*aprasiddha-kalpanā*), and he pronounces it 'to be not reasonable' (*na etat nyāyyam*).[14] However, one must not condemn speculation as such, for as was discovered after the first flush of critical thought, without it philosophy itself is not possible. There are, no doubt, good and bad speculations, although, as always, good things may sometimes become bad while bad things never become good.

13. Kant, *op. cit.*, p. 47.
14. Śaṅkara, *Commentary on the Brahma-Sūtra*, 3.2.32.

The ground beyond, already close at hand, is that in which everything takes place, the seeking, the rise of the sense of the abyss and the urge to transcend. It is what is called *Brahman*. Here we are given the real meaning of the transcendent as that which comprehends and encompasses what otherwise remains uncomprehended and unencompassed. But because it is already at hand the word 'reach' or 'attain' is used metaphorically in the same manner in which the idea of the self absconding from itself is used. But "metaphor" must be taken seriously, as, structurally, it coincides with consciousness itself, and has the same orientation to the transcendent. Metaphor is the speech proper to consciousness understood the way we have outlined it.

Brahman and the Question of Being and Knowledge

Transcendent *Brahman* clearly offers a new foundation for considering philosophy's two most vexing questions, i.e., those posed by the verbs 'is' and 'is not', and 'to know'. It will not be henceforth legitimate to pursue the meanings of these verbs to some so-called ontological foundations of their own. *Brahman* has already taken us beyond *whatever* meanings we may independently arrive at for the verbs 'to be' and 'to be not'. We ourselves have no logic by which to come to a point where we can decisively say that ultimate reality is what is and not what is not, or for that matter, to the contrary. The logos operative here comes wholly from *Brahman*, and that presents us with a radical situation expressed in this way : if it is the case that ultimate reality may be either being or non-being, then it is only Being. The conditional part is formulated according to our logic but the consequent is according to the logos that resides in transcendent *Brahman*. Otherwise, we will have only a meaningless tautology such as "if it is either being or non-being then it is either being or non-being". But that is not the case. Now substitute 'God' for *Brahman* and we get the same proposition. Thus, if God can be said to exist or not exist then he can only be said to exist. This, one should think, is the ontological ground for the existential leap of faith which, therefore, is not ungrounded. That by which this is so must be called the principle of the annullment of the alternative to Being, and it belongs only to the transcendent. However, by no means can it be generalized in the form, "if *something* is either being or non-being then it is only being". That kind of complete ungeneralizability is what shows forth as the uniqueness of the logos of the transcendent.

The choice of Being over against non-being was expressed by the *Chāndogya Upaniṣad,* when it posed this question long ago and then declared: "How could Being come from non-being? But, my dear, this was Being itself in the beginning, one only without a second."[15] In our ordinary thinking, being is met by its other, namely non-being. Where do we find being that is not so met by its opposite? It is obtained in *Brahman,* which is only Being, hence said to be one without a second. Interpreting this Upaniṣadic statement, Śaṅkara declares that *Brahman* is being alone (*satkevala*) and it responds only to the notional word 'being' (*sacchabda-buddhi-mātra-gamyam eva*).[16]

However, we do not know Being (in the sense of *Brahman*) through analogies of being. In that respect it always remains hidden. But it comes to us in the self-revelation of *Brahman* through the logos (*vāk, śabda*) that belongs to *Brahman.* Nevertheless, analogy there is, that is, between the self-revelation of *Brahman* and the way things present (reveal) themselves to us. The determining notion is self-luminosity. *Brahman* is immediate to us through its own self-shining, analogous to the self-presentation of things by the light of their own presence. This ideal is fundamental to Vedānta. Citsukha, a late medieval writer, has a classic formulation for this: "although not known, it (*Brahman*) is the only entity that is fit to be called immediate (to us) as in the case of a pot sitting out there."[17] We may call this the "analogy of revelation" (*analogia revelationis*), which may very well be what underlies the "analogy of being" (*analogia entis*). The examples of seen things (*dṛṣṭānta*) [as analogies of revelation], Śaṅkara observes, are necessary, for without them [the highest secrets] "are not known even to the gods" (*devairapi durjñeyatvam*).[18] The source of analogical knowledge is, however, the logos, not our conceptions.

15. *Chāndogya Upaniṣad,* 6.2.2.

16. Śaṅkara, *Commentary on the Chāndogya Upaniṣad,* 6.2.1, 2.

17. *avedyatve sati aparokṣavyavahārayogyatvaṁ...yannaivaṁ tannaivaṁ yathā ghaṭa,* Citsukha, *Tattvapradīpikā,* Ch. 1.

18. Śaṅkara, *Commentary on the Kena Upaniṣad,* 4.4.

On the ground of revelation the question whether we can know the ultimately real is already answered. *Brahman* is what we know but do not know that we know. Therefore, the real questions are : "How is it that we do not know that which is alone fit to be called immediate to us ? Is it because the self-shining light works for us as obscuring and concealing darkness ?"

Here one must consider what is to be understood by "thinking" ? Now do even these questions, although the only real ones, necessarily mark out the domain of thinking to the end that answers must be found for them ? Or rather, are they merely for the purpose of rousing thinking so that it may reach a destiny not at all determined by them ? For Vedānta it is clearly the latter. That is the reason why it views knowledge, in the sense of gnosis (*jñāna*), to be the true end to which thinking is directed. The directing of thinking to gnosis is the "function" of the logos and it is exactly the same as the revealing. Thus Vedānta does not believe that thinking can ever be the subject-matter of thinking except as a secondary "activity".

Thinking as a secondary "activity" pertains to the proposition, "the world is what we do not know but *think* that we know". The world (Sanskrit, *iagat*, etymologically, that which is of the nature of movement), is metaphysically speaking, a constant and unsteady shifting between two false poles of "is" and "is not". Because ordinarily, it serves as the ground of thinking especially in respect of the question of being, it calls for critical investigation. And, therefore, the thinking based on it is similarly to be investigated, but in itself is not directed to gnosis.

Transcendent Void, and the Questions of Being and Non-Being and Knowledge

Now having briefly set forth the view of the transcendent in terms of the Vedāntic doctrine of *Brahman*, let us take a look at the Buddhist doctrine of *Śūnyatā* in the same manner. *Śūnyatā*, the Void, let us make clear again, represents an ultimately concerned effort to grasp the meaning of the transcendent as underlying the thought about reality. In this connection we repeat an earlier statement : "Buddhism has convincingly demonstrated that, far from turning back to consciousness's empirical ground with a sense of defeat, thought can actually be stretched to the dimensions of an impossible task, namely to make the abyss devoid of determinate characteristics (*niḥsvabhāva*) itself serve the cause of transcendence, thus to hold it under its power and spell."

Whatever is said about the abyss of indeterminateness can also be said about the transcendent, and what is over and above that can never be said, thought or imagined, nay, *must not* be said, thought or imagined, lest one fall into the trap of views (*dṛṣṭi*), all of which are mutually falsifiable and hence falsifiable all together. This accounts for the celebrated silence of Buddha on the question of the transcendent when urged to describe it otherwise than in terms of the indeterminate abyss of our experience. It is entirely possible that the silence was a symbolic recognition of the fact that there is more to the transcendent than the abyss absolutized as the Void. But the express teachings of Buddha and his followers urge us to turn our thought to the Void and not to what may be even beyond it. All existential and salvific knowledge comes from meditating on the Void. And what one does not and cannot know one must not speak about, as it obviously does not contribute to salvation (*nirvāṇa*). Therefore, the Void itself must be taken as the transcendent by the test that it is that which contributes to salvation. Nāgārjuna, the greatest of the Buddhist thinkers, declares, "there is no non-Void entity (*aśūnyodharmaḥ*)."[19] Other great Buddhist writers like Āryadeva and Prajñākaramati concur. The latter adds that knowledge of the Void is the only thing that profits the soul, leaving no need for considering a self-existent reality (beyond it).[20] At the same time it would be, for us, a mistake to conclude that the Buddhist thinkers were negative towards there actually being something beyond even the Void. They were

19. *aśūnyo hi dharmaḥ kaścinna vidyate*, Nāgārjuna, *Mādhyamikakārikā*, 24.19.

20. *hetupratyaya-sāmagrīṁ pratītya jātasya parāyattātmalābhasya pratibimbasyeva kutaḥ sasvabhāvatā*, from *Bodhicaryāvatāra Pañcikā of Prajñākaramati*, quoted by T. R. V. Murti in *The Central Philosophy of Buddhism*, London. George Allen & Unwin, 1960, p. 229 fn.

neither negative nor positive. They were no more than inculcating the salvific self-sufficiency of the Void with regard to the existential question, "What is ultimately real ?"

If the absolutized abyss or the Void itself serves as the transcendent there arises no question of any bridge such as the *ātman* spanning it, because it is itself self-comprehending and all-encompassing. Actually, when Buddhism says that there is no *ātman* this is what it really means. As for the questioning self, the soul to be saved, it somehow remains, primarily as the focal point of all the unresolvables. As their bearer, its salvation is a legitimate concern.

It is clear that in a system such as this there is no place for the logos, at least as explicitly set forth by Vedānta, in conjunction with transcendent *Brahman*. Therefore, it is thrown into thought without the logos. It need not be expressly said that in our present context of discourse that thought, whatever it is, must not be confused with speculation. As for critical reason, although an important accessory to thought, it is not itself thought. We have to understand this in the context of the common tradition of which Buddhism and Vedānta are the two most important branches : accordingly, thought means meditation (*dhyāna*).

There can be an interpretation of meditation which accords with "pure" thought for two reasons, negative and positive, respectively. (1) Negatively, its character of independence of anything else, either formal or material, and of any kind of data-support or logistical support. (2) Positively, using Heidegger's definition of Socrates as the purest thinker of the West, its character of putting oneself in the "draft" or "current" of "what addresses itself to thought."[21] While we do not turn attention to the differences in Heidegger's interpretation of pure thought and *dhyāna* as pure thought, let us profit by learning the positive truth common to both. That is what is well expressed by the idea of "putting oneself in the draft or current" of "what addresses itself to thought". It is just that much that we need and will take. As for what it is that addresses itself to

21. Cf. Martin Heidegger, *What is Called Thinking* ? translated by J. Glenn Gray, New York, Harper, 1954, p. 17.

thought in respect of Buddhism and Vedānta the answer can already be anticipated. For Buddhism it is the reality of the Void; for Vedānta it is the logos that has its source in *Brahman*, taking up residence in thought thus to direct it to gnosis.

Accordingly then, Buddhism deals with being and non-being and with knowledge in terms of the Void. So then, "if the transcendent is either being or non-being", then what is the consequent ? Not "being", not "non-being" (both precluded) but "both being and non-being" (regarded as an absurd conclusion), or "neither being nor non-being" (also regarded as an absurd conclusion). In this way the full frame of the four-cornered dialectic is expressed as "is", "is not", "both is and is not" and "neither is nor is not". These are the four possible views (*dṛṣṭi*). Hence the dialectic develops in this manner because there is no annullment to the alternative to Being, which would not be possible without the logos that resides in the transcendent as understood by Vedānta, but develops freely, and even absurdly in a calculated way. The very absurdity of it is intended to challenge logic, and without the logos, logic has no ground to stand on. That this frame is a complete expression of the foundation of the conditional, i.e., "if the transcendent is either being or non-being" is stated by Nāgārjuna's greatest commentator, Candrakīrti, who writes "the four-cornered frame is based on the two views (of being and non-being)."[22] The classic formulation is given by Nāgārjuna in the following stanza in an almost algebraic fashion :

> All is suchness, not-suchness, both suchness and
> non-suchness
> Neither not-suchness nor suchness, that is the
> teaching of the Buddha.[23]

The same four-cornered frame can be approached in another manner, i.e., as an exhaustive list of the four ways in which we

22. *dṛṣṭidvayopādānam upalakṣaṇārthaṁ catasras tu etā dṛṣṭayaḥ* Candrakīrti, *Prasannapadā* (*Commentary on Mādhyamika-kārikā*), 27.2.

23. *sarvaṁ tathyaṁ na vā tathyaṁ tathyam cātathyam eva ca naivātathyaṁ naiva tathyaṁ etat buddānuśāsanam, Mādhyamikakārikā,* 18.8. *Note* : This kind of revelation of Reality is truth and hence "commandment" (*anuśāsanam*).

view the transcendent : as like, unlike, both partially like and partially unlike, and as neither like nor unlike (that is to say in terms of an otherness which totally defies the categories of similarity and dissimilarity to) what we know as being. Surely, we can draw instances from the history of metaphysics, both Eastern and Western, to exemplify all these four angles or point-limits (*koṭi*) of views. The view based on analogy (like what we know), the view based on the irrational principle as also the *via negativa* (unlike what we know), the view based on the dialectics of becoming (like and unlike what we know), and the view based on the final limit situation, or a possible radical dialectic (neither like nor unlike what we know) have all been well represented in metaphysics. Buddhism argues that the voiding of the whole frame *in toto* through criticism goes hand in hand with meditation on the Void.

Nowadays, among certain scholars there is a tendency to regard the four-cornered frame as a formal criticism of views and also to compare it with the way Kant dealt with the antinomies of reason by means of the transcendental deduction of its categories, which is by taking them to their limits. There is, no doubt, a certain formal similarity, which, however, must not be made too much of. In Buddhism, the four-cornered frame is simply the clinical bed in which the unresolvable questions are laid for examination and through diagnosis confirmed that they are unresolvable. The question is, where is the source from which they come ? The answer is, from consciousness by virtue of its structural orientation to the transcendent, implicit in which is the encounter with the abyss. Therefore, they come as existential signals. They are not just theoretical viewpoints. The abiding questions of metaphysics, namely, those about ultimate reality and eternity become the subjects of infinite brooding. But the contradiction of having to resolve the problematic of ultimate reality in terms of the flux, that of eternity in terms of time are felt as inescapable. Therefore, everything is absorbed into the Void (which is not just Nothing). The Void is the transcendent and is what is ultimately real, certainly for salvific purposes. Finally, although here there is a refusal of the logos there is still an infinitely powerful spiritual adventure, not to say an adventure of thought, that takes one to the farthest limits that one can go to without the logos. In this respect it does not lack authenticity. And it is fully the equal of Vedānta in representing in its completeness a powerful spirituality and a challenging approach to Reality.

Concluding Remarks

Now, we have all along tried to let transcendent *Brahman* and transcendent Void be seen as they are, as the two expressions of ultimate reality in the two most important branches of a common tradition. And how interesting it is that at times they should appear to be setting forth the same vision, and absolutely contrary visions at other times ! Scholars have been swayed to one side or the other by this fact. But the truth can be understood only by diving deep below the surface. And only so can these two approaches to the transcendent be of benefit to our contemporary metaphysical task.

Using the transcendent as the problematic of Ultimate reality, as we have done, a typological distinction as between *Brahman* and *Śūnyatā* becomes unavoidable. And it cannot be swept under the fact that the common term *paramārtha satya* is used for both. Which of them has handled the problematic more effectively and coherently ? That is a question which can not be avoided. The answer, however, can now be made explicity by employing this decisive criterion : whichever of them has fully accounted for the aspects of the problematic most crucial to the other and yet has surpassed it, is qualified to be considered the more effective and coherent. With this criterion we can see that transcendent *Brahman*, by completely comprehending the abyss, has removed the possibility of the abyss being absolutized as the transcendent Void and hence surpassed it. On the other hand, it has been maintained by the Buddhist philosophers that the Void is the dispersing (though not the grasping) of that, namely, being, of which they consider *Brahman* to be the absolutization. And so according to them such absolutization has to be inauthentic. The problem here is that they sought to disperse what they ought to have grasped.

The reason for doing this lies in the way they approach being, and with it all similar matters like eternity and the soul. They see nothing that is not of the nature of the Void. When they approach being in order to grasp it they see the equal claim also of its other, namely non-being, that counters it, and thus they are led on to the four point-limits, which only serve to disperse being and ultimately to disperse themselves through their own relentless self-application.

Transcendent *Brahman* is the complete comprehension of the abyss, which means also that it is the grasp of being. But the grasp of being is not accomplished within the abyss, for already the abyss itself has been comprehended. And the grasp of being is nothing other than the annullment of the alternative to Being, and such annullment is the nature of transcendent *Brahman*. The possibility of reaching a knowledge of Being comes only via the logos, which has its source in *Brahman*.

It is the clearest implication of transcendent *Brahman* that this knowledge (gnosis) is what is already there. Our efforts to know it, which is what metaphysics is, or in a larger sense, what philosophy as a whole is, is no more than clarifying this supreme truth to ourselves, or more appropriately, removing the veil of darkness that obscures it from our view. The same logos which reveals gnosis as itself the nature of the disposition of ultimate reality to us also directs our thinking to it. This is the ground of absolute certainty and all other certainties are but a flash of it. And it frees metaphysics and makes it a joyful task.

Transcendent *Brahman* is not only Ultimate Reality in the sense of knowledge but also in the salvific sense, and the two are by no means to be held separately. The difference from Buddhism in this respect is worthy of note. It is seldom realized that in Buddhist philosophy there is difficulty in working out a clear internal coherence between the Void as ultimate reality and a salvific absolute, *nirvāṇa*, which is sometimes spoken of in terms identical with the Void and sometimes in different terms. This salvific absolute of *nirvāṇa* is often described in positive terms as perfectly blissful reality beyond all anxiety, beyond the flux. It is called the goal.

Buddha himself is reported to have said, "There is, O monks, a not-born, a not-become, a not-created, a not-formed. If there were not this not-born, not-become, not-created, not-formed there would be no escape, no way out of this phenomenal bondage".[24] Metaphysically, however, can this salvific absolute be said to be the same as the Void or not said to be the same ? Surely, in affirming the reality of *nirvāṇa* there is acknowledgement of *gnosis*, a fact well enough adumbrated in Buddhist mysticism as *prajñā-pāramitā* (transcendent knowledge). But there is the insuperable problem of attaching *gnosis* to the Void. The Void is a *that* but is it a *what* ? That is where the problem lies.

In the last analysis, it seems mysticism could get away with a *that* and shirk the question of a *what*. But we must be able to conduct thought outside mysticism too. It is in this respect that the transcendent *Brahman* of Vedānta shows its greater strength in comparison with its Buddhist counter-part, a strength which derives from the adherence to the logos, i.e., as *vāk*, or *śabda*, which makes all our thinking cohere with our experience, mystical as well as other, by reason of its coherence with its ground which is gnosis itself understood ontologically. Buddhist idealism, however, resorts solely to dialectics, the more revolutionary part of it being negative in character, which of course, will be effective as long as we have some given structure (paradoxically enough, in the last resort unrecognizedly logos-based) existing merely for the purpose of being demolished. But the positive part of the dialectics will have to merge with mystical gnosis, if not with some *positivist*, substitute, as nowadays attempted by modern would-be Buddhists. Fortunately, however, genuine Buddhist mysticism continues as a possibility, even at the pain of not raising the question of coherence, that is to say of the logos. And it is good as far as it goes.

24. Cf. *Udāna*, 8.1.

Four

THE NOTION OF AVIDYĀ ("IGNORANCE") IN VEDĀNTA

The notion of *avidyā*, "ignorance" (better translated, "agnosis"), has a very important vogue in the Vedāntic system, one that is more crucial and central than in other Indian systems. This fact is indeed well-known and is not a novel piece of information. That it goes hand in hand with the notion of *māyā*, from which in many ways it is hardly distinguishable, is also well-known. The important question is, what is its precise nature? When that question is answered, its distinction from *māyā* (not so much in the resultant metaphysical function performed as in respect of genesis and formation) will automatically become clear. However, to show how it is different from, or the same as, *māyā* is not the purport of the essay but merely to understand it for itself.

To begin with, in order to achieve a preliminary understanding of the notion of *avidyā* in Vedānta, it would be useful to compare it with the Greek approach to ignorance. Comparing the two with each other is useful because the framework in which the problem was dealt with in both traditions was the logos, but no doubt differently conceived.

For the Greeks the logos ultimately reflected itself in man's reason. And reason is not a private faculty but a universal reality, which not only bound being to thinking but also joined everyone together. There was, of course, knowledge to be reached, which is the ultimate justification for the existence of philosophy. Heraclitus' cosmic oracles, Pythagoras' mathematical insights and Parmenides' wisdom pertaining to the logic of Being simply gave assurance as to this knowledge which in itself was, however, always elusive and held to be elusive. In front of it, the claim made by others to possess knowledge concretely stood eternally self-condemned, and was shown to be nothing but opinionated sense-delusion. The difference between the two was kept alive through dialectic, an activity made possible by the logos.

The Socratic interlude, which came as the new, great landmark in philosophy, as Plato depicts it, while still holding fast to the opposition between real knowledge (reserved only for the gods and eternally elusive from man's grasp) and sense-delusion or mere appearance, ushered in the revolutionary use of ignorance itself as a subject of man's genuine knowing. Plato's Socrates disclaimed himself to be a knower of anything but his own and everybody else's ignorance—a fundamentally new start in philosophy, valid not only historically but at all times. This of course entailed the rejection of opinionatedness, or *doxa,* on the one hand and the eternal but never fulfilled quest for the truth on the other hand, through that unique Socratic (and Platonic) variant of dialectic known as dialogue, which is a veritable innovation inasmuch as it made philosophy an activity of human persons in earnest discourse. But the Socratic knowledge of ignorance undoubtedly comprehended, by reason of the irrepressible *eros* and *orexis* of the soul, the seeds as well as the promise of transcendent knowing, in the way the gods themselves know. This involved a further step which marks Plato's own unique contribution to philosophy. But through it all the amazing manner in which Socrates had turned ignorance itself upside down so as to be the cornerstone of the new foundation for philosophy has persisted.

Now turning to the Indian world, although the counterpart of the notion of ignorance in that world, expressed by the word *avidyā* (or *ajñāna*), does often appear in all the systems, it is in Vedānta that it is given a fundamental place. In other *āstika* systems except Sāṁkhya and Yoga the treatment it receives, especially in Nyāya-Vaiśeṣika, is rather inane and superficial.

But in Vedānta, unlike in Greek philosophy, the counterpart of ignorance, namely *avidyā,* has to be taken in conjuction with transcendent knowledge (*vidyā,* or *jñāna*). In Vedānta the transcendent knowledge is held to be entirely within human capability to achieve, but under terms that it has itself set up. The achievement of it is the union with the Absolute, and nothing less than that is philosophy's goal, which in the words of Śaṅkara "is the vision of the ultimate truth wherein is no distinction between knowledge, what is to be known and the knower," (*jñāna-jñeya-jñātṛ-bhedarahitaṁ paramārthatattva-darśanam*).[1] Here *avidyā* is different from ignorance which is to be turned upside down and serve as the cornerstone of philosophy. Rather it is something to be overcome and destroyed together with its constructions. So then *avidyā* is always to be seen from the gnosis end, always pre-supposing gnosis.

Here the difference between the Greek-Western conception of the logos and the Indian conception of the same as *vāk,* or *śabda*, also comes to light. The Indian logos is two-fold, consisting of, on the one hand, the word (*śruti*, or Veda), mediating gnosis, and, on the other, the immanent power within the soul, which stirs the desire to know, leading man to the point where he can perceive what has been revealed, with clarity and intuitive certainty. The latter, no doubt, entails reflection upon human consciousness, in the conduct of which there is assured phenomenological freedom, even to the point of putting the revealed knowledge itself under *epoché*. The eventual goal of the process is the thorough co-ordination of revealed knowledge and phenomenological reflection, a task which the logos itself takes over. In this task the logos unfolds itself symphonically through the various *pramāṇas*, or so-called means of knowledge.

All this of course makes Vedānta appear more like theology than philosophy—then again theology not so much in the Greek sense, strangely enough, as in the Christian sense. The Greeks never reckoned with any kind of revelation in the sense of the word of God or *śruti*, inasmuch as, for them, transcendent knowledge was taken to be eternally elusive, but in a way that nonetheless unconditionally held on to the logos, thus calling out to man, who as philosopher responded by ever straining forward to reach reason through dialectic—and dialogue. [There is an intriguing parenthetical question in respect of theology and philosophy, which, however, we are not going to take up here, but will just mention: In due deference to Western spiritual-intellectual history, we ask, what is it that made possible the inflow of philosophy into Christianity in the Greek sense and the frequent

1. Śaṅkara's *Commentary on Māṇḍūkya-kārikā*, 4.1.

outflow of philosophy from Christianity both in the Greek and modern senses, in spite of Christianity's adherence to revelation? One wonders whether, paradoxically, it is due to Christianity's own essential side-stepping of gnosis, despite some vivid exceptions, and to its putting in its place a practical substitute like faith (*pistis*)—to follow here Kant's model of philosophizing—that it was able to condone pursuit of transcendent knowledge in whatever way it was open to particular philosophers, not excluding huge speculative undertakings, and yet obey its own immediate imperative of largely concentrating on matters of practical reason, even existential reason. By the same token, however, there is no need to draw the conclusion that the grounding of gnosis has to lead a system to philosophical stagnation and dead-end, open to further movement only through scholastic self-repetition or mysticism. The possibility of thought as such coming forth from gnosis is ever there to be discovered through projects that are both hermeneutical and dialectical (but under the logos).][2]

A Preliminary Understanding of Avidyā

The most striking feature of Vedānta's (as well as Sāṁkhya's and Yoga's) treatment of *avidyā* is to regard it as a real thing (*vastu satattvam*), in the sense of phenomenon at least, and as a positive thing (*yathā...sapatnaḥ*) despite its being characterized by negation.[3] This elementary understanding is subjected later to highly sophisticated qualifications in Vedānta, and Vedānta parts company with the other systems too.

The Advaitic doctrine of *avidyā* has three main aspects, as pertaining respectively to what may be called metaphysics, theory of knowledge and spiritual life, although they cannot be neatly distinguished from one another. Perhaps one may ask, ought

2. The author in his own way has made an effort to face up to the hermeneutical-dialectical task of laying out the path from gnosis to thought in his recent book *Gnosis and the Question of Thought in Vedānta* (The Hague, Martinus Nijhoff, Publishers, 1985).

3. Cf. *Vyāsa Bhāṣya on Yoga Sūtra*, 2.5. Compare also with the discussion of the negative compound (*nañ-samāsa*) in the grammatical work *Pātañjala Mahābhāṣya*, and in the ṭīkā on the *Vākyapadīya* concerning it.

not the theory of knowledge be central insofar as the word itself suggests that ? The answer is that it need not be so, because of the various uses of the word 'knowledge'. (Let us withhold the original Sanskrit word or words for 'knowledge' for a moment, and we will directly turn to it.) It is used metaphysically, cognitively and morally-spiritually. In any case, the theory of knowledge has no primacy in the use of 'knowledge' in Advaita Vedānta.

Let us speak briefly about the word or words for 'knowledge'. But first of all let us recognize the fact that in the Indian tradition as a whole words are not subjected to any monopoly, that is to say, no word is reserved for any special meaning. All words have to be read in their contexts. That initial understanding will help to avoid much puzzlement, and this elementary observation is made due to a legitimate concern. The most obvious word for 'knowledge' is *jñāna*, and it is ubiquitous. At its highest level it is one of the words by which *Brahman* itself is defined, e.g., *satyaṁ jñānam anantaṁ brahma, Taittirīya Upaniṣad*, 2.1.1. Can we call this the ontological use of the word? Perhaps, that is so insofar as we consider *Brahman* ontologically. Below this level of meaning is what may be called the metaphysical level, which is where there is a world to be thought about in respect of its ground, where there are beings like humans, which seek to know *Brahman* as well as themselves. Here we may translate *jñāna* by *gnosis*. In the Upaniṣads and the Vedānta tradition generally the most favoured equivalent for *jñāna* in this sense is *vidyā*. Now, further down the ladder, *jñāna* is used often for 'cognition', not only in non-Vedāntic literature, not to speak of its frequent occurrence even in the sense of sensual perception. An apt synonym for this, customarily employed in the literature, is *pramā*.

The word *avidyā* is used in Advaita Vedānta primarily as the negation of metaphysical gnosis (*jñāna*, or *vidyā*), as opposite, as absence of, gnosis and as wrong knowledge. No doubt, *ajñāna* is a proper synonym for it. Now it is clear that *ajñāna*, or *avidyā*, is never to be construed as the negation of *jñāna* when it constitutes a definition of *Brahman*, which, as we have observed, is the highest level use of that word. To ascribe such a meaning to *ajñāna* or *avidyā* would entail the notion that there is something that negates, or is other than, *Brahman*, a notion absolutely inadmissible.

As it has become amply clear that the word *jñāna* or *vidyā*, when negated by the negative prefix *a*, is primarily metaphysical, a term like 'agnosis' can be used (with some caution) as the closest philosophical translation for *avidyā* (*ajñāna*). However, caution is necessary because of the word agnosticism, with a different history. In the word agnosticism the import is decidedly cognitive though negative, and as such is directed at the transcendent with a question mark against it and thought to be inaccessible to cognition and hence "unknowable". At the bottom end of the scale, *jñāna*, in the sense of cognition (*pramā*), can not only be negated but opposed. Here *ajñāna* would, however, mean merely non-cognition (*apramā*). We are, then, really concerned with the metaphysical level only, which as far as the usage of the word *jñāna* is concerned is the middle one. But then, we must be prepared for the shock registered by the unexpected suggestion that metaphysics belongs to some middle level rather than the highest. We can, however, only repeat the statement that metaphysics is what arises where there is a world to consider and beings like humans, who want to know *Brahman* as well as themselves and the world. Hence metaphysics is always based on the world, whose ground is being sought. It cannot be said that *jñāna* in its highest sense as an essential definition of *Brahman* suggests *Brahman* as the ground of the world unless the question as to the ground of the world implied in the notion of Being (*sat*) has already preceded. So then as a prod to metaphysics it is not *jñāna* but its absence that has a part to play in the shape of the ignorance of Being, to overcome which there is a demand.

Avidyā, or *ajñāna*, must be confined primarily to the metaphysical realm of the knowledge *of Brahman* (but does not apply to *Brahman as* knowledge, *jñāna*), and only secondarily does it apply to the sphere of cognition, whether of *Brahman* or of any other object. But Advaita Vedānta does not assume that the sphere of cognition is independent of the metaphysical realm of knowledge. The dependence of the latter upon the former becomes evident through reflection upon the experience of non-cognition. It is one thing to generalize from this experience and possibly project it upon a transcendent reality with a question mark, and consequently decide upon agnosticism, but it is quite another thing to learn some metaphysical truth about knowledge from it. The latter alternative will point to the metaphysical truth that knowledge comes to us as what has already undergone a primordial division of itself from itself, resulting in its boundless extensiveness and interminability except through the forced and extraneous act of judgement. We must call this condition *avidyā.* Yet *avidyā* is what it is, or seemingly is, by reason of this primordial division of knowledge. So we may conclude that something of knowledge which is other than the infinite extensiveness and interminability, namely a *pointedness,* still remains in *avidyā* although in a concealed manner. It is this concealed pointedness that makes *avidyā* an ever-forming structure. But because the structure of *avidyā* is ever-forming, and because it is infinite extensiveness and interminability, cognitions are created and destroyed, and we have even such a thing as cognition of cognition (obviously produceable *ad infinitum*). The structure of *avidyā* itself is borne by the concealed pointedness, which makes it possible for us to draw connecting lines between cognition and non-cognition and at the same time demarcating lines between "true" and "false" cognitions. This is of course what makes it possible for us to make a philosophic inquiry into such a thing as *avidyā* even if we take it in the limited sense of non-cognition. *Avidyā* itself has to be a knowable in the empirical sense, both discursively and intuitively, both being covered by cognition (*jñāna,* or *pramā*) in our present sense. Yet *avidyā* remains *avidyā,* a universal and all-pervasive structure, which does not permit any kind of cognition to be an exception. For this reason all cognition, insofar as it is within that structure, can only be analogical in character. That which all cognition is referred to analogically is never made manifest inasmuch as it is the pointedness concealed by *avidyā.* These truths are learnt by dwelling upon the experience of non-cognition. Such dwelling will lead us, through cognitions which can serve as analogies, to the pointedness concealed within *avidyā.* The question then is, what is it that the cognitions are analogies of ? It will suffice to suggest gnosis (*jñāna,* or *vidyā*).

Phenomenology of Avidyā as Non-Cognition

Among the great Vedānta scholastics, Madhusūdana Sarasvatī, is the one most noteworthy for his painstaking and penetrating analysis of our experience of non-cognition, and it is quite phenomenological in approach. In the celebrated inquiry into *ajñāna-vāda* in his great work, *Advaita Siddhi*, he first asked what it means when one says : "I do not know myself and others; I do not know the meaning of what you say" (*tatra cājñāne 'ham ajño mām anyaṁ ca na jānāmī' 'ti pratyakṣam, tvaduktamarthaṁ na jānāmī 'ti viśeṣataḥ pratyakṣam.*).[4] Madhusūdana, however, in true scholastic spirit took *ajñāna* to be something, the existence of which needs to be proven. To prove the existence of *ajñāna* he employed the chief *pramāṇas* of Advaitic epistemology. The propositions already quoted above belong to the *pramāṇa* of *pratyakṣa* (perception). As for *anumāna* (inference), Madhusūdana begins the analysis with a citation from the *Vivaraṇa*, stating that a valid cognition is such that its object is covered with a veil, which it breaks through, and that, even though broken through, the veil does exist. Further, *ajñāna* is to be thought existent because it is devoid of the signs of non-existence, that is to say, it is *abhāvavilakṣaṇa*. In turning to the scriptural (*śruti*) evidence, he begins by providing an analysis of a passage out of the *Chāndogya Upaniṣad:* "Just as those who do not know the field walk again and again over the hidden treasure of gold and do not find it, even so all creatures here go day after day into the *Brahma*-world and do not find it, for they are carried away by untruth," (*tad yathāpi hiraṇya-nidhiṁ nihitam akṣetrajñā upary upari sañcaranto na vindeyuḥ, evam evemāḥ sarvāḥ prajā aharahar gacchantya etaṁ brahma-lokaṁ na vindanti anṛtena hi pratyūḍhāḥ*).[5] Likewise, the *pramāṇa* of postulation (*arthāpatti*) is held to be warranted by the fact that the ordinary consciousness of difference between the individual self and *Brahman* cannot be explicated without

4. *Advaita-Siddhi* (from the section entitled *ajñāna-vāde tatra pratyakṣa-pramāṇopapattiḥ*), published by Pandurang Jiwaji, Bombay, Nirnayasagar Press, 1937, p. 548.

5. From *Chāndogya Upaniṣad*, 8.3.2; translation by S. Radhakrishnan, *The Principal Upaniṣads.*

the hypothesis of *ajñāna* (*na ca jīvasya brahmabhedenaiva tādṛgaprakāśopapattiḥ*), as stated at the very opening.

Madhusūdana endeavours to prove the existence of *avidyā*. In doing so he is merely identifying and describing the fundamental philosophic problem, without dealing with which we really do not get started on the road to the knowledge held out to us by the logos. *Avidyā* is a fact to be recognized and understood. But this does not mean that it is also the ultimate object of philosophic inquiry. But the purpose of understanding it is that it may be removed—and it is removable. It is by no means what should be known (*jñeya, jñātavya*) *per se:* that only *Brahman* is. In the effort to know *avidyā* we are only trying to know what is really there to be known, i.e., *Brahman*. But the nature of existence, the nature of the world and the nature of thought itself require that we recognize and understand *avidyā* in order that we may know *Brahman*. The true constitution of the condition under which we exist and seek to know is something to be understood in order that we may know what is free of that condition.

Is there something free of that condition ? Theoretically, that question cannot be answered by 'yes' or by 'no' if in putting it we assume the condition that we have called *avidyā* to be an absolute. If such were the case that question must perpetually hang in the air. However, there is something self-contradictory about regarding the condition called *avidyā* to be an absolute, for then it would be required for it to be what is free of itself, beyond itself. This is part of the self-contradiction involved in making any relativity an absolute. But there is no reason why we should not let that question hang in the air, even strangle itself by the self-contradiction, viz., that of regarding the condition to be free of an absolute. Clearly, this kind of talk is metaphorical, for questions do not experience the pain of strangling by self-contradiction. The pain is experienced only when taken up into thought. In the Upaniṣadic declaration of *Brahman* the answer to the question, "Is there something free of *avidyā*?" is to be found. But to assume that the declaration is the answer to this question, or to a number of other questions co-ordinate with it, is quite incorrect, as, in fact, it not only logically succeeds but *also* precedes the questions. Because it does succeed the questions, however, one may receive the impression that Vedānta rushes to the rescue of the questions, or less metaphorically speaking, to the rescue of the thinking which experiences the pain of contradiction within it. However, this impression can only be partially true, for the declaration also precedes even such thinking. In any case, the removal of pain generated by such contradictions of thought is only an incidental consequence, and not by any means a contemplated result of the reception of truth.

As mentioned already, there are several other questions coordinate with this question, such as these : "If there is something beyond the condition called *avidyā*, that should be known, what is it ?" "Why is it that we do not know what should be known ?" These questions are all unresolvable (*avyākṛta*), to borrow the Buddhist terminology, because they get tangled up in hopeless knots. If they are resolved in one way they generate further antinomies which will undo the original resolution. But the truth is, every ultimate question is an unresolvable, gets tangled up in inextricable difficulties. Existence itself is the leading and the basic one among the unresolvables. It is the one to which all the others always return, and yet not finding a solution even there, are set again ever and anon on their unending journey. In that situation there are four distinct paths open to us : (1) persist in finding an ultimate resolution, (2) make one of the resolutions ultimate, (3) declare the fact of unresolvability itself as ultimate and (4) learn from the fact of unresolvability the way to think, not, however, in submission to that fact, but in obedience to an ultimate truth which will provide a perspective on that fact itself. Clearly, Vedānta has inherited the fourth alternative. As in the original question, in these coordinate questions too the removal of the pain in thought generated by its own contradictions is only an incidental consequence, and not a contemplated result of the reception of the ultimate truth.

Avidyā and the Desire to Know

The condition called *avidyā* is, however, one that potentiates the desire to know (*jijñāsā*). One may grasp this desire entirely within that condition with no apparent relation to the ultimate truth called *Brahman*, merely as made up of moments in thought, ridden with unresolved contradictions though they be. One may terminate the apparent endlessness of these moments by imposing on them a sequential order from the point of view of some practical reason such as the consideration of justice (*dharma*), the good end (*svarga*), and such like, which would, according to Pūrva Mīmāṁsā, be embodied in ritual and moral conduct (*karma*). The *Brahma-Sūtra* rejects such an approach. Hence, as expressed by the great Śaṅkara *Commentary*, it begins by advancing a revolutionary meaning to the moment called "then" (*atha*) as the moment before all moments of thought. The desire to know is shown to be a valid beginning of philosophy only insofar as it is metamorphosed into the desire to know *Brahman* (*athāto brahma-jijñāsā*). The desire to know *Brahman* is no longer a variety of the mere desire to know; rather the desire to know *Brahman* is what re-structures and re-orients the mere desire to know. It is thus that *Brahman*-knowledge is wrested out of *avidyā*. Further, the desire for the knowledge of *Brahman* causes the mind to be taken away from the unresolvables and helps to concentrate thought on that which alone is worthy to be known, i.e., *Brahman*. What follows from there is set forth as a completely revolutionary enterprise. The moment before all moments of thought is gnosis, which is capable of making thought henceforth its reflection.

Gnosis must be understood in the metaphor of light, and thought likewise in the metaphor of reflection of light. The stuff of *avidyā*, which is darkness searching for a light it knows not, and possibly even refuses to recognize, will indeed continue so as to make thought to be a reflection of light in darkness an abiding possibility. Thought in Vedānta, while it remains a reflection of the light of gnosis, also participates in the "darkness" of *avidyā* which, nevertheless, is a quest for light. Therefore it simultaneously enjoys knowing and suffers not-yet-knowing. There is that in thought which belongs with gnosis, that is light, and also that which belongs with *avidyā*, which is the struggle, the pain, the sweat and the journey through the dark woods.

The darkness of *avidyā* potentiates the desire to know, although not necessarily the desire to know *Brahman*. When a person living in darkness knows that he is, he already has an indirect knowledge of light. But insofar as *avidyā* potentiates the desire to know, and insofar as what it potentiates is capable of being re-structured and re-oriented, *avidyā* is not mere darkness, but so to say a darkness which is capable of being dissipated by gnosis (*jñāna-nivartyatvam*).

Avidyā itself furnishes some of the basic material for thought and sustains thought by the desire to know that it potentiates. In Vedānta, which understands thought from its essential order, that is, as the reflection of gnosis in *avidyā*, the connection with *avidyā* which supplies the basic material for thought and sustains it by the desire to know that it potentiates, is necessarily retained. Otherwise, we cannot meaningfully speak of thought. But thought so understood by Vedānta must also reconstitute the thought which within the order of *avidyā* is merely a product of the material it supplies and the desire it potentiates. The first step which Vedānta as a system has traditionally undertaken in this respect is to try to remove any formal or material contradiction between its gnosis and the so-called means of knowledge, or *pramāṇas*. This way the connection between the two orders of thought is vitally preserved. This in itself does not seem to be the very height of philosophy but, nevertheless, as an essential ground has an inalienable place in philosophy, for after all, anything we say, however profound, must have that rational character which makes discourse possible. Advaita Vedānta employs the infinite virtuosity of the science of *pramāṇas* successfully to this end. But essentially it is gnosis that unfolds itself symphonically through the *pramāṇas*. The use of this science with virtuosity is also necessary because the gnosis which is the foundation of its own order of thinking is clearly outside the epistemic sphere, and against it, therefore, a question mark had been placed. Hence the demonstration of non-contradictability (*abādhitatva*) is an essential act in the course of the reasoned view that Advaita has been obliged to undertake. Further, insofar as what has been necessary for it to do has also been eminently possible, an extremely beneficial character of the nature of reasoning—and of the *pramāṇas*—has been exhibited.

The principle of non-contradictability is necessary also because of the analogical character of all our perception of truth.

In fact, this principle itself is no more than analogy—to the knowledge of the non-dual *Brahman*, which we must, in terms of our description earlier, regard as the pointedness concealed by *avidyā*.

Avidyā and the Cosmos

We have said earlier that *avidyā* is a universal and all-pervading structure, and that it must be taken primarily in the sense of the metaphysical realm of knowledge (in the negative form, of course). The structure makes its claim upon our thought in terms of the questions we characterized as unresolvables. For this reason, *avidyā* inevitably becomes the principle by which to interpret the coming to be of the world. This is where Vedānta is unique. No other system, Eastern or Western, uses the structure of agnosis for cosmology. By the 'world' is meant that which is extended through name and form (*nāma-rūpa*), hence an ordered cosmos rather than chaos. The world is cosmos because the things which constitute it are given individual and general (or universal) names and marked by their forms. The world is interpreted as "cosmos constituted of names and forms imagined by *avidyā*," (*avidyā-kalpita-nāma-rūpa*). This is unique among cosmological theories. Sāṁkhya and Yoga do not follow Vedānta, and the latter turns its criticisms against them. *Avidyā* is the basis of name and form, which are the constituting seeds of the cosmos. That there is a cosmology based on *avidyā* must seem puzzling and even strange. But it will become comprehensible when we realize that this Advaitic cosmology is oriented towards gnosis (*vidyā*).

This cosmology's orientation to gnosis is merely making explicit what is seen as lying concealedly in the cosmos, and in fact, according to Advaita, this is the most satisfactory account of the cosmos. The world itself is seen in terms of *avidyā*. This structure of the world is *avidyā* because it manifests itself as that which conceals gnosis (*vidyā*), and hence *a+vidyā*. Gnosis has no other way of manifesting itself except as that which is concealed by *avidyā*. *Avidyā*, as the concealer of gnosis, has nevertheless its own function assigned by the logos, which is what expresses itself in the desire to know. The logos which expresses itself in the desire to know potentiated by *avidyā* itself we may call the seeking side of logos, which makes reflection of gnosis in *avidyā* possible once gnosis has been delivered by the revealing logos. The cosmos itself is characterized by this desire; otherwise it will not be cosmos.

In the *Commentary on the Brahma-Sūtra* Śaṅkara develops *avidyā* cosmology primarily as criticism of the Sāṁkhyan cosmology based on *prakṛti* (Nature), which has a vague orientation to gnosis but without reckoning with *avidyā*. Here one sees a partial affinity, which is what moved Śaṅkara to choose Sāṁkhya for the favoured position of chief opponent (*prathama malla*).

The common orientation to gnosis shared by Advaita and Sāṁkhya is expressed by the concern for what should be known (*jñeya*, *jñātavya*), though what should be known is not the same for both, wherein lies the difference. Advaita believes that knowing what it is that should be known must come in the context of, and as answer to, the *avidyā*-based questions stated earlier, i.e. "Is there anything free of *avidyā* ?"; "If there is, what is it, inasmuch as it is that which should be known ?" and "Why is it that we do not know what should be known ?" Sāṁkhya, on the contrary, without taking *avidyā* and the questions based on them into consideration, speaks of something as what should be known in terms of a sheer cosmology of causality, that is of seeing the world as an effect whose cause is sought to be known. For Sāṁkhya the knowledge of the cause of the world spectacle is the basis of the knowledge that discriminates between that cause and the pure, conscious spirit which neither causes nor is caused. Both these together constitute the Sāṁkhyan version of gnosis. So clearly Sāṁkhyan cosmology is oriented towards gnosis too, but without *avidyā* having been taken into consideration.

Not only by reason of the orientation of cosmology to gnosis but also by reason of the formal similarity in the view of cause-effect relationship, Advaita finds the closest affinity among all the *darśanas* with Sāṁkhya. Sāṁkhya regards *pradhāna* (Primordial Matter) as the cause (*kāraṇa*) of the effect (*kārya*) called the world. The effect is not considered a new thing but the cause itself in a different form. This view is expressed by the doctrine of the identity of cause and effect (*satkārya-vāda*), shared by Vedānta and Sāṁkhya. Śaṅkara writes : "The doctrine that *pradhāna* is the cause is at least minimally accepted by Manu and other knowers of the Vedas by reason of the support it gives to *satkārya-vāda*" (*pradhāna-kāraṇa-vādo vedavidbhirapi kaiścit manvādibhiḥ satkāryatvādyaṁśopajīvanābhiprāyeṇa upanibaddhaḥ*).[6] Śaṅkara agrees with Sāṁkhya that what we know in the effect (*kārya*) is the cause (*sat*).

But then, what is the *sat* to be known ? Here arises the critical difference. The word *sat*, used in the sense of cause, has the more primary meaning of Being, and so actually in the cosmological context it means the Being which is the only (material) cause. Advaita maintains that this Being, than which there is no other (material) cause, and therefore to be called cause '*per se*, must be known in its essential transcendence over the cause-effect situation of cosmology itself, in fact over the whole metaphysical situation involving the relation between Being and the world. This situation has to be explained in terms of *avidyā* which is what brings it about. Hence "causation" pertains to *avidyā*. In fact, *avidyā* is the "causation factor", as distinguished from *sat*, which is the "cause". [These two terms "causation factor", and "cause" we put in inverted commas in order to show that they must not be taken literally. We could have called them instrumental cause and material cause respectively but for the fact that these terms would signify literal meaning and be confused with other accounts of what is instrumental and what is material.]

What is the *sat* which should be known ? That is the principal question on which Advaita registers its fundamental difference from Sāṁkhya. Sāṁkhyan dualism regards *pradhāna* (Matter, no doubt, but not anything material)[7], which is co-eternal with, and totally independent of, the other ultimate principle, *puruṣa* (Spirit), to be the *sat*, or Being, which is the (only) material cause of the World. Śaṅkara repeatedly argues, "The word *sat*, does not indicate *pradhāna*; The word *sat* does not indicate the

6. *Brahma Sūtra Bhāṣya*, 2.2.17.

7. *Note*: Both in the Indian and the Greek traditions primordial Matter is conceived as nothing material. Matter, *hyle*, for Aristotle especially was approachable by using material things as analogies. Today it is very true of Dialectical Materialism.

non-intelligent *pradhāna*" (*na pradhānaṁ sacchabda-vācyam*; *na acetana pradhānaṁ sacchabda-vācyam*).[8] Elsewhere he states, "It is not possible to accept the non-intelligent *pradhāna* as fancied by Sāṁkhya to be the cause of the world" (*na sāṁkhya-parikalpitam acetanaṁ pradhānaṁ jagataḥ kāraṇaṁ śakyaṁ vedānteṣu āśrayitum*).[9] He shows that the word *sat* is only applicable to *Brahman*. Śaṅkara quotes the Sāṁkhyan view that *pradhāna* is the *sat* that should be known (*jñeya*), because only by knowing the difference between the *guṇas* (strands, or qualities), which constitute *pradhāna*, and *puruṣa* could spiritual liberation (*mukti* or *kaivalya*) be facilitated. Śaṅkara explains that this view is a misconception mainly predicated on the wrong definition of the word *avyakta* (unmanifest or unclear), which the Sāṁkhyans believe signifies *pradhāna* in its unmanifested state.

Sāṁkhya bases its case for defining *avyakta* as *pradhāna* on the few passages in the Upaniṣads where the word is mentioned, principally *Kaṭha*, 1.3.11 (*mahataḥ param avyaktam*, beyond the great intelligence is *avyakta*); *Kaṭha*, 2.3.7 (*mahato avyaktam uttamam*, higher than the great intelligence is *avyakta*). Śaṅkara contends that in these statements only the mere word *avyakta* occurs, while it is neither defined as *pradhāna* nor indicated as what should be known (*jñeya*). Accordingly, commenting on the sūtra, *jñeyatva avacanāt ca* ("And because it, viz., *avyakta*, is not mentioned in the scripture"), he states : "Only the word *avyakta* occurs. Here *avyakta* is not spoken of as what should be known (*jñeya*) or as what should be meditated upon (*upāsitavya*). Nor would it be reasonable to maintain that what is not specifically instructed in the Scriptures could pertain to the highest end of man. Therefore the word *avyakta* does not mean *pradhāna*" (*pada-mātram hi avyakta śabdaḥ neha avyaktaṁ jñātavyam upāsitavyaṁ ceti vākyam asti. na ca anupadiṣṭa-padārthajñānaṁ puruṣārtham iti śakyaṁ pratipattum. tasmāt api na avyakta-śabdena pradhānam abhidhīyate*).[10]

The Sāṁkhyan contention that *avyakta* is *pradhāna* is motivated by the desire to show what it is that is *jñeya*, i.e., that it is

8. *Ibid.*, 1.1.7,8.
9. *Ibid.*, 1.1.5.
10. *Ibid.*, 1.4.4.

pradhāna. Sāṁkhya, accordingly, advances the view that knowing *pradhāna* is mandatory for realizing the highest end of man, i.e., *mukti* or *kaivalya*. This Śaṅkara meets with a very fundamental argument, namely, that what is not specifically given as instruction in the scriptures cannot devolve upon the question of the highest end of man, or *puruṣārtha*.

It is demonstrated that *pradhāna* is a fictitious notion, to advance which Sāṁkhya equates it with *avyakta*, whereas *avyakta* means no more than what is unclear. What is unclear must not be regarded as positive being (let alone positive Being). Hence the notion of *pradhāna* is a mere fiction. There is no evidence for its reality. In fact, over against the Sāṁkhyans, Śāṅkara is the realist, as it is he who, affirming the actuality of the world, wants to see it grounded on what is unconditionally and absolutely real, namely, *Brahman*, rather than on a hypothetical being like *pradhāna*. [Vedānta generally believes that there are only two grounds on which something real can be asserted : the logos as the Word and the logos in human consciousness.] Śaṅkara argues that *avyakta*, may not be taken to stand for the fictitious notion of *pradhāna*, and also that such a notion does not in any case indicate the goal of our quest insofar as that quest, in the agreed opinion of all Indian systems, has to do with the highest end of man. Thus he concludes, "Therefore, *pradhāna* is not what is to be known nor is it what is defined by *avyakta*" (*tasmāt na pradhānasya atra jñeyatvam avyaktaśabda-nirdiṣṭatvaṁ vā*).[11]

There is something generic about Śaṅkara's criticism of the doctrine of *pradhāna* in that it can be applied to a whole lot of other similar doctrines, perhaps to a whole lot of what is taken as metaphysics in both East and West. (This is a normal characteristic of much of his writings.)

Following Śaṅkara's lead we must be able to understand *avyakta* in its mere literal sense alone, i.e., as what is merely unclear and no longer as the unmanifest *pradhāna*. But *avyakta* is taken quite seriously by Śaṅkara and it is shown to have a vital role to play in our quest.

As to what it is that should be known (*jñeya, jñātavya*), that should be desired to be known (*jijñāsitavya, vijijñāsitavya*), the

11. *Ibid.*, 1.4.5.

answer is directly forthcoming from the Upaniṣads: it is *Brahman*. However, it is not an answer really until the logos via which it comes is grasped. The real task, then, is to generate understanding of that logos, or a true insight of it, which is what is connoted by the word *prajñā*. [We are here referring to the Vedāntic, not the wider, use of it. The Buddhists, for instance, employ it without recognition of its logos base.] What should be known is that which both makes itself known via the logos and is desired to be known, again, via the immanent function of the logos. In both respects the Sāṁkhyan Matter principle does not qualify.

The logos basis underlying the answer to the question points to *Brahman*, rather than to the Matter principle. This is brought out in an arresting *sūtra* in the context, 1.4.5: "If (Sāṁkhya) were to proclaim (that *pradhāna* is what should be known), (then the answer is) no, for only the *prājña* (i.e., the possessor of the logos of understanding) is that, on account of the expressed speaking of the logos" (*vadati iti cet na prājño hi prakaraṇāt*). Śaṅkara in his comment on it identifies the *prājña* (the possessor of the logos of understanding) with the Supreme *Ātman*, or *Brahman* (*prājño hi paramātmā*).[12]

What is to be Known, and the Problem of Avyakta or the Unclear

Now, having set forth what is *jñeya* according to Advaita, let us now turn to the word *avyakta*. The mutually agreed upon primary understanding of *avyakta* is that it denotes the antecedent seed stage of this world in which it is not manifested by names and forms (*jagat idam anabhivyaktanāmarūpaṁ bījātmakaṁ prāgavastham avyakta-śabdārham*).[13] Śaṅkara argues that the antecedent condition of the world is not some sort of mindless, blind mechanism but something that can only be imputed to a conscious creator who thinks the world into being. It is that same dependence which guarantees that the released souls (*jīvas*) are not again thrown back into the *saṁsāric* (transmigratory) cycle, a matter about which Sāṁkhya can say nothing. Therefore, "the dependence of this antecedent condition" upon the conscious

12. *Note* : We must set aside the usual, pedestrian translation of *prakaraṇa* as "chapter" instead of "the expressed speaking of the logos", as we think is appropriate in this profoundly ontological context.

13. *Ibid.*, 1.4.3.

creator "must be necessarily so" (*sā ca avaśya-abhyupagant-avyā*).

In view of this dependence Śaṅkara replaces *pradhāna* as the definition of *avyakta* with two words, *avidyā* and *māyā* (*avyaktā hi sā māyā; avidyā hi avyaktam*). It is the same principle that is called *māyā* and *avidyā*, the one with respect to the imputed creative power of *Brahman*, and the other with respect to the seeds of *saṁsāric* becoming ensconced in name and form. Śaṅkara writes, "This potential power of the seed is of the nature of *avidyā* and is signified by the word *avyakta* and, having the supreme Lord as its ground is of the nature of *māyā* and is the great sleep in which transmigratory souls unaware of their form continue to slumber on" (*avidyātmikā hi bījaśa-ktiravyakta-śabda-nirdeśyā parameśvarāśrayā māyāmayī mahā-suṣuptiḥ*).[14] In the sense of *avidyā* or *māyā* sometimes *avyakta* is signified by the word *ākāśa* (cosmic, spatial container) or by the word *akṣara* (the imperishable).

The souls' unawareness of their own form (*svarūpa-pratibo-dharāhityam*), is *avidyā*. In this lie the seeds of *saṁsāric* becoming (*saṁsāriṇo bījā*). The seeds are defined as names and forms. The same names and forms when used by the supreme creator-Lord and willed as power for the creation of the entire expanse (universe) of transmigratory existence is properly called *māyā*. To quote Śaṅkara, "The names and forms which are imagined through *avidyā* and which are, as it were, the self of the omniscient Lord, and which are indefinable as identical with or different from the *tattva* (i.e., *Brahman*) and are the seeds of the entire universe of transmigratory existence are the *māyā*-power and the nature of the Lord" (*sarvasyeśvarasya ātmabhūta iva avi-dyākalpite nāma-rūpe tattvānyatvābhyām anirvacanīye saṁsāra-prapañca-bījabhūte sarvajñasya īśvarasya māyāśaktiḥ pra-kṛtiriti*).[15]

Now a matter of the greatest importance must be mentioned here. At an earlier place we said: "There is that in thought which belongs with gnosis, that is light, and also that which belongs with *avidyā*, which is the struggle, the pain, the

14. *Loc. cit.*
15. *Ibid.*, 2.1.14.

sweat and the journey through the dark woods." Also: "In Vedānta which understands thought from its essential order, that is, as the reflection of gnosis in *avidyā*, the connection with *avidyā*, which supplies the basic material for thought and sustains it by the desire to know it potentiates, is necessarily retained." These statements acquire a new significance in the cosmological context right at this point of our discussion, which is this: that of thought which belongs with *avidyā* has both a macrocosmological and microcosmological significance. Just as divine thought uses the names and forms of *avidyā* for the creation of the world, so human thought as microcosmology uses *avidyā*.

The *Chāndogya Upaniṣad*, (6.2.3) has it: "It *thought*/desired, 'let me become many' " (*tad aikṣata bahusyāṁ prajāyeyeti*). The *Aitareya Upaniṣad* (1.1) has it: "He thought/desired, 'let me create the worlds' " (*sa aikṣata lokān nu sṛjā iti*), and so on.

No doubt, *in all Eastern views* (*not just Indian*), *perhaps all ancient views, thought appears to be fundamentally interiorizing microcosmological process*. The same process of the world's creation, continuance and end is microcosmologically recaptured in mind, re-enacted and re-lived through thought, which for most traditions is participation in gnosis, with other elements of gnosis such as discrimination, renunciation or even voluntary identification with the cosmos, added. But *Vedānta is unique in arguing that this microcosmological character of thought is not gnosis but agnosis,* and yet under certain provisos it sanctions and even sanctifies it. And it also shows that this agnosis-based microcosmological part of thought is also comprehended by the logos. That is precisely the reason why the homology with the divine model of creation through thinking, desiring, or beholding is so important. The Sāṁkhyan suggestion of *pradhāna* as Being, or Cause, at the source of creation is rejected on account of this. Hence, *īkṣater na aśabdam*, "It does not think because it is devoid of the logos", *Brahma Sūtra*, 1.1.5.

Now, exactly in the way in which *avidyā* is used as material for thought, it is used by the supreme Lord as material for creation of the world. *Avyakta* is *avidyā*, and it is material for creation but is not *sat*, as *avyakta* (=*pradhāna*) is regarded by Sāṁkhya.

The fact that names and forms have been there without beginning and the fact that they have been there because they have been used by the supreme Lord are inseparable. Their existence is their use.

The condition of the souls' unawareness of their own real essence is to be understood cosmologically. Experience is cosmos and cosmos is experience. Experience is by no means some individualized abstraction. When we perceive the world we normally realize that there is a world out there which is both the object of our perception and at the same time that which contains us as a part of itself. If this paradox does not lead us to think of an experience which is cosmic in nature, of which our own experience is but a manifestation, it is difficult to see how we can meaningfully speak of experience at all. Is it possible that in contemporary epistemology we may have cut thinking off from the concreteness of cosmic experience?

We have tried to show that cosmology in Advaita is much more than giving an account of the cosmos. It is giving an account of it in such a way as to illuminate the nature of thought itself. *Avidyā* binds thought and cosmos together. The metaphysics of knowledge which *avidyā* is—as we stated at the outset—has its simultaneous application to thought and to cosmology.

Some more things may be said about philosophy as such, in relation to *avidyā*. But let us turn to one single issue. We naturally understand philosophy to be first and foremost the asking of questions about everything and about itself at the same time. We also normally push everything into the lap of philosophy and philosophy, likewise, into the lap of everything. But why philosophy and why everything? Why should we ask the questions which constitute philosophy and why should there be a world? We need a satisfactory answer to the question "why" in both respects.

We may say, as philosophy usually assumes, "there is that which constitues a problem". This *that which constitutes a problem* is traditionally pushed into the lap of the cosmos, or the world, and the cosmos, or the world, in turn converted into *that which constitutes a problem.*

Here another dimension of causality (*kāraṇa*) arises. This is expressed by the questions, why there shoutd be that which constitutes a problem, and why there should be a world. These *why* questions represent a more fundamental dimension of causality (*kāraṇa*), which again may be, although misleadingly, equated with "the final cause". Why should *saṁsāra* (that is, the cycle of cosmic existence, from which *mukti* is sought) ever have been; why should suffering, perplexity, longing, desire, fear, pain ever have been?

But these questions are extremely difficult. One way to see their extremely subtle character is to put them in the context of two alternative, general approaches to causality which are exhibited in the Indian tradition as elsewhere. These approaches are necessitarianism and contingency respectively. Śaṅkara in his great *Commentary* after he has quit criticizing the Sāṁkhyan versions of causality turns to Vaiśeṣika atomism (*paramāṇuvāda*) and Buddhist aggregationism (*samudāya-vāda*). True enough, we must not force these two doctrines into the mould of necessitarianism and contingency, but it is equally true that these doctrines have thrusts which can be correctly described by these terms. (Śaṅkara's criticism of Vaiśeṣika and Buddhist doctrines runs the whole gamut of causality. No doubt about it, and it is by no means focussed solely on the *why* questions.)

As for the necessitarianism contained in the doctrine of atomism, the centre of it is the doctrine of inherence (*samavāya*). The *Commentary on the Brahma-Sūtra* at 2.2.11-17 contains some trenchant criticisms of "inherence" and the "necessary relation" of inherence (*ayutasiddhatva*) between cause and effect. According to this doctrine of the Vaiśeṣikas cosmology is merely following the logic of inherence (*samavāya*) and its concomitant principle of contact (*saṁyoga*), whereby for example, white cloth comes out of white thread. Cosmology as an account of the cosmos is also not at the same time an account of thought. Mind (*manas*), one of the substances (*dravyas*), thinks partly because it is its nature and partly in obedience to "inherence" and "contact". Necessity governs thought. And thought has nothing to do with trying to resolve the contradictory signals it gets from such a realm as *avidyā* envisaged by Advaita. Vaiśeṣika too has its view of *avidyā* as being "merely the failure to perceive the causes of effects which exist as beings and are perceivable" (*tadyadyevaṁ vivrīyate satāṁ paridṛśyamāna-kāryāṇāṁ kāraṇānāṁ pratyakṣeṇa agrahaṇam, avidyā iti*).[16] The world as effect comes and goes by necessitarian laws and thought too likewise comes and goes. Beyond that, the questions, "why the world", "why thought" cannot be answered. Superficially speaking, the Vaiśeṣika theory that effects are different from the cause (*asatkārya-vāda*) might appear not to warrant necessitarianism. But this theory does operate under necessitarian laws like inherence and contact.

At the other end stands aggregationism (*samudāya-vāda*) of Buddhism, and this is deemed the paradigm expression of the view that the world is a contingent, in fact a fortuitous, occurrence. *The Commentary* at 2.2.18-27 deals with this theory and its inadequacy. *Samudāya* is the method of explaining *saṁsāra* and so *duḥkha* (sorrow) through the causal chain of co-dependent origination (*pratītya-samutpāda*) beginning with the first link, which the Buddhists themselves call *avidyā*, progressing to impression, name, form, the tabernacles of the six (five sense organs and *buddhi*), body, touch, desire, activity, birth, species, decay, death, sorrow, etc. [Śaṅkara himself details them in 2.2.19.] Śaṅkara asks, "If *avidyā*, etc., are themselves the cause of the aggregates, then how can they, which depend upon the aggregates for coming into existence, be themselves the cause of the aggregates?" (*yadī tāvad ayam abhiprāyaḥ avidyādayaḥ saṁghātam antareṇa ātmānam alabhamānā apekṣante saṁghātam iti, tataḥ tasya saṁghātasya nimittaṁ vaktavyam*).[17] This theory of aggregation is undoubtedly the most daring attempt to explain the *why* questions—obviously in a way true to the classical form, concealed in the *how* question—through contingency. Only by dialectics such as Śaṅkara provides can what is hidden be brought out.

But Śaṅkara in criticizing these two doctrines, of the Vaiśeṣikas and Buddhists respectively, points the way to something other than necessitarianism and contingency, on the basis of which the questions, "why the world?", "why thought?" can be raised—

16. *Ibid.* 2.2.15.
17. *Ibid.*, 2.2.19.

and that is *avidyā*. *Avidyā* not only produces the contradictory signals, which are the materials for thought, but also accounts for the structure of the desire for knowledge. And it becomes illumined darkness by being the medium in which reflection of gnosis takes place.

Five

THE MACRO-MICRO-COSMOLOGY APPROACHED THROUGH A GĪTĀ TEXT

Text :

ūrdhvamūlam adhaḥśākham
aśvatthaṁ prāhur avyayam
chandāṁsi yasya parṇāni
yas taṁ veda sa vedavit.

adhaś co 'rdhvaṁ prasṛtās tasya śākhā
guṇapravṛddhā viṣayapravālāḥ
adhaś ca mūlāny anusaṁtatāni
karmānubandhīni manuṣyaloke.

na rūpam asye'ha tatho 'palabhyate
nā 'nto na cā 'dir na ca saṁpratiṣṭhā
aśvattham enaṁ suvirūḍhamūlam
asaṅgaśastreṇa dṛḍhena chittvā.

...*The Bhagavadgītā*, 15.1-3.

Translation :

"They say [that there is] an indestructible *aśvattha* tree with roots above and branches below, whose leaves are the Vedic hymns : who knows it is a knower of the Veda.

"Its branches spread below and above, being nourished by the *guṇas* (i.e., the strands that constitute *Prakṛti*, or Nature), objects of perception being its twigs. Its [adventitious] roots are produced below, in the world of man, bound to *karma*.

"Its form is not obtained here as thus or thus, nor its end, nor its beginning, nor the ground [on which it is planted] once this *aśvattha* tree, so well nourished [though it is] , has been cut down with the mighty sword of non-attachment."

The question is, although the *aśvattha*, described here is the "Cosmic Tree", as all interpreters, both ancient and modern, agree, in what sense is it that ? Is it in the ordinary sense of the visible universe only or perhaps in that sense, no doubt, *plus* in the sense of something more fundamental, that subtle human world which pervades the visible universe, tasted and felt in consciousness in the form of temporality, death, rebirth, etc., for which the word *saṁsāra* stands?

The symbol of the *aśvattha* calls for an exegesis. Parallels with the Cosmic Tree in other parts of the world known to us through the history of religion can mislead one into thinking that the *Gītā* is talking about the visible universe, its creation, implying the creator behind it, etc. The context of our exegetical effort here is some statements by R. C. Zaehner, which reveal a profound misunderstanding. Prof. Zaehner seeks to counter-balance the Cosmic Tree with the belief in one God, Viṣṇu-Kṛṣṇa, which he sees to be the essence of the *Gītā* teaching any-way ! So he believes that here "the disciple is first asked to cut down the Tree of primordial creativity (*pravṛtti*) and then asked to take refuge in the very author of that Tree, 'from whom all things proceed (*pravartate*)' (10.8)". He also sees this as an important example of "mystical religion", as he adds, "this is, however, typical of mystical religion and the Muslim mystic, for instance, takes refuge in God's mercy against his wrath. In Hinduism it is not the divine wrath that hides the eternal from the eyes of the worshipper but his 'divine *māyā*' (7.14), his creative activity which conceals the timeless peace which is 'his changeless [all] highest' mode of his being (7.24)".[1]

Etymology of the word aśvattha

In the *Atharva-Veda* there are references (5.4.3; 19.39.6) to the *aśvattha* being the home of the gods and being in the third heavenly sphere, viz., the *Varuṇa-loka*[2]. The *Taittirīya Brāhmaṇa*,

1. R. C. Zaehner, *The Bhagavad-Gītā*, with a commentary based on original sources, Oxford at the Clarendon Press, 1969, p. 362.

2. *aśvattho devasadanas tritīyasyām ito divi tatrāmṛtasya cakṣaṇaṁ devāḥ kuṣṭham avanvata*. (The *aśvattha* is an abode of the gods; it grows in the third heaven; this tree which confers immortality was acquired by the gods.)

(3.8.12.2) says, "the tree is called *aśvattha* because *Agni* or *Yajña-Prajāpati* fell from the sphere of the gods (i.e., the *Deva-loka*) during the *pitṛyāna* (i.e., the path of the fathers), and taking the form of a horse (*aśva*), remained invisible in it for a year." Several etymologists have argued that *aśvattha* means horse-stable, because the horses of the sun took rest under it in the *Yama-loka* (the sphere of *Yama*) during the night of the *pitṛyāna*.

In the commentaries on the *Gītā* particularly in those of Śaṅkara and his followers—we find a radical philosophical etymology—as is usually the case when certain significant words are involved. Śaṅkara's comment on *Gītā* 15.1, explains it as follows : *na śvo 'pi sthātā iti aśvattham, kṣaṇa-pradhvaṁsinam aśvattham*—not abiding even till tomorrow (*śvaḥ*), destroyed momentarily—hence the word *aśvattha*.[3] It is further described as *saṁsāra-māyā*—the *māyā* of the cycle of *saṁsāra*.

Madhusūdana Sarasvatī in his exposition (*vyākhyā*) of Śaṅkara's comment carries it even further as he defines the word thus : *āśuvināśitvena na śvo 'pi sthātā iti viśvāsānarham aśvattham*—on account of quick perishability and not deserving to be relied on, not abiding even till tomorrow—hence the word *aśvattha*. Śrīdhara makes this derivation even more emphatic, as he has it : *vinaśvaratvena śvaḥ prabhātaparyantam api na sthāsyati iti viśvāsānarhatvād aśvatthaṁ prāhuḥ*—they call it *aśvattha* because it is unreliable on account of the fact that it will not abide even till tomorrow morning.

Now it would appear on the surface, that the etymology of Śaṅkara and his followers is far-fetched, but when we remember that there are so many links between *śvaḥ* (tomorrow), *aśva* (horse) and *āśu* (quick, fast and also—in the *Ṛgveda*—horse) it ceases to look fanciful. It will be recalled that "the horses of the Sun" (*Chronos*) stands for time in Greek mythology also, and hence the association of the horse—and the sun—with speed and time will become irrepudiable. "The horses of the

3. *Note* : Quotations from Śaṅkara's *Gītā* commentary and the sub-commentaries of Ānandagiri, Madhusūdana Sarasvatī and Śrīdhara are taken from the combined text edited by W. Laxman Shastri Pansikar, Bombay, Pandurang Jawaji, 1936.

sun resting during the night of the soul's progress in the path of the fathers (*pitṛyāna*)" eventually becomes identified with the god of time (*Kāla*), who emerges finally as the mythological god of death. We are at this point inevitably brought to the *Kaṭha Upaniṣad* where the imagery of the upside down tree occurs—evidently earlier than in the *Gītā*—the revealing god here being *Yama*, the official deity who presides over death. When we bear all these associations in mind, the objections of recent writers including B. G. Tilak (*Gītārahasya*, English translation, p. 1136) that Śaṅkara's etymology is far-fetched will cease to be valid. Śaṅkara would seem not to be speaking from mere imagination even as Tilak suggests.

Aśvattha is no doubt tree but the word *vṛkṣa* (tree) as such is used only once in the *Gītā* (10.26)—*aśvatthaḥ sarvavṛkṣāṇām* ("of all trees [I am] *aśvattha*") in the same way in which (Kṛṣṇa speaking of himself) "of *Ṛṣis*, I am Nārada, of *Gandharvas* I am Citraratha, of *Munis*, Kapila", meaning either the primordial, the original or in some ways the most puzzling and mysterious member of each class of significant beings. In the Upaniṣads the word appears several times, e.g., *Kauṣītaki* 1.3 and 5; *Chāndogya*, 6.9.1; 6.11.1; *Bṛhadāraṇyaka* 3.9.27 and 28; *Taittirīya*, 1.10.1; *Śvetāśvatara*, 3.9; 4.6 and 7; 6.6. In fact, strangely, it does not occur in the *Kaṭha Upaniṣad*, in which the parallel passages to the *Gītā* text are found.

The word *vṛkṣa* (tree) has also been subjected to etymological treatment by Śaṅkara in his *Kaṭha Upaniṣad Bhāṣya*, *a propos* the text in the the *Upaniṣad* 2.3.1,[4] which has a notable similarity with the first *Gītā* passage about *aśvattha* (15.1). Śaṅkara writes : *vṛkṣaśca vraścanāt* (the word *vṛkṣa* [is used] owing to cutting down). This etymology is given in the context of expounding *saṁsāra-vṛkṣa* (*saṁsāra*-tree). Gopāla Yatīndra in his *Ṭīkā* (sub-commentary) expands Śaṅkara's etymology even further : *saṁsāra eva vṛkṣaḥ saṁsāravṛkṣaḥ vṛkṣa-śabda-*

4. *ūrdhva-mūlo 'vāk-śākha eṣo'śvatthas sanātanaḥ tad eva śukraṁ tad brahma, tad evāmṛtam ucyate. tasmin lokāḥ śritāḥ sarve tad u nātyeti kaścana. etat vai tat*, "With roots above and branches below (stands) this timeless *aśvattha*; that alone is the pure; that is *Brahman*; that alone is said to be immortal. In it all the worlds rest, and no one ever goes beyond it. This indeed is that."

pravṛttinimittam āha vraścanāt iti.[5] "The tree [is] that which is indeed *saṁsāra*, that is the *saṁsāra*-tree; the word *vṛkṣa* is spoken because of instrumentality of becoming [that is] due to its being cut down". Despite this kind of etymological elaboration, it is well to bear in mind that actually in the Upaniṣad text in question neither the word *saṁsāra* nor the term *saṁsāra vṛkṣa* nor the notion of cutting down appears. On the contrary, the tree here is apparently *Brahman*. In the *Gītā* the tree is *saṁsāra*. Is there, then, a contradiction between the *Gītā* meaning and the *Kaṭha* meaning ? Frankly, no, because *saṁsāra* is derived from lower *Brahman*, which is nevertheless *Brahman*. Lower *Brahman* can be seen in terms of *saṁsāra* as well as ultimate Brahman.

In this context we must inquire into the meaning of *chandāṁsi* (the Vedic hymns) in line 3 of the *Gītā* 15.1, where it is said that they (the Vedic hymns) are its (i.e., the *aśvattha's*) leaves (*parṇāni*). Śaṅkara writes : "The *saṁsāra-vṛkṣa* is qualified thus : Its leaves are the leaves as it were of *Ṛk, Yajus and Sāma* (i.e., the three Vedas) and they protect, or cover (*chad*), the *saṁsāra*-tree." He defines *chandāṁsi* in the following manner : *chandāṁsi chādanāt* (because of the function of covering they are called chandāṁsi).[6] Here we may refer to the *Chāndogya Upaniṣad* 1.4.2; "Verily, the gods when they were afraid of death entered the three-fold knowledge [for refuge]; they covered themselves with Vedic hymns (*chandobhir achādayan*). Because they covered themselves with these, therefore the hymns are called *chandas* (*chandasāṁ chandas*)." In the fourth line of our principal text in question, i.e., the *Gītā* 15.1., it is said, "he who knows this is a knower of the Veda" (*yas tam veda sa vedavit*), implying that the knowledge pertaining to the *saṁsāra*-tree is an inferior knowledge of covering and refuge and also knowledge, otherwise not attainable, of something which calls for such refuge, namely the ontic terror.

5. *Kaṭhopaniṣad, with Śaṅkara's commentary and its Ṭikās*, (*Ānandāśrama samskṛta granthāvalī* No. 7.), Poona, 1965, p. 109. This etymology is from the *Nirukta* of Yāska, 2.6.

6. Śaṅkara's *Gītā* Commentary (15.1).

The Kaṭha text and the Gītā text compared

It has become necessary for us to compare the two texts in the two respective scriptures where similar descriptions of the *aśvattha*-tree occur. Two points of contrast are inevitably to be noted. (1) the *aśvattha* spoken of in the *Kaṭha* is *Brahman* itself, no doubt in its cosmic aspect, (2) there is no reference to cutting it down in the *Kaṭha*. With regard to the *Gītā* text the case is quite the contrary. The fact that the two passages are so strikingly similar and yet so different has puzzled several modern interpreters. It may very well be, as Zaehner holds, that one of them—the *Kaṭha* one most likely—is the original and the other in a modified copy. Zaehner is right in observing no contradiction "between the Cosmic Tree and the immortal Being which is its source."[7] The question is, are the two texts different, as it were by accident, while they ought to have been identical ? Or, rather, is it possibly the case that these differences in the texts represent two aspects of the same truth concerning *saṁsāra* ? Radhakrishnan observes: "The tree of life has its unseen roots in *Brahman*. The tree, roots and branches represent *Brahman* in its manifested form. While the tree of life is said to be imperishable *Brahman*, the *Bhagavadgītā*, which uses this illustration, asks us to cut off the tree of existence by the potent weapon of non-attachment."[8] The tree of *Brahman* represented in the one, not depicted as cleavable, is pictured in the other as the tree of existence eminently deserving to be cut down.

Śaṅkara in fact seems to assume that, far from being intentionally opposed or accidentally different, the texts are co-ordinated in the same ultimate ontology. Hence while interpreting the *Gītā* passage, he moves towards the *Kaṭha* passage with this observation : "[It is called] *ūrdhvamūlam* (with roots above) because of subtlety with respect to time, because of causality, because of eternality and because of *mahat-hood*. Hence the unmanifest *Brahman* is said to possess the power of *māyā*. That (i.e., the unmanifest *Brahman*) is its (i.e., the tree's) root. Hence this *saṁsāra*-tree has its roots above."[9]

7. Zaehner, *loc. cit.*

8. Radhakrishnan, S. (ed.) *The Principal Upaniṣads*, London, George Allen & Unwin, Ltd., 1953, p. 642.

9. *ūrdhvamūlaṁ kālataḥ sūkṣmatvāt kāraṇatvāt nityatvāt mahattvācca*

Śaṅkara quotes a Purāṇa text, which is in fact a text (47:12-14) of the *Aśvamedha parva* of the *Mahābhārata*,[10] being part of the *Anugītā*. The discrepancies between the Śaṅkara quotation and the original are purely verbal, and inconsequential. The main reason for quoting the *Mahābhārata* text is to show that the reality represented by the tree is the lower (*saprapañca*) *Brahman*, and even so *Brahman* is the ground, or the real being of the tree, and, vice-versa, the tree is the resort of *Brahman*. Ānandagiri observes in this context that the tree is grounded in *Brahman*, and also *Brahman* dwells in the tree and that because the tree cannot be cut without that knowledge it is called timeless and enduring.[11]

Now there is the mention of a tree in the *Śvetāśvatara Upaniṣad*, 3.7-9. The question is, is there any connection between the *aśvattha* (the *saṁsāra*-tree) or the tree of *Brahman* and the tree in this particular Upaniṣad passage ? The two seem wholly unrelated to each other except for the fact that the word 'tree' occurs in the latter too. Yet Zaehner thinks that in both the same concept of the tree exists, performing the same function.

ūrdhvam, ucyate brahma avyaktaṁ māyā-śaktimat, tanmūlasyaiti so 'yaṁ saṁsāravṛkṣa ūrdhvamūlaḥ.

10. *avyakta-bīja-prabhavo buddhi-skandha-mayo mahān;*
mahāhaṁkāra-viṭapa indriyāntara-koṭaraḥ.
mahābhūta-viśākhaśca viśeṣa-prati-śākhavān;
sadā-parṇaḥ sadā-puṣpaḥ śubhāśubha-phalodayaḥ;
ājīvaḥ sarvabhūtānām brahmavṛkṣaḥ sanātanaḥ.
etat chittvā ca bhittvā ca jñānena paramāsinā;
hitvā cāmaratām prāpya jahyādyau mṛtyujanmanī;
mirmamo nirahaṁkāro mucyate nātra saṁśayaḥ.

—From the *Mahābhārata, Aśvamedhikaparvan* (Critical edition, Poona, 1960).

Trans.: "The great tree of *Brahman* is timeless, having risen out of the seed of the Unmanifest, with *buddhi* (intelligence) for its trunk, the great ego for its branches, the senses for its sprouts, the great elements for its sub-branches, the sense-objects for its side-branches; ever covered with foliage and ever bearing flowers, producing fruits pleasant and unpleasant, it is fed upon by all creatures. Having felled it and split it with the sword of knowledge and attaining freedom from attachment to things that cause death and (re) birth, (the person) who is without the sense of "mine" and "I" attains *mokṣa* : as to this there is no doubt."

11. *brahmaṇā adhiṣṭhito vṛkṣo brahma-vṛkṣastha api*
jñānaṁ vinā chettum aśakyatayā sanātanaḥ ciraṁtanaḥ.

He further assumes that the theistic interpretation of the cosmos, which he obviously sees as implicit in the *Gītā*, the *Kaṭha* and the *Anugītā* texts, has been made explicit in the *Śvetāśvatara* text; *apropos* the last of which he observes "it is God Himself who is the Tree."[12] The last mentioned text does not support his interpretation as the actual statement in the *Upaniṣad* runs as follows : *vṛkṣa iva stabdho divi tiṣṭhaty ekas tene 'daṁ pūrṇaṁ puruṣeṇa sarvam* (the *Śvetāśvatara*, 3.9b)—"The one stands like a tree [established] in heaven; by Him, that is, by *puruṣa* [is] all this filled."[13] "Tree", it is quite clear, is employed here purely as a simile for describing how the One stands. The fact "all this" (*idaṁ sarvam*), the universe, is juxtaposed with "tree" is utterly without the particular kind of significance implied in Zaehner's interpretation. There is no reason at all why he should have been led to the *Anugītā* passage on the *aśvattha* from here as we note in his text. The two are thematically dissimilar.[14] The *aśvattha* is a huge symbol for the *saṁsāra* and hence for the lower *Brahman*, in terms of which *saṁsāra* becomes something meaningful in spite of its transitoriness and its destiny of having to be cut down.

The Philosophical Meaning of the aśvattha—Some Preliminary Proposals

The reason why the *aśvattha* appears to be important enough for a close scrutiny is that it stands as a symbol for the human cosmos (not so much the physical cosmos), the world of man, the *saṁsāra*, representing the endless round of birth, death and rebirth as well as old age, sorrow and bondage. The ancient thinkers were intensely aware of Ultimate Reality as such, that is *Brahman*. And they were aware also of the world of becoming. The two cannot co-exist as two separate and equally true parts of reality. Nor can the two be treated as if there is no

12. Zaehner, *Op. cit.*, p, 362.

13. Zaehner translates incorrectly : "Like a sturdy tree firm-fixed in heaven he stands, the One, the Person, this whole universe fullfilling". *op. cit.*, p. 363.

14. There is mention of "tree" in many places, and there are different kinds of trees; and at every instance "tree" occurs it is not necessary to assume that the *aśvattha* of the *Gītā* is intended.

meeting at all. On an empirical basis what we know as life—along with birth, death, rebirth, old age and all other things which go with them—belongs to becoming. Yet the ancient thinkers found becoming to be not self-explanatory. The principle whereby it can be understood is the transcendent'*Brahman*, *para Brahman*. But as the *principle* of explanation *para Brahman* has been already taken one step down from its pure transcendence to the status of a structure : hence *apara Brahman*. This of course does not even imply any kind of dialectical self-alienation in a Hegelian thesis-antithesis manner. *Brahman* simply does not become. But insofar as the empirical basis of our understanding is the world of becoming *Brahman* must serve as the principle underlying it. The employment of *Brahman* as the principle in this manner is what gives rise to the concept of being. As a concept it is always answer to a question, whereas Ultimate Reality *per se* is not answer to any question, much less a question. It is a *that* first and then a *what*. Insofar as becoming is the question, being (*sat*) is the answer. *Saṁsāra* is the name for the total framework of becoming, constantly under the existential pressure to be put as a question. *Brahman*, the ground, is provided as the answer. This way we have an ontology not by virtue of any pressure that being puts upon becoming—there is no such pressure and indeed apart from becoming taken problematically there would be no need for the concept of being at all. There is, on the contrary, a pressure that comes from within the realm of *saṁsāra*, of becoming, and that is an existential pressure calling for an answer. Hence *Brahman* is to be understood as the ground of the tree of *saṁsāra*, and the tree inevitably grows downward. That tree is the *aśvattha* of the *Bhagavadgītā*. This has been pointed out by the present author in his book *Religion as Anxiety and Tranquillity*.[15] The symbol of the *aśvattha* then would seem to be a characteristic way of

15. "The true foundations of Indian religious perspectives are the tranquillity structres mediated through the teaching (*dharma* in Buddhism and different *darśanas* in Hinduism): and the structures of suffering are placed as appendix to them, to be always seen from the tranquillity end like the upside down tree of the *Bhagavadgītā* with its roots above and branches below.", *Religion as Anxiety and Tranquillity : An Essay in Comparative Phenomenology of the Spirit*, The Hague and Paris, Mouton, 1972, p. 80.

articulating ontology as an answer to the question that *saṁsāra* poses. Hence it is not to be construed as something "typical of mystical religion" as is done by Professor Zaehner.

It is in view of this ontology that *aśvattha* is called both *saṁsāra* tree and the tree of *Brahman*; and the two apparently different significances attached to the tree in the *Gītā* and the *Kaṭha* are not really contrary to each other. Because of this ontology, the concept of God enters into it naturally, not in any partisan manner, however, to be construed as an expression of theism, so to say as against *Advaita*, as Professor Zaehner seems to see it. The concept of God is always natural and ontologically necessary for the *Advaita*. *Brahman* the ground or the root of the *saṁsāra*-tree is in that relation to be necessarily referred to as God. Hence there is no contradiction between Madhusūdana saying *saṁsāra-vṛkṣasya hi mūlam brahma* (*Brahman* is the ground of the *saṁsāra*-tree) and Śrīdhara saying *saṁsāra-vṛkṣasya mūlamīśvaraḥ śrī nārāyaṇaḥ* (Īśvara, Śrī Nārāyaṇa, is the ground of the *saṁsāra*-tree).[16] Again, God mediates between two eternities, one that belongs intrinsically with *Brahman* and another that belongs with becoming: hence the distinction between the *svarūpanityatā* (of *Brahman*) and the *pravāhanityatā* (of the cosmos). In terms of the former the *aśvattha* is perishable; in terms of the latter it is unending, ever-enduring.[17]

The Philosophical Significance Based on Survey of Further Texts

In order to understand the context in which the symbol of the tree is *saṁsāra* it will be well to go back to the Vedic texts. By doing so we will be able to perceive more clearly than otherwise two important philosophical truths contained in the *aśvattha* symbol, as we will learn of its very early genesis also :

1. The upside-down tree is no new innovation, its inverted position having been there from the genesis of the concept in the Vedas as representing, no doubt, clear anticipations of an

16. In their respective sub-commentaries on the *Gītā*, in the *aśvattha* text.

17. Madhusūdana writes, *sa ca saṁsāra-vṛkṣaḥ svarūpeṇa vinaśvaraḥ pravāha-rūpeṇa ca anantaḥ*; and Śrīdhara likewise writes, *sa ca saṁsāravṛkṣo vinaśvaraḥ pravāharūpeṇa nityaśca, loc. cit*, in both cases.

ontology of the cosmos (basic to cosmology), re-appearing in the *Gītā*, the *Kaṭha* and the *Mahābhārata* (the *Anugītā*), expressing essentially what has been vastly more elaborately set forth in Vedānta philosophy in subsequent times.

2. The ontology of the cosmos is something which goes hand in hand with a particular kind of self-knowledge, or wisdom, used as a sword, is what enables one to deal with the world: knowledge is also detachment—hence *asaṅgaśastreṇa dṛḍhena* (the *Gītā*) or *jñānena paramāsinā* (the *Anugītā*).

Let us consider these two philosophical points as presented in Vedic literature.

1. In the *Ṛgveda* 1.24.7, we have a very striking *mantra*: It is the oldest one referring to the tree. Ṛṣi Śunaḥśepa, while describing Varuṇa's greatness speaks of a tree that the latter planted in the bottomless (*abudhna*) with its roots above and branches below:

abudhne rājā varuṇo vanasy-
ordhvaṁ stūpaṁ dadate pūtadakṣaḥ
nīcīnāḥ sthur upari budhna eṣām
asme antar nihitāḥ ketavaḥ syuḥ.

(King Varuṇa placed the orb of a tree in the bottomless in a downward position, with his holy power. Of these, roots remained above. They are the clues (*ketavaḥ*) concealed inside us.)

The domain of Indra is described as transcendent, not accessible even to the high-soaring birds (metaphorically standing for the flight of the intellect). But the clues are inside us. The poem goes on to describe how Varuṇa made the path for the sun to traverse.

This symbol of the tree is also evidently linked with the *Ṛgveda*, 10.72.3, a poem connected with Bṛhaspati, where the famous image of *Uttānapada* (what has feet upward) occurs; it goes as follows:

devānāṁ yuge prathame
'sataḥ sad ajāyata
tad āśā anvajāyanta
tad uttānapadas pari.

(In the first epoch of the gods the existent arose from the non-existent. Afterwards arose the directions, whereafter [there grew] around [it] what has feet upwards.)

These two are the most express references to the tree (or the cosmos) with roots above (or feet upwards) and the body (or boughs) downwards. There are several other less express ones, which must be omitted from this investigation.

We meet with the upside down tree in the *Chāndogya Upaniṣad* (6.12.1) in the form of the *nyagrodha*.[18] The word *nyagrodha* is made of two parts *nyag* (downward) and *rodha* (growing). Mārkaṇḍeya Ṛṣi also is said to have seen *Īśvara* sitting on the branches of the *avyaya* tree (*vaṭavṛkṣa*, or *nyagrodha*)—at the time of the great Deluge. The great tree (*mahān nyagrodha*)—called so because it is the cosmos itself—, it is declared in the next verse, had arisen out of that extremely minute entity residing imperceptibly within the fruit and the seed— (*etam aṇimānaṁ na nibhālayase...eṣo 'ṇimna*, etc.).

2. Now, the relation between the ontology of the cosmos and knowledge must be considered. Knowledge here is definitely an inward-turning knowledge (which is the essential meaning of *jñāna*), a wisdom by means of which one achieves an existential disconnection from the things which bind one to *saṁsāra*.

In the context of the tree planted by Varuṇa, described in the Śunaḥśepa hymn, the question is, what is above, namely the bottomless, where the roots are placed ? We learn that it is light.[19] The root of the tree is in the region of light. But for

18. The object of inquiry is the fruit of the tree rather than the tree itself.

nyagrodha-phalam ata āhareti; idam, bhagava, iti;
bhindhīti; bhinnam, bhagava, iti;
kim atra paśyasīti; aṅvya ivemā dhānā, bhagava, iti;
āsām aṅgaikāṁ bhindhīti; bhinnā bhagava, iti;
kim atra paśyasīti; na kiṁ cana bhagava, iti.

(Bring hither a *nyagrodha* fruit; this my Lord. Break it. It is broken my Lord. What do you see here ? Extremely small seeds, my Lord. Break one of those. It is broken, my Lord. What do you see here ? Nothing at all, my Lord.)

19. The hymn of Śunaḥśepa was sung by him, we learn from the *Aitareya Brāhmaṇa* (the *Ṛgveda* does not recount the story) where he, the young boy that he was, was bound to the stakes to be sacrificed by Varuṇa; by this hymn he prays to Varuṇa for freedom and light (wisdom), and he found the answer : search within.

gaining light man must seek clues within: the seeing of light is wisdom. Man comes to light by means of the inward quest, that is to say, the searching of consciousness.

The theme of searching within for knowledge—and freedom—comes fully to light in the Upaniṣads (and re-stated in the *Gītā*, no doubt). It was echoed faithfully by Śaṅkara.[20] Cutting down the tree of the cosmos is not refusing to see it, but rather seeing it in the Self: he who sees so truly sees.[21]

The tree of the Cosmos is not only mysterious but also fearful—not an object of comfort but of dread. And knowledge of the tree must comprehend the dread too; dread is an element of human and cosmic consciousness which must be brought to the open through knowledge. The *Kaṭha Upaniṣad* verses (2.3.2-3) following the one concerning the *aśvattha* speak about it. In describing this there occurs the metaphor of the great fear, the upraised thunderbolt (*mahad bhayaṁ vajram udyatam*) for the way the cosmos and its forces impress man. They who know it become immortal (*ya etad vidur amṛtās te bhavanti*), says the *Kaṭha* text.

Professor Zaehner does not omit to note the *Kaṭha* theme of fear in his exposition of the *Gītā* text under consideration, as he observes: "It may paralyze through fear, yet it is, nonetheless, the ladder by which and through which the immortal can be found."[22] But surely, the fear here described is not an indivi-

20. *ātmā tu satataṁ prāpto 'pyaprāptavadavidyayā*
tannāśe prāptavad bhāti svakaṇṭhābharaṇaṁ yathā.

(The Self is ever present, yet due to ignorance it remains unrealized, as a man looks for his ornaments which he is wearing on his neck.)—*Ātmabodha* of Śaṅkara, stanza 44. See *Ātmabodha* (Self-knowledge), ed. Swami Nikhilananda, Madras, Sri Ramakrishna Mutt, 1962, p. 207.

21. *samyagvijñānavān yogī svātmanyevākhilaṁ jagat*
ekaṁ ca sarvamātmānam īkṣate jñāna-cakṣuṣā.

(The yogī endowed with complete wisdom sees the entire universe in his own self; through the eye of knowledge he sees everything as one.)—*Ātmabodha*, Stanza 47. See *Ibid.*, p. 210.

ātmaivedaṁ jagatsarvamātmano 'nyanna vidyate
mṛdo yadvad-ghaṭādīni svātmānaṁ sarvam īkṣate.

(He knows the entire universe to belong to the Self, and to be nothing other; he sees everything to be of the Self just as things like pottery to be clay.)—*Ātmabodha*, Stanza 48. See *ibid.*, p. 211.

22. Zaehner, *Op. cit.*, p. 362.

dual fear, but one of a cosmic nature, governing the very principle by which the forces of the universe are sustained. This the *Kaṭha* verses in question make abundantly clear. Agni, Indra, Vāyu, Death (the physical forces as well as the deities) do their work through fear of Him (*Ātman*, *Brahman*). Śaṅkara clarifies that the universe itself trembles in *Brahman* (*parasmin brahmaṇi saty ejati kampate*).

Yet the knowledge which comprehends the dread that moves the entire cosmos and all the forces in it—thus generating a genuine self-knowledge pertaining to man's situation in the universe of becoming—also liberates him from that dread. The dread is there in the first place as a vague, unclarified individual experience—an unexplored sense of the wrongness of existence[23]—which afflicts man, but its true ontological genesis and depth, its cosmic character, must be explored by means of knowledge. This constitutes part of the essential theological knowledge that Vedānta not only permits but warrants. To know the depth and the universality of dread, the point at which it touches the divine is an indispensable act of religious knowledge.[24] It must be complemented by another act of religious knowledge, that of taking refuge in God. Hence the *Gītā* enjoins :

> *tataḥ padaṁ tat parimārgitavyam*
> *yasmin gatā na nivartanti bhūyaḥ*
> *tam eva cā 'dyaṁ puruṣaṁ prapadye*
> *yataḥ pravṛttiḥ prasṛtā purāṇī.*[25]

(Therefore, that path must be followed, from whence those who have walked it never return. And in Him, that Primal Person, I take refuge, from whom has flowed this ancient current [of the cosmos].)

Gnosis is both the comprehension of Dread and the flight for Refuge,—fully these, and yet more. The thrust of knowledge

23. This theme is elaborated phenomenologically in the author's book, *Religion as Anxiety and Tranquillity*.

24. *na rūpam asye 'ha tatho 'palabhyate*
nā 'nto na cādir na ca saṁpratiṣṭhā.
(Its form is not perceived here, nor its end, nor its beginning, nor its foundation.) The *Bhagavadgītā* 15.3.a,b.

25. *Ibid.*, 15.4.

according to the Upaniṣads and the *Gītā* is not exhausted by these, however.

The experience of the dread and the taking of refuge are two coordinate steps, both being of the character of gnosis (*jñāna*), and focussed on the Divine. In both respects, Śunaḥśepa is the true Vedic prototype. And strangely, perhaps not so strangely, but rather as we should expect, the substance of this knowledge is built into the constitution of the cosmos, as the Vedas are its leaves—and the Vedas have meant shelter, refuge. And here we recall the *Chāndogya Upaniṣad* 1.4.5, where we read that "the gods fearing death took refuge in the three-fold knowledge (*trayīṁ vidyām*), i.e., the three Vedas". The Vedas were their cover, hence they are known by the word *chandas.* Knowledge has a paradoxical location in the cosmos. It is not alien, and yet it is alien, particularly insofar as it is the sword with which to cut it down. But in the quest for understanding it must lead one inevitably to the complex doctrine of the Word—the world itself comes from the Word, which is another side of the matter.[26]

Lastly, the purpose of doing this particular piece of exegesis has been to show that the real significance of the *aśvattha* symbol is something other than what is described by Professor Zaehner as "typical of mystical religion" and is not something into which an ultimate and terminal devotional theism can be read.

Professor Zaehner is right in calling attention to the theistic emphasis, but it is also necessary to make sure that that legitimate emphasis must not lend support to the view that the theism here is of a terminal, or ultimate, kind. The exegetical placing of the *aśvattha* is only one example of how the *Gītā* theism must be seen.

26. *Brahma Sūtra*, 1.3.28. But it is *Brahman*, not the Word, which is the material cause of the world.

SIX

TIME, WITHIN LOGOS AND WITHOUT : AS IN GRAMMAR VEDĀNTA AND MĀDHYAMIKA

"Time" was traditionally part of cosmology, from which naturally it was taken over by physics. But through Christianity (St. Augustine, mainly) it was brought into a mutuality of internal relation with history. Mysticism has had its own approach to time, one that took on new philosophical significance through the duration (*la durée*) concept advanced by Bergson. Phenomenology and existentialism have, in our present epoch, furnished another, revolutionary angle from which to understand it.

The Eastern (in our present case, the Indian) world has had its own diversity of approaches to time. We pick out two interesting Indian views that emerged from their respective religio-philosophical matrices so that we may look at them, to do so being the purpose of this short essay. These two are the ones held by that version of Vedānta known as Grammar Philosophy, stemming from Bhartṛhari's *Vākyapadīya*, for one, and for the other, the Mādhyamika branch of Buddhist philosophy, sourced in Nāgārjuna's *Mūlamadhyamaka-kārikā.**

A comparison of these two views, which were enunciated in roughly the same general epoch of Indian history, could prove instructive, and that for more than historical reasons. Now, we notice in the one a mixture of cosmology and salvation concern

*The *Mūlamadhyamaka-kārikā* text is from the *Madhyamaka-śāstram*, edited by P. L. Vaidya, Darbhanga, the Mithila Institute, 1960. The *Vākyapadīya* text is the one edited by K. A. Subramania Iyer, Poona, Deccan College (*Kāṇḍa* I, 1966; *Kāṇḍa* III, part 1, 1963; *Kāṇḍa* III, part 2, 1973). *Bhartṛhari* by the same author (Poona, Deccan College, 1969) is also referred to, and its textual material cross-referred with the *Vākyapadīya* text.

(which latter may be brought within what we nowadays call the existential), while in the other the salvation concern predominates without any definite cosmological interst. [Mādhyamika itself generally is not noted for its cosmological interest, unlike the other great Buddhist School, Vijñānavāda-Yogācāra.]

The General Framework

Nāgārjuna and Bhartṛhari, who lived about 150 years apart, the one around 300 A.D., and the other from the middle of the 5th to the end of the first decade of the 6th as now believed, are very different kinds of thinkers. Nāgārjuna was a Buddhist, the greatest of all Buddhist thinkers by common consent, while Bhartṛhari was a grammarian of the Vedic-Vedāntic tradition, and surely one of the greatest. [The official Vedānta of Śaṅkara, however, criticized Bhartṛhari's theories.] In fact he was the last great thinker of a great grammatical tradition coming from hoary antiquity. Nāgārjuna is an extremely subtle and original mind, while Bhartṛhari, though no less subtle, is strikingly more comprehensive, and as for originality, he preferred to stand under the umbrella of the three great (*munitraya*) of his tradition, Pāṇini, Kātyāyana and Patañjali.

As for any possible connections between the critical tradition which flowed from Nāgārjuna, and Bhartṛhari's work, that is not our objective, although a distinguished scholar like T. R. V. Murti (in *Central Philosophy of Buddhism*, p. 2) suggests that, like Gauḍapāda and Śaṅkara himself, Bhartṛhari too not only thought within a philosophical climate dominated by *Śūnya-vāda* and *Vijñāna-vāda* but may have been actually influenced by them at least in respect of some techniques.

A comparative study of these two great figures (i.e., in terms of their writings) could be as broad or as restricted as one wants it to be. In our case now we restrict it to the issue of time in their respective fundamental texts.

The ground from which each speaks and the ways of their public thinking as revealed in the texts, which some might choose to call by the name method, are very important for any comparison. In Nāgārjuna's case the ground is far from explicit, clearly by the design. But it is reasonable to suggest that it is what is elsewhere called Ultimate Reality (*paramārtha satya*) as *Śūnyatā*, comprehended, nevertheless, within the term *nirvāṇa*. As for Bhartṛhari, the ground is totally explicit in the sense that it is explicitly identified by the name *Brahman* as well as in the sense that that name is covered by the logos (*śabda*) which underlies all names and all words. Hence *Brahman* is ultimately identified as *Śabda-Brahman*, or *logos-Brahman*. It is equally important to see how the ground extends into, or withholds itself from extending into, the ways of public thinking, consisting of concepts embodied in the texts in question.

It is inevitable that the public thinking should be facilitated by splitting up the subject-matter into a number of topics. To take the *Mūlamadhyamaka-kārikā* first (in deference to chronology), it contains twenty-seven topics elaborated into twenty-seven respective chapters. Its "method" may be described, for a start. The ground from which it speaks refuses to extend itself to the domain of public thinking, and that refusal is reflected in the special kind of critical examination (*parīkṣā*) of the different, logically inter-related, alternatives with respect to the issues of every topic. The technique involves pushing every alternative to its utmost limit, to the end, and with the result, that that which is diametrically opposite to it will automatically come forth for the same kind of critical consideration. The diametrically opposed alternatives, or the pairs of such alternatives, become the four corners of a symmetrical structure (the *catuṣkoṭi*) although in fact a mere lateral symmetry of two diametrically opposite principal alternatives, such as being versus non-being, will essentially suffice. It is quite reasonable to consider this technique as a variant of what can broadly be called dialectic.

In the case of the *Vākyapadīya*, the ground extends itself into the domain of public thinking, embodied in that text unreservedly. That is how it is with *śabda*, both in the sense of the *Śabda-Brahman* and in that of just language. This is naturally so because it is a work dealing with sentence (*vākya*), and word (*pada*). The subject-matter is single, i.e., *śabda*, or the logos. As the ground of thought, it is Ultimate Reality, that is *Śabda-tattva*, or *Brahman*, which are the same. As the logos that manifests it it is language (sentence and words). The manifestation of the logos and our own efforts to understand it are co-respondent activities. This is stated in 1.44. "*Dvāvupādāna-śabdeṣu śabdau śabdavido viduḥ. eko nimittaṁ śabdānām aparo arthe prayujyate*". (The knowers of the logos know two basic things in the logos, of which one is the cause—of its manifestation—and the other is what has to do with—our efforts to obtain—meaning, or in other words, comprehend what language conveys.) In this way Grammar is seen as a total activity, coincident with religion and philosophy, distinguishable only in respect of its pursuit of the way of the logos as its special department. The vision of its specialized pursuit in the total activity is described by Bhartṛhari as he splits up the single subject matter of *śabda* into provisional parts, which are of four kinds, i.e., meanings, words, relations, such as cause and effect, fitness, etc., and uses or purposes (1.26-29). The description is comprehensive, parailelling the complex dynamics of human consciousness—and Bhartṛhari, true to his tradition, pays heed to them from the start. In language as in consciousness, the whole has to be handled but has also somehow to be done through the parts. All in all, Bhartṛhari's public thinking is an activity in which the logos is self-referent and self-involving, both in the sense of its own manifestation and in the sense of our efforts to understand it.

The Basic Differences Between the Two Approaches : And Nāgārjuna's View of Time

The issue of Time is only an instance of useful study in contrast between the two great thinkers. However, we may also find some hidden unity somewhere at some remote end, that is, when we arrive at the question of Ultimate Reality, which is ground for both, although in the case of the one its presence can only be signified by its refusal to enter the domain of public, conceptual, thinking, while in the case of the other the same is signified by its entry into that domain as the logos. It is worthwhile to try and see if this thesis can be at least tentatively exemplified by a quick look at the treatment of Time in the two texts in question.

The ground which (in the case of the *Mādhyamika-kārikā*), refuses to be extended to conceptual thinking, and (in the case of the *Vākyapadīya*) does so extend itself is depicted appropriately at the beginning of both texts. The Nāgārjuna text has the famous eight negatives (in the invocation) : *anirodham, anutpādam, anucchedam, aśāśvatam, anekārtham, anānārtham, anāgamam, anirgamam,* "No arrestation, no generation, no cancellation, no perpetuation, no unity, no diversity, no advent, no departure". The Bhartṛhari text describes it thus : *anādinidhanaṁ brahma, śabdatattvaṁ yadakṣaram,* "*Brahman*, is without beginning and end; it is the Logos-Being, free from decay".

Where the ground has been completely withheld from conceptual thinking paradoxical things happen. Most of all, the basis for making any distinction between that which withholds itself and that from which it is withheld disappears. That is the ultimate *rationale* for the identification of *nirvāṇa* with *saṁsāra,* or so to say the absolute with the relative, in Nāgārjuna's thought. This rationale is also necessary as the tacit justification of the very critical examination which constitutes the *kārikās,* or according to it any philosophy whatsoever, for otherwise it would be nothing but a self-indulgent exercise in what it knows to be self-contradictory. It is in the light of this that we should try to understand Nāgārjuna's examination of Time (Ch. 19 of the *Kārikā*).

Time is a relativity among the past, present and future, and as such it is merely temporality, as we should say. Temporality as such destroys the promise of Eternity which Time carries. And so the only eternity that there is is the eternity of constant passage, the stream of moments. The real Eternity of which Time is the promise (in the language of Sāṁkhya and Vedānta, *kūṭasthanityatā*) is undelivered, while what is delivered is the mere eternity of passage. The rationale requires that what is undelivered—the *kūṭastha*—must also be denied while denying the power of the bearer of the promise to deliver what is undeliverable. The failure of Time to be what it promises to be is what moves Nāgārjuna to say, "therefore Time does not exist", *tasmāt kālo na vidyate* (19.3).[1]

In what other sense could Time's existence be called into question ? For, after all what consists merely in the passage of

1. *Madhyamaka-śāstram*, p. 163.

moments is not regarded as non-existent and its constitution as the relativity among past, present and future is not something that is encountered contrary to our expectation but to Time's promise of Eternity, which, however, we already know to be self-belying. We may reckon this to be Nāgārjuna's fundamental problematic with respect to Time. There are also other ways of looking at Time, both in Nāgārjuna and in those who came after him, and not just through this fundamental problematic. The causality concept was introduced duly (Chapter 20). Thus, it is argued that Time is not a cause of the world as it is, subsisting through the succession of moments. The greatest warrant for the rejection of Time's causality appears to be to deny that the attainment of *Nirvāṇa* is the "result" or end-product of a process. Hence these *kārikās* (20.9,10)[2] :-

> *niruddhe cet phalaṁ hetau heto saṁkramaṇaṁ bhavet*
> *pūrvajātasya hetośca punarjanma prasajyate.*

(The effect being, as it is, the transition of cause which has already passed away, [then] it follows that that would be the rebirth of the cause that had a previous existence.)

> *janayet phalamutpannaṁ niruddho 'staṁgataḥ katham*
> *tiṣṭhannapi kathaṁ hetuḥ phalena janayet vṛtaḥ.*

(How can a cause that has already passed away give rise to an effect which already exists ? How could a cause which is simultaneous with the effect give rise to it ?)

The view is shared with Vedānta that *mukti, nirvāṇa*, is not something to be attained as the result of a process as that would go counter to the very character of salvation. Commenting on this, Candrakīrti repeats the definition of the ground (Ultimate Reality), which Nāgārjuna has introduced in the invocation, and describes it thus :

> *aprahīnam asaṁprāptam anucchinnam aśāśvatam*
> *aniruddham anutpannam etā nirvāṇam ucyate.*

(What is neither given up nor attained, what is neither annihilation nor perpetuity, what is neither destroyed nor generated—these are said to be *nirvāṇa*.)

2. *Ibid.*, p. 171.

Bhartṛhari's View of Time

In Bhartṛhari, "Time" (*kāla*) occurs in the context of the fundamental topics we have already mentioned, i.e., meaning, word, relation and use, or purpose. Time arises here as a special notion along with *dravya* (Substance), *guṇa* (Quality), *dik* (Place), *sādhana* (Means) and *kriyā* (Action). Of these, Place, Means, Action and Time are made into a group, based, of course, on the features of the central part of speech, namely, the verb (itself called *kriyā*), from which other parts of speech derive. These four fundamental categories (if we may borrow this term) are the dynamics, or powers (*śaktis*) of the verb—and of all parts of speech—, although in truth they are only powers of the logos (*śabda*), and are nothing by themselves, as stated in the opening *kārikā* of *Dik-samuddeśa*,

> *dik-sādhanaṁ kriyā kāla iti vastvabhidhāyinaḥ*
> *śakti-rūpe padārthānām atyantamanavasthitāḥ.*[3]

(Such named things as direction, means, action and time are, in respect of their substantial powers, utterly ungrounded.)—*Kāṇḍa* 3.6.1.

Bhartṛhari's treatment of time is rather elaborate compared to Nāgārjuna's—and indeed his whole work is elaborate and comprehensive. His treatment of Time is found mostly in the first *kāṇḍa* and in the topical section *kāla-samuddeśa* (along with a number of *samuddeśas*) in the third *kāṇḍa*. He lists a number of other views which he rejects. Most important of all is the Vaiśeṣika view according to which time is a substance (*dravya*). The Vijñāna-vāda understanding of Time as a construct of the mind and the Sāṁkhyan understanding of it as a potentiality of the *guṇas* are also described and rejected. So many more are mentioned.

For Bhartṛhari Time is the most important of the powers of *Brahman* (or *Śabdatattva*). *Kālaśakti*, or Power of Time, is mentioned as early as the third stanza of the whole text. The *vṛtti* (later comment) on that calls it *svātantrya*, or free creative power, or *kartṛśakti*. It is the cause of genesis and succeeding modifications and of the six transformations (*janmādayo vikārāḥ*

3. *Vākyapadīya*, III, part 1, p. 209; *Bhartṛhari*, p. 437.

ṣaḍ bhāva-bhedasya yonayaḥ[4]). Accordingly, Time is a cooperative cause (*sahakāri-kāraṇam*[5]) of everything. It is further stated that it is the operator of the machine called the cosmos (*tamasya lokayantrasya sūtradhāraṁ pracakṣate*[6]). Also, as to why some things happen and some things do not happen, the explanation has to be sought in the power of Time, which prevents certain events and permits certain others in the universe (*pratibandhābhyanujñābhyāṁ tena viśvam vibhajyate*[7]). Here is a well worked out cosmic economy. Destruction too is due to Time, not only origination and subsistence (*utpattau ca sthitau caiva vināśe cāpi tadvatām*)[8].

Verbs merely express the dynamics of actions (that is primarily the power of Time). Past, present and future are not the only terms which express this. There are also "quick" and "slow" which determine actions, as well as "after" and "before". All of these are applicable to events which already have happened as well as to ones which are yet to happen. In other words, there is a much wider range of relativities affecting Time than past, present and future. Naturally, for conceiving all these, the grammarian is much better equipped than the dialectical thinker. To this task he brings the techniques of discerning meanings which are their own steady signifiers (*arthāḥ sthitalakṣaṇāḥ*) as well as of discovering other meanings which can be obtained through exegesis, or *apoddhāra*[9].

Time is one and the divisions—and qualifications—are merely attributed to it. And yet they are signs of its existence and act as proofs thereof. The very fact that things are remembered is proof of the existence of Time (*kāla-saṁkrānta-rūpatve 'bhūditi vyavahārāt kālasiddhiḥ*)[10]. Likewise, the fact that we can conceive of events yet to come, like reflection in a mirror, is also proof of Time's existence (*bhāvināṁ caiva yadrūpaṁ tasya ca pratibimbakam; sunirmṛṣṭa ivādarśe kāla evopapadyate*).[11] The argu-

4. *Vākyapadīya*, I, p. 18.
5. *Ibid.*, p. 19.
6. *Vākyapadīya*, III, part 2, p. 42; *Bhartṛhari*, p. 438.
7. *Loc. cit.*; *Bhartṛhari*, *loc. cit.*
8. *Vākyapadīya*, III, part 2, p. 41; *Bhartṛhari*, p. 439.
9. Ref. *Bartṛhari*, pp. 220-21.
10. *Vākyapadīya*, III, part 2, p. 55; *Bhartṛhari*, p. 441.
11. *Vākyapadīya* III, part 2, p. 56; *Bhartṛhari*, p. 441.

ments advanced are the exact opposite of those in *kāla* and related *parīkṣās*, of the *Mūlamadhyamaka-kārikā*. Actions which are complete give the name 'past' to Time. But then, how can something which is no longer here give a name to anything ? The answer is : objects produced by action in time gone by are preserved (as present) in memory (*smṛti*), and give the name "past". Past actions are remembered and expressed in appropriate words. So then, past, present and future (like quick and slow, and before and after) are the evidence of Time's existence but are not the constituents of Time. They are the *aṅgas* (parts) but Time is the *aṅgin* (the whole preceding and exceeding the parts). Bhartṛhari works out a scheme, through the category of *aṅgāṅgi-bhāva*, the relation of parts to the whole, the application of which to Time is one of his unique contributions.

All this is part of the explanation of the cosmos, and what we have is a dynamic non-dualism of an all-comprehending logos. Events in Time and parts and divisions of Time are seen as evidences of one eternal Time, and yet not as constituted of passing moments. This theory is a special way to see Time. It is the obverse side, as it were, of looking at Time as the unfulfilled and unfulfilable promise of Eternity. Rather Time is Eternity immanent. In this way Bhartṛhari seems to combine through Time several fundamental things—cosmology, of course, the existential concern, and also the vexing problem of providence.

However, while his philosophy, including his conception of Time is squarely based on the logos, it is clear that it moves in a very different direction from Śaṅkara's Vedānta. For Bhartṛhari, the logos, being itself ultimately *Brahman*, makes everything real, Time included, too real and without truth-provoking paradoxes, from the Śaṅkarite point of view. It would appear, nevertheless, that, though non-paradoxical and even non-dialectical, his efforts to base Time on the logos must ultimately be seen as being motivated by the very laudable desire to combine cosmology with a positive scheme for fulfilling the existential concern for salvation, while giving an account of providence operating in the world's affairs at the same time, and within the same "Time". The power of Time is totally subject to the logos and the logos is *Brahman*. And so ultimately *Brahman* is in control, a fact which can, thanks to the logos, be rationally contemplated and expressed through the human power of speech without palpable limits. And, so as a different kind of Vedānta, it makes a vital point, which need not be regarded as being at variance with Śaṅkara's, in spite of the difference in their general directions.

Seven

SOME UNIQUE CHARACTERISTICS OF SELF-KNOWLEDGE IN VEDĀNTA

Introduction

Wisdom in traditional cultures is usually an amalgam of several kinds of knowledge, among which perhaps cosmology is dominant. Of course, there is also the concurrent cosmization of man and humanization of the cosmos going on hand in hand within this wisdom. Certain cultures of antiquity also had included some elementary forms of self-knowledge within it.

However, it is only in two significant developments in the ancient world—the Socratic in Greece and the Upaniṣadic in India—that self-knowledge as a distinct theme acquired decisive significance. Also, while these two developments are marginally similar, in a deeper sense they are very dissimilar. In the Delphic command *Gnothi seauton* (know thyself) the word *seauton* is a reflexive pronoun meaning 'oneself', 'thyself', in the accusative case. On the contrary, in the Upaniṣads the Self (*Ātman*) is substantive Being, universal as well, no doubt. In the Delphic "know thyself" the actual human personal being (or beings) in his (their) human-ness is addressed as such, with no suggestion that the boundary of being human can or must ever be crossed in the quest for self-knowledge. H.-G. Gadamer clarifies this point well when he observes: "The Delphic demand "Know thyself", meant "Know that you are a man and no god".[1]

Because of the outward resemblance between that Upaniṣadic quest formulable in the words *ātmānam viddhi* (Know the Self), and the Greek *Gnothi seauton* (Know thyself), many scholars have succumbed to the temptation of seeing them as essentially

1. "On the Natural Inclination Toward Philosophy", *Reason in the Age of Science*, previously mentioned, E. T., Cambridge, Mass., M. I. T. Press, 1982, p. 150.

the same in meaning. But in fact, the two are quite different. In the more than 50 places where *ātmānam* (the self) occurs in the canonical Upaniṣads it is mostly as the accusative singular of the substantive noun *ātman,* and only in rare places does it have the sense similar to *seauton* (accusative case of the reflexive pronoun *auton*). As for the word *ātman*, it has had from its inception the connotation of both self and soul, and it is the unique characteristic of the Sanskrit language that both meanings should be contained in the same word. No doubt, it is not the case that these connotations are completely isolable from each other. To isolate them so would be very artificial. It is nonetheless true that in certain hermeneutical contexts they are to be distinguished. The leading cases in point are those which stress *ātma-vidyā* (knowledge of the *ātman*), an expression which if translated should be phrased as *knowledge of the Self,* for the sake of clarity, and certainly not as *knowledge of the soul.* Again, *ātma-vidyā* of the Upaniṣads, if it is to be understood properly, must be approached from the perspective of the all-important theme of identity between the individual *ātman* and the universal *Ātman* (same as *Brahman*). [In order to distinguish between the two we must resort to the cumbersome practice of writing the one with a lower case *a* and the other with a capital *A*.] The substance of Self-knowledge in the Upaniṣads is knowing *that*, the individual *ātman* (one's own self) and the universal *Ātman, parama Ātman* (the Highest Self, i.e., *Brahman*) are identical. Now while it has the formally expressible character of *knowledge that* and the intrinsically inexpressible character of intuitive realization, in the form of a demand made by the logos (*vāk*) itself, it belongs to a class of its own, along with all things which are primordially and unmediatedly of the logos, necessitating both speech and silence. It remains the unspeakable, however, always sustained through speaking.

Self-Knowledge and Identity in the Upaniṣads

In respect of *ātma-vidyā* (self-knowledge) as the theme which derives its interpretable meaning from the central identity postulate[2] of the Upaniṣads the meaning of the term *ātman* must

2. The greatest of the statements of identity is "That thou art" (*tat tvam asi*) repeated nine times in *Chāndogya Upaniṣad*, 6.8.7—6.13.3.

be apprehended as 'Self'. But that meaning emerges solely within the hermeneutics of that postulate, which, however, is the apex of the entire Upaniṣadic teachings. Ordinarily and conventionally, the term, pre-Upaniṣadic in origin, may mean either soul or, in some cases, the Supreme Spirit, or God. Especially is this case in some of the Brāhmaṇas, most notably the *Śatapatha*. We may consider the usage in the sense of 'soul' or Supreme Spirit, continued in the Upaniṣads, to be essentially theological or metaphysical. But, in the Upaniṣads it is metamorphosed into something different in meaning wherever the identity theme impinges: in those instances it has to be read as 'self'. The meaning of 'self', by the same token, also derives from the unique identity thesis of the Upaniṣads. Self-knowledge, therefore, is knowledge of the Self, focussed on the act of placing oneself, thanks to what *vāk* has said, at the decisively important point of the identity of the *self* with the *Self*. This is the point at which *vāk* simply defies theology or metaphysics in the hitherto or elsewhere prevailing sense and forces everything theological or metaphysical to be re-oriented to something utterly new.

The revolutionary nature of the conception of the *ātman* notwithstading, it would not be proper to attempt to completely distance it from theological beliefs and metaphysical speculations pertaining to the soul and the supreme Spirit. Are those beliefs and speculations true? The answer is, they are true inasmuch as they are grasped from the vantage point of all truths, i.e., the oneness of the self with the Self. That is the unique feature of Vedāntic hermeneutics which makes true (or false) all kinds of theological and metaphysical doctrines.[3] In the concept of truth there is then, hermeneutically approached, a difference as between *that which can be made true* and *that which makes true*. The Upaniṣads put forward the identity truth as that which *makes true,* as distinct from doctrines, based on belief or spe-

3. *Note*: Buddhism repudiates theological and metaphysical doctrines, Vedic and others, whereas the Upaniṣads re-orient them towards their being made true or their being made false. The doctrines of the soul and the Supreme Spirit offer the most concrete instances of the divergent approaches. In denying the *ātman* does Buddhism deny it in the sense of the Self ? But how can one be said to deny something that is outside the purview of one's thought ?

culation, which *can be made true.* Some of these doctrines have the distinct aspect of the relation between the souls and the Supreme Spirit. As a striking instance we read (*Bṛhadāraṇyaka Upaniṣad,* 2.5.15) using the same word *ātman* in both senses: "In this *Ātman* (Supreme Spirit) are all beings and *ātmans* (souls) held together" (*asmin ātmani sarvāṇi bhūtāni...sarva eta ātmanaḥ samarpitāḥ*).

Further, the doctrines are made true not by any means by the arbitrary decision by *vāk*. On the contrary, they must exhibit their own disposition in that direction by the testimony of introspective knowledge, so that *vāk* works from within the inner recesses of thought itself. That is why the Upaniṣads speak of "the *Brahman* (i.e., *Ātman*) that is immediately present and directly perceived" (*yat sākṣāt aparokṣāt brahma*), "the self in all" (*ya ātmā sarvāntaraḥ*) (*Bṛhadāraṇyaka Upaniṣad,* 3.4.1,2). Intuitive truth, gained through introspection, is what puts itself in the stream of that which makes true.

It is Śaṅkara who, through his *bhāṣyas*, teaches us that the meaning of 'Self' is concealed in the truth of identity, which he sees as the essential import of all the Upaniṣadic passages. Even when there is no express declaration of identity it is implicitly there, and even the bare descriptions of *Ātman* (i.e., *Brahman*) are indelibly stamped with it, and the meaning of 'Self' emerges from this stamp. Śaṅkara argues that even the description "not this, not this" (*neti, neti*) really has the purpose of teaching identity.[4] This is feasible, he suggests, because identity is conceptually and formally defined as the total absence of any relations—and relations imply separateness. Separateness is

4. See comment on *Bṛhadāraṇyaka Upaniṣad,* 2.3.6.
"If the student wants to teach the transcendent nature of the individual self—which is free from all differentiations of limiting adjuncts, then only can this assertion [about the teacher's instruction] be fulfilled. Because instructed in this way, the student knows himself to be *Brahman*....If, on the other hand, the individual self is one, and what is described as 'Not this, not this' is something else, then the student would understand just the reverse of the truth, viz., that *Brahman* is something and that he is something else. He would not know only himself as 'I am *Brahman*'," *The Bṛhadāraṇyaka Upaniṣad with Śaṅkara's Commentary,* trans. Swami Madhavananda, Mayavati, 1950, p. 342.

determined by species, quality and distinguishing marks. To negate such things is to assert identity.

Human Existence Interpreted as a Project in Self-knowledge

To re-iterate what we have discussed so far, Self-knowledge is depicted in the Upaniṣads as the knowledge of the oneness of Universal *Ātman*, (i.e., *Brahman*) and the individual *ātman*. The dialectics of it is expressed by Śaṅkara in the following words: "As long as the knowledge of the Self which is to be sought after has not arisen, so long the self is a knower, but the same knower will turn out to be the Self sought after, free from all evil and blemish", (*anveṣṭavyātma-vijñānāt prāk pramātṛtvam ātmanaḥ, anviṣṭaḥ syāt pramātaiva pāpma-doṣādi-varjitaḥ*).[5] Here we have in these words the rudiments of a view of human existence as a project in Self-knowledge.

Man may be defined as the being called to self-knowledge. This call may be apprehended as the one thinkable reason why there is some on-going activity attributable to Reality, directed to the world's redemption. It is akin to what St. Paul seems to have in mind when he writes "All creation groaneth and travaileth to wit for the redemption of Man."

No doubt, all speculation about "purpose" of the universe does reflect that primordial pattern in our thinking which we have earlier described as the concurrent humanization of the cosmos and cosmization of man. In every kind of archaic religion the pattern of thought is executed in projects of redemption with the aid of analogies, and at a lower level with the aid of metaphors carried over from speech through thought to action. No execution of purpose seems to be able to surpass this limitation. The ideology of Self-knowledge as depicted in the Upaniṣads seems to be one exception not bound by this limitation. It does not depend upon analogy and metaphor, as the very definition of knowledge (*jñāna*, *vidyā*) suggests its transcendence over them. Śaṅkara argues that "the purpose implicit in all cosmogonies merely buttress the sole purpose of knowing the oneness of the Self" (*sṛṣṭyādi-vākyānām ātmaikatva-darśanārtha-paratva-upapattiḥ*).[6]

5. *Commentary on Brahma Sūtra*, 1.1.4.
6. Comment on *Bṛhadāraṇyaka Upaniṣad*, 1.4.7.

Man really exists only by living towards this highest end. And the notion of "end" must still be entertained in view of the project of Self-knowledge.

The identity of the Self is not a bare idea, not an abstraction, because it is reached by overcoming the differentiating attributes of two concrete beings (not just two heuristic ideas), that is, the soul and the Supreme Spirit. These two beings have every reason to be considered dualistically so that Vedānta commentators like Madhva are entirely justified in their own limited way. But they are limited by not being able to grasp the meaning of 'Self' because they are not able to grasp identity, for in identity alone is the self Self—till then we have only a Supreme Spirit and individual souls. Identity of the Self is shown as the infinite plenitude of Being, and as the only ground for Being to be no longer chained to beings or to *a* particular being.

The first step in the overcoming of duality is to let the sense of the Self in the word *ātman* come to the fore, replacing the senses of soul and Universal Spirit as separate beings. In this way and in this way only can the same Self be apprehended as both the sought after and the seeker (*anveṣṭavya-ātmā/anviṣṭa* and *ātmā pramātā*). So we repeat Śaṅkara's statement: "As long as the knowledge of the Self which is to be sought after has not arisen, so long the Self is a knower, but the same Self will turn out to be the Self sought after."

The two realms to be re-interpreted in the project of Self-knowledge

When Śaṅkara speaks of Self-knowledge he takes into account two realms, one ordinary, everyday consciousness—something we have to use—and the other one that in which Self-knowledge has already manifested itself as a possibility. How wide the latter realm is it is difficult to determine. But some points of incidence where the possibility of Self-knowledge has actually manifested itself are concretely known: these are called by the names *śruti*, *śāstra* and *āgama* (the last meaning what has come of its own accord). The Upaniṣads are regarded as the paradigm expression of it. Where else it could be found is a wholly different matter.

No doubt the existence of such means of knowledge as *āgama* introduces a strange element into Vedānta as a philosophy and it is not easy to circumvent it. But Śaṅkara provides some help in understanding this predicament at least partially. *Āgama* is supposed to have authority to teach. In respect of the concept of authority (*pramāṇa*) Śaṅkara argues against the orthodox (*Pūrva-Mīmāṁsā*) view and shows that it is nothing but "a functional capacity to generate knowledge of the Self" (*ātmajñānotpādanam*) and that there is no other criterion.[7] In this sense there really is no such thing as "authority". As to what is instrumental to the manifestation of the possibility of Self-knowledge, in principle no limit in scope can be set for it.

These two realms mentioned, Śaṅkara takes with utmost seriousness, and in arriving at a clear concept of Self-knowledge he employs the method of exegeting both consciousness and the texts, sometimes successively and sometimes simultaneously. The secret of success lies in the complete integration of the two. He does take special care to point out why we should regard the former realm with respect, for "as long as the self is not realized, appeals to everyday consciousness and means of proof are valid, as the self is assumed to be what everyone takes it to be, to the extent of treating it as just body" (*dehātma-pratyayo yadvad-pramāṇatvena kalpitaḥ laukikaṁ tadvad eva idaṁ pramāṇaṁ tu ātmaniścayāt*).[8] Therefore, Śaṅkara is as much an interpreter of consciousness as he is of the texts of the Upaniṣads. To interpret revelation and human consciousness simultaneously, empirically by stripping the latter down to the absolutely given and the *sui generis*, and then building it up by correlating with revelation—and that without benefit of dogma—is a unique feature of Śaṅkara's thought.

The truth of Self-knowledge can, theoretically speaking, be reached by understanding ordinary consciousness and what it really conceals. There are a number of positive suggestions in the Upaniṣads themselves, which Śaṅkara picks up.

Examples: analysis of four states of consciousness in Māṇḍūkya; describing the five sheaths (*pañcakośa*) of matter, life, mind, intellect and bliss;[9] direction for progressive self-

7. *Loc. cit.*
8. Commentary on *Brahma Sūtra*, 1.1.4.
9. *Taittirīya Upaniṣad*, 2.1.1—2.5.1.

reflection like repeatedly looking into a mirror;[10] analysis of the structures of desires.[11] The last mentioned is particularly interesting because Self-knowledge is described as the desire to know what is hidden within the inner space within 'the small lotus flower' (*puṇḍarīkaṁ veśma*) which resides in the city of Brahman (*Brahma-pura*) i.e., *puruṣa*, i.e., man. 'Inside' is merely a figure of speech, for the Self has no inside or outside (*anantaram, abāhyam*).[12]

Consciousness must understand itself as constituted of different layers of cover which hides the spaceless Self 'within'. Śaṅkara in different places forces consciousness to reach an understanding of itself in this manner. The definitive scheme for the act of self-understanding by consciousness is given in his Preface to the *Commentary on Brahma Sūtra.* He begins by faithfully giving an analysis of consciousness as having a structure of *viṣaya* and *viṣayin* (two terms which we have no recourse but to translate as 'object' and 'subject' respectively). These two belong to the respective spheres of operation of *yuṣmat* (the base form of the pronoun 'you' and its declensions) and *asmat* (the base form of the pronoun 'I' and its declensions), and have natures as opposed to each other as darkness and light. All the same, there is in this structure a certain pre-disposition or tendency to confuse between the subject and the object. Accordingly, it is found to be a characteristic of everyday conduct of man (*naisargika-lokavyavahāra*) to superimpose each of these and its properties upon the other, resulting in such a consciousness as 'I am this', 'this is mine' (*aham idam, mama idam*). Such mutual superimposition (*adhyāsa*) is due to the pervasive factor of false knowledge (*mithyā-jñānam*). This false knowledge is so pervasive that one's knowledge of one's own self (*pratyagātman*) is itself conditioned, even though in the smallest degree, by objectivity. "One's own real self is not a non-object absolutely insofar as it is denoted by the word *asmat* (the base form of 'I') and because also it is directly and immediately intuited (*na tāvad ekāntena aviṣayaḥ asmat-pratyaya-viṣayatvāt aparokṣatvāt ca pratyagātma-prasiddheḥ*). [It may be noted that in this context the terms *pratyagāt-*

10. *Chāndogya Upaniṣad,* 8.7.1—8.12.6.
11. *Ibid.*, 8.1.1—8.4.3
12. Cf. *Bṛhadāraṇyaka Upaniṣad,* 2.5.19; 3.8.8.

man and *aparokṣa* are used simply in the empirical sense.] Even in the intuition of one's own self there is no discrimination between subject and object. Upon non-discrimination is based man's notion of being a doer (*kartā*) and experiencer (*bhoktā*). Such is the natural condition of everyday consciousness, which is described as false consciousness of 'I' and 'mine' (*aham mam iti abhimāna*). However, this false consciousness is the only context into which the teaching on Self-knowledge can be introduced, which would be applicable under no other condition.

Not only in this Preface but in different places in all of the twelve (or thirteen?) commentaries Śaṅkara periodically returns to the analysis of consciousness. But analysis for him is *exegesis*, that is an activity undertaken for the sake of bringing to clear daylight its deepest essence, which is none other than the being in whom the potentiality for Self-knowledge resides. This potentiality is described as "the desire for knowledge (*jijñāsā*)" of the Self. [But wherever there is a chance of the Self being misunderstood as the individual soul the alternative term *brahman* is used in its place. Hence it is clarified that the desire for knowledge of the Self is desire for knowledge of *Brahman*.]

The certainty of the sense of one's own existence is the potentiality for Self (or *Brahman*)-knowledge that consciousness carries. It is in that light that Śaṅkara makes his famous statement which has often been mistakenly compared to the Cartesian formula of *cogito ergo sum*. "Everyone", writes Śaṅkara, "knows his own existence, no one thinks that he does not exist" (*sarvohi ātmāstitvam pratyeti, na nāham asmīti*). This statement has nothing at all to do with methodological doubt. This is not a device for deriving the existence of the world and God from a ground of something that is held indubitably certain of itself. (Śaṅkara feels no need to reinvent the world or to disinvent it.) Śaṅkara repeats the idea (in 1.1.4.) in a slightly modified form: "Not this, not this—that is the Self; it cannot be denied because it is the self of him who denies it" (*sa eṣa neti neti ātmā, ityātmaśabdāt ātmanaśca pratyākhyātum aśakyatvāt; ya eva nirākartā tasyaiva ātmatvaprasaṅgāt*).

It should be apparent that the context in which these enunciations have been made is the debate with Pūrva-Mīmāṁsā which denies that the Self (or *Brahman*)-knowledge is the highest "end" of man. The latter argues that the concept 'self' is beyond the scope of knowledge, because it has to be either already known or unknown. Śaṅkara replies that this logical predicament is inapplicable because Self is a well-known which because of that very fact is *what should be desired to be known.* Pūrva Mīmāṁsā fails to take into account the highest testimony of consciousness, but it regards such things—and the concept 'Self' —to be merely auxiliary to injunctions pertaining to what is to be done (*vidhiśeṣatvam*). It is noteworthy that in this controversy Śaṅkara puts himself squarely in the company of all other schools, materialist, Buddhist, Sāṁkhya, Vaiśeṣika, etc., all of whom are willing to consider experience as a central principle in philosophy and to admit at least a functional conscious self, as a question, if nothing else. By listing them all[13] he implicitly assumes that in one way or another the acceptance of a "self" that exists is a common denominator for them. But he outlines his difference from them: (1) they do not know the deepest implications of this testimony because they do not know what the real nature of the self is; (2) they fail to realize that knowledge of the self at a level befitting profundity is the highest call of man. To know the self is the highest "end" of man, because, as the *Bṛhadāraṇyaka Upaniṣad*[14] says, it is dearer than everything else (*preyo'nyasmāt sarvasmāt*), is more interior (*antarataram*). Commenting on this Śaṅkara writes: "That which is most dear deserves to be attained by the utmost exertion" (*yo hi loke niratiśaya-priyaḥ sa sarva-prayatnena labdhavyo bhavati*).

Śaṅkara never surrenders the role of empirical introspection as something that leads to Self-knowledge. With regard to the object referred to by the pronoun 'I' (*ahaṁpratyaya-viṣaya*) or, so to say, the "ego", one must rather use it as a tool—the only tool that we really have—for discovering someone who stands behind it. Ego is an objectified subject (or subjectified object). In the last resort the object referred to by the subjective pronoun 'I' and the object referred to by the same pronoun in its base form *asmat* (i.e., *asmatpratyaya-viṣayaḥ*) are different only in the degree of objectification.

13. Cf. *Commentary on Brahma Sūtra*, 1.1.1.
14. *Bṛhadāraṇyaka Upaniṣad*, 1.4.8.

Object and subject (*viṣayaḥ,* and *viṣayin*) like 'I' and 'you' are co-ordinately predicating (*samānādhikaraṇyam*) and really inseparable (*apṛthaksiddham*). They are like the concepts 'transcendent' and 'immanent' which occur together. These constitute the structure of empirical consciousness. Both subject and object are products of the intercourse between truth and falsity (*satyānṛta-mithunīkaraṇam*). Subject is only provisionally treated as though it is exempt, but ultimately it is not. Śaṅkara shows that introspection should be able to get beyond (or behind) even empirical consciousness, to that which underlies it, i.e., to transcendentally-grounded subjectivity. This is what he calls *sākṣi,* witness, a concept already given currency, in a way not different from Śaṅkara's usage, by Sāṁkhya. The *sākṣī* can only be perceived by differentiating it from the objectified subject (or the subjectified object) referred to by the pronoun 'I' (*aham-pratyaya-viṣaya-kartṛ-vyatirekeṇa*).[15]

This is beyond the sway of object-subject (*viṣaya-viṣayin*) co-ordinate predication. This witness is described as the only seer, only knower, etc., in the language of the Upaniṣads.

If the potentiality for Self-knowledge already resides in the *sākṣī* its possibility is manifested by the logos. Such manifestation is through the texts, specifically the Upaniṣads. Beyond the fact that the Upaniṣads have been found to be capable of generating Self-knowledge (*ātma-jñānotpādakam*) they hold no other authority. The *Chāndogya Upaniṣad* expresses this well through a simile—and it is hard to see how any other kind of account will be effective in this respect—: "Just as, my dear, one might lead a person away from [the city of] the Gāndhāras blindfolded and abandon him in a desolate place and just as that person would cry out towards the east or the west or the south or the north saying 'I have been left here blindfolded, I have been left here blindfolded'. And as, if someone removed his blindfold and told him, 'In that direction are the Gāndhāras, go in that direction', thereoupon being informed and capable of judgement he would, by inquiring from village to village, arrive at Gāndhāra; even so does one here who has a teacher know 'I shall remain

15. *Commentary on Brahma Sūtra*, 1.1.4.

here only so long as I am not released. Then I shall reach the goal' ".[16]

Śaṅkara suggests that the Upaniṣads are the teacher: that has been the accepted view in the tradition also. However, one circumstance of defining the Upaniṣads as the source of information about Self-knowledge must always be remembered: that is when Śaṅkara contrasts their contents with the contents of the earlier, ritualistic sections of the Vedas. In one place in the *Chāndogya Upaniṣad* itself (7.1.1-5) the scope of the texts which have no capacity to provide information about Self-knowledge is extended to a wider variety of books and sciences of the day. These texts unlike the Upaniṣads are ruled out as incapable of guiding us to Self-knowledge.

If we follow the simile of the blindfolded man, the Upaniṣads are merely like a passer-by. How the passer-by happened to pass-by is a very difficult question. But somehow the way-farer who can guide always *happens* to pass by. The horizon of these texts is merely the horizon of the possibility of Self-knowledge manifested in the appropriate medium, viz., through words.

They are, however, of the nature of revealing logos, not to be differentiated as this or that statement. All teachings of the Upaniṣads, according to Śaṅkara point to one thing only: the unity of the individual self with the Supreme Self, expressed by the paradigm formula: "that thou art" (*itaśca tattvamasi vākyaṁ vastu-paramevetyāha sarvopaniṣaditi*).[17] There are indeed many similar statements in the Upaniṣads such as "I am *Brahman*", "this *ātman* is *Brahman,*" etc. But it is clear that they all are essentially the same in form and meaning. But then there are some others which describe the Supreme *Brahman* (*Ātman*) differently: e.g., "not this, not this". Śaṅkara argues, as we have already explained, that this text too, as well as others, is same in meaning as "That thou art." In this context also he repeats the assertion that all the Upaniṣads teach the identity of the individual self with the Supreme *Brahman* (*Ātman*) (*ātmanaḥ parabrahmatvam*) and that the real import of the teaching is to deny the suggestion that "*Brahman* is one and I am another" (*anyadado brahma anyo aham asmīti*).

16. *Chāndogya Upaniṣad*, 6.14.1,2.
17. *Commentary on Chāndogya Upaniṣad*, 6.16.3.

Śaṅkara maintains that if there is no unity of meaning in the texts it would be impossible to see them as revealing word. This unified meaning is that of the identity of the individual self and the Supreme Self, and that meaning does not rest with the text but belongs to the logos (*vāk*). And as observed before, the identity is what holds the meaning of the 'self' and releases it from the conventional meaning of 'soul', and it is brought out through exegesis of the texts. Exegesis simply brings out the meaning that is struggling to be delivered.

Now comes the question of the integration of the two realms, consciousness and text. We may repeat that the potentiality for Self-knowledge resides in the Self witnessed to by *sākṣī*, but the possibility is manifested in the text. The potentiality becomes an actuality by the guidance of the text. *Sākṣī* can never pre-empt that role. It is strange that the possibility of Self-knowledge should be manifested in the texts, but again, not so strange because the possibility is borne by the logos. Like a way-farer the text will come and go, simply leaving the direction-giving words with the lost man. All the Upaniṣadic statements, however diverse they appear, give the same direction, because the logos is the same. The text is exactly like the object-subject structure of empirical consciousness. It too is called what is bodied (*śārīrakam*).

Redefinition of man from the end of Self-knowledge

We have already said that Vedānta understands man as the being called to Self-knowledge. Accordingly, the only way to carry out the understanding is to find man placed in the stream of Self-knowledge, which is the beginning. So, we must forget man. Of course if he is forgotten he will be found again.

We, therefore, do not impose any previously existing definition of man upon 'Self-knowledge' as is mostly customary in philosophical anthropology. In fact, we push 'man' aside, putting the Self (*ātman*) in its place, who again is defined only as "not this, not this". The fact that from the moment the identity truth is stated we begin defining the individual self exactly in the manner of the Supreme Self as "not this, not this" tells everything that is to be told.

Supposing we assume, as we normally do, that Self-knowledge is an activity of man (whom we already know), let us see where it will lead us. There is an extra-ordinary passage in *Bṛhadāraṇyaka Upaniṣad* 1.4.9: "They say, men think 'by *Brahman*-knowledge, we shall become all.' Well what did that *Brahman* know by which it became all?" This passage bespeaks a certain tendency among some who have already accepted the Upaniṣadic doctrine of Self-knowledge but think of it, nevertheless, as an activity of man, modelled on Pūrva-mīmāṁsā. The occurrence of the term 'man' (*manuṣya*) here is extremely important. Commenting on this, Śaṅkara writes, "the term 'man' is used for declaring a special competency" (*manuṣya-grahaṇaṁ viśeṣato adhikāra-jñāpanārtham*). "It is commonly believed that men are beings marked by a special ability to strive for ultimate well-being and felicity (that is to say that they are destiny-seekers)" (*manuṣyā eva hi viśeṣato abhyudaya-niḥśreyasasādhane adhikṛtā ityabhiprāyaḥ*). This view of Self-knowledge Śaṅkara rejects on the ground that it makes Self-knowledge out to be the result of an action just like any other action (*karmaphalena tulyam eva*) and therefore transitory (*anitya*).

So "what did *Brahman* know by which it became all"? This means *Brahman* did not know any other as there is no other. "Man" insofar as he is that which is other to itself (*anātma*) should not be that to which "Self-knowledge" refers.

Man is to be placed in the stream of Self-knowledge and re-defined. Utterances like "That thou art", "I am *Brahman*" do precisely place man in that stream. Man, as thus re-defined, fleetingly shows himself in that stream. The *Bṛhadāraṇyaka* passage which speaks of "not this, not this" actually refers to the fleeting manner in which the human phenomenon (*puruṣa*) shows itself and compares it to the glowing of the fire-fly or tongue of fire or "flash of lightning" (*sakṛd-vidyuttam*).

It also answers the question, "if the Self is self-identical where do we go from there?" Vedānta does not depict Self-knowledge as an abstract idea but as that which is the greatest fullness and plenitude. Self-knowledge is the great feast of the Self. The question is, riding on what shall man enter the banquet hall? No doubt, Self-knowledge remains the eternal prospect which does not mean that it is something placed in a future. And, finally, all the techniques of meditation, etc., recommended as means (*sādhana*) to Self-knowledge must simply be taken for what they are to thought, as testimony to that prospect. They also testify to the fact that Self-knowledge is real and not just metaphorical. The prospect is real but the means must not be taken at its face-value. In fact, if so taken they might even contradict the reality.

EIGHT

THE QUESTION AS TO THE JĪVAN-MUKTI "IDEAL"

The *jīvan-mukti,* or liberation-in-life "ideal", has been customarily enshrined as the highest vision of life in the Indian tradition. Its sublimity is unquestionably self-evident enough not to require any special effort to justify it. In any case the interest that lies underneath the writing of this brief essay is not its theological or philosophical dimension but simply the historical problem as to its origin and development.

Even very careful scholars read this "ideal" of *jīvanmukti* back into the origins of classical systems (especially Sāṁkhya-Yoga and Vedānta, the latter even more so). For instance, M. Hiriyanna, generally a model of conservative carefulness, states in respect of *Sāṁkhya-kārikā* that it 'explicitly admits' the ideal of *jīvan-mukti,*[1] and in expounding Śaṅkara's teaching on liberation he suggests that Śaṅkara favoured the *jīvan-mukti* ideal.[2] In contrast, I argue that while the material for this notion can be found in the classical texts and in Śaṅkara, its origin as an articulated ideal lies outside them, in fact in certain texts of popular spirituality.

Many models of the saint's life and of liberation have come from popular spirituality, including the *jīvan-mukta, bodhisattva* (in Buddhism), *parama-haṁsa,* and *avatāra.* But all these are particularizations, which it is the prerogative of popular spirituality to produce. Primary texts like the *śruti* will not particularize. Nor will someone like Śaṅkara do so; his work is to "show" *śruti.* Inasmuch as a particular ideal is part of popular spiritua-

1. M. Hiriyanna, *Outlines of Indian Philosophy* (London: George Allen and Unwin, 1956), 279.
2. *Ibid.*, 380-82.

lity it addresses itself to some basic common belief with wide currency and seeks to challenge it, reform or supplement it, in a revolutionary manner. And in this way it also particularizes what it addresses.

It is normal for all religions, including Hinduism, to believe that spiritual salvation comes after death. In the Indian religious traditions, however, which believe in the transmigratory chain, 'death' has had to be something more than the cessation of the present life, and therefore had to be the "final death", or *atyanta-viyoga*. Thus the *Nyāya-mañjarī* is by no means exceptional, but only echoes the commonly held notion, when it says : "Only when the nine factors of incarnate existence (listed as will, aversion, pleasure, pain, cognition, effort, *dharma, adharma,* and *vāsanā*) are destroyed will *mukti* occur; that is, only after absolute death will *mukti* occur" (*tad evam navānām ātmaguṇānām nirmūlocchedo 'pavargaḥ iti yaducyate tadevedamuktaṁ bhavati tad atyantaviyogo 'pavargaḥ iti*)[3]. [In this quotation there is the concept, peculiar to *Nyāya,* that is, the absence of cognition or knowledge in *mukti,* which we must not take account of.] This latter is the norm and is called *videha-mukti.*

The final shedding of the body and liberation are equated with each other. In other words *mukti* and the *videha* state are identical, and there never has been a contest about that in the normal religious life. This fact still holds good. However, the radical notion of gnosis known diversely as *jñāna, vidyā,* and *sāṁkhya,* etc., entered the religious realm, first through the Upaniṣads, and continued in different ways through a number of subsequent texts, eventually organized into the twin traditions of Sāṁkhya and Vedānta such as we know them. Now, insofar as the notion of gnosis became the governing one it appropriated *mukti* directly, leaving the issue of the final atrophy of the body to the realm of Necessity, which in its physical aspect was called *prakṛti* and in its moral aspect *karma,* the two together constituting the twin law of Necessity.

3. *Nyāya-mañjarī* of Jayanta Bhaṭṭa, *Taduttarabhāga,* ed., by Pandit Ganganath Sastri (Banaras : Medical Hall Press, 1895), 508; also *Nyāya-mañjarī* of Jayanta Bhaṭṭa, by Pandit Suryanarayana Shukla (Banaras : Chowkhamba, 1934), *Taduttarabhāga,* 77.

Gnosis brings about liberation directly and without having to wait upon the workings of Necessity either in the aspect of *prakṛti* or of *karma*; yet it does not totally disregard them. The Upaniṣads have generally worked out the various implications of gnosis, including, most importantly, its power to bring about freedom. In several places in the Upaniṣads the possibility of attaining *mukti* "here" (*iha*) (i.e., in this present life) through *vidyā* (*gnosis*) is stressed. For instance, in *Muṇḍaka* 2.1.10b, we read, *etad yo veda nihitam guhāyām so'vidyāgranthim vikirati iha* —"He who knows that which is kept hidden in the cave breaks loose from the bonds of *avidyā* "here" (i.e., in this life) itself."[4] *Bṛhadāraṇyaka* 4.4.14 has it, *ihaiva santo'tha vidmas tad vayam* —"Verily even while we are *here* we may know this."[5] A few passages before this, at 4.4.7, it is said, "When all the desires that dwell in the heart are cast away, then the mortal becomes immortal, then he attains *Brahman* 'here' (*atra*)."[6] Commenting on the verse previous to it (i.e., 4.4.6) Śaṅkara stresses the possibility of attaining *mukti* through gnosis in this life itself insofar as a knower freed from desire can become *Brahman* even here (*sa ca vidvān āpta-kāmaḥ ātmakāmatayā ihaiva brahma bhūtaḥ*), suggesting that *mukti* does not depend upon the time when the body falls away (*na śarīrapātottarakālam*), because it is nothing but the actualization of a reality, and not an event.[7]

Now, although the foundational texts themselves nowhere use the term *jīvan-mukti*, it is clear that the idea can be worked out from what they say. Nor is the opposite term *videhamukti*, used by them anywhere, although, undoubtedly, the later coinage of both these terms is justified on the authority of these texts. However, it is fascinating to find that the passages in the

4. Reference for text in transliteration : S. Radhakrishnan (ed.), *The Principal Upaniṣads* (London : George Allen and Unwin, 1953), 682. Translation is my own.

5. *Ibid.*, 276.

6. *Ibid.*, 273.

7. *tasyaivam akāmayamānasya karmābhāve gamana-kāraṇābhāvāt prāṇā vāgādayo notkrāmanti nordhvaṁ krāmanti dehāt. sa ca vidvān āpta-kāmaḥ ātma-kāmatayā ihaiva brahma-bhūtaḥ, Bṛhadāraṇyakopaniṣad . . . Śāṁkara-bhāṣya-sametā*, ed. by Ramachandra Sastri (Banaras : Vani Vilas Press, 1954), 611.

Bṛhadāraṇyaka cited occur in the course of the long discussion between Yājñavalkya and Janaka, the king of Videha (no doubt a historical kingdom). We do not wish to insinuate a pun into the word *videha* in such an august conversation, which could most probably have not been intended. However, it is not without some incidental interest that it is Janaka, king of Videha, who has been usually extolled as the supreme example of *jīvan-mukti,* and that the *Bhagavadgītā* (3.20),[8] although not employing the word, implies the idea.

Pun or no pun, there still remains the possibility of considering Janaka Vaideha (Janaka of Videha) since the Upaniṣad here refers in both ways to him. *Bṛhadāraṇyaka,* 4.4.7, part of which is quoted above, speaks of the body (*śarīra,* synonym for *deha*) comparing it to the cast-off slough of a snake lying on an anthill, lifeless, whereas the immortal life (*prāṇa*) is *Brahman.* Śaṅkara sees in this passage the meaning of what is meant by the body to be shed as attendant upon *mukti.* He defines it as one of attitude of the physical selfhood governed by desire and *karma* (*kāma-karma-prayukta-śarīrātma-bhāva*).[9] The stress of the Upaniṣads, as exemplified by the Yājñavalkya-Janaka discourse, is that if the right attitude prevails one can be spiritually free from the body even though one is still in the body. Such seems to be the essential import of the word *iha,* or *atra* ('here'), used in many places.

The citations from the *Bṛhadāraṇyaka* we have just made constitute part of one of the two most famous discussions on *mukti* in the Upaniṣads. The other is the Uddālaka-Śvetaketu dialogue in *Chāndogya,* 6th chapter.[10] To relate the contents of this chapter to the problem of *mukti,* section 14, verse 2, is especial-

8. *karmaṇai 'va hi saṁsiddhim*
āsthitā janakādayaḥ
lokasaṁgraham evā 'pi
saṁpaśyan kartum arhasi.

Reference for text in transliteration, S. Radhakrishnan (ed.) *Bhagavadgītā* (London : George Allen and Unwin, 1963), 139.

9. *Kāma-karma-prayukta-śarīrātma-bhāvena hi pūrvam saśarīro martyaśca, Bṛhadāraṇyakopaniṣad . . . Śāṁkarabhāṣya-sametā,* 621.

10. *Chāndogya Upaniṣad* 6.1.1-6.16.3. Reference : Radhakrishnan (ed.), *The Principal Upaniṣads* (see n. 4 above), 446-67.

ly important. It concludes with the words, "In the same manner does one here, who has a teacher, know within himself 'I shall remain here only so long as I shall not be liberated and reabsorbed'" (*evam eva iha ācāryavān puruṣo veda, tasya tāvad evaṁ ciram yāvan na vimokṣye atha sampatsya iti*).[11] The expression 'so long as' (*yāvad tāvad*) indicates that waiting is the essential meaning of the word 'here' (*iha*), that is, in this life. There is much to be said for interpreting 'here' as that which is already under the control of gnosis and accordingly as a waiting for *mukti.* The only question is whether this waiting for *mukti,* insofar as it is under the control of gnosis, is itself *mukti,* and if so in what sense ? We can say that one of the basic characteristics of Vedānta is that, under gnosis, there is the possibility of that kind of waiting for *mukti* which is itself *mukti,* but that it is so in such a way that the 'waiting' will not be rendered meaningless. Briefly put, to be in *mukti already* and still to *await* it is the distinguishing feature of Vedānta's teaching on gnosis.

Śaṅkara's *bhāṣyas* are an aid in putting the different sides of the matter together. There are four places where he treats the matter thoroughly. Two of them are in the context of the two Upaniṣadic passages I have mentioned (*Bṛhadāraṇyaka,* 4.4.6 and *Chāndogya,* 6.14.2), and the other two are in the context of *Brahma Sūtra*, 3.4.51 (on the topic *iha*, or 'here', hence called *aihikādhikaraṇam*) and 4.1.15 (on *karma* that has not begun to produce fruits, hence called *anārabdhādhikaraṇam*).[12]

On *Bṛhadāraṇyaka,* 4.4.6 which declares the possibility of one's attaining *Brahman* here, Śaṅkara writes as follows :

> That man of realization, who has attained all the objects of his desire since they are but Self to him, has become Brahman in this very life...This man of realization is Brahman in this very life although he *seems* to have a body. Being but Brahman he is merged in Brahman. Because he has no desires that cause the limitation of non-Brahmanhood, therefore being but Brahman, he is merged in Brahman in

11. *Ibid.*, 464.

12. *Brahmasūtra-Śāṁkarabhāṣyam*, ed. by Mahadeva Sastri Bakre and W. Laxman Sastri Pansikar (Bombay : Pandurang Jivaji, Nirnaya-Sagar Press, 1934), 820f., 849f.

> this very life, not after the body falls. A man of realization after his death undergoes no change of condition; he does not become something different from what he was in life, for the only difference is that he is not connected with another body.[13]

This idea that *mukti* is possible here, in this life, is expressed also under *Brahma Sūtra,* 3.4.51 on the word *iha,* or 'here'—*aihikam api aprastuta-pratibandhe tad darśanāt*[14] ('In the absence of any hindrance [*mukti* is possible] even here, i.e., in this life'). Hindrance (*pratibandha*) consists of the functions appurtenant to the body. In other words, those functions are no longer any hindrance. *Mukti* is possible here, in this life (*samāna-janmani*). However, Śaṅkara makes it clear that 'here', 'in this life' has no unique existential force. 'Here' and 'in this present life' are not special, for *mukti* has nothing to do with any particular time, place or cause (*na deśa-nimitta-viśeṣam api saṁkīrtayati*). All that it means is that *mukti* is indifferent to factors like, time, place and cause, that gnosis is able to bring about *mukti* at any time, in this or in any subsequent life, and the fact that one is still in the body is no hindrance. Since *mukti* always entails ultimate liberation from the body, whether in this birth or any subsequent one, it has to take place during some bodily existence, this or any other subsequent one. The only difference is that it can take place 'here' in this present life as effectively as in any subsequent life because of gnosis, which can destroy all the *karmas* that are yet to fructify and consequently put an end to all future bodily existences.

However, the *karmas* that have already begun to fructify, the present body being their fruit, cannot be destroyed and therefore even after realizing unity with *Brahman,* that is, after attaining *mukti* through gnosis, the present body has to live out its time. This fact is clearly brought out in *Chāndogya,* 6.14.2, as well as in the corresponding *sūtra* (4.1.15). The closing words of the

13. *The Bṛhadāraṇyaka Upaniṣad,* with the Commentary of Śaṅkarācārya trans. by Swami Madhavananda (Mayavati : Almora, Advaita Ashrama, 1950), 720. Cf. *Bṛhadāraṇyakopaniṣad... Śāṁkarabhāṣyasametā* (see n. 7 above), 611.

14. *Brahmasūtra-Śāṁkarabhāṣyam,* 820f.

Chāndogya passage are "The man with a teacher knows 'I shall remain here only so long as I am not ultimately liberated (from the body) and re-absorbed' " (*evam eva iha ācāryavān puruṣo veda tasya tāvad eva ciraṁ yāvan na vimokṣye atha sampatsya iti*).[15] Śaṅkara speaks about the delay (*kāla ciram*) expressed by the phrase *so long as* (*yāvad tāvad*). 'How long' is the delay in being re-absorbed ? The answer is 'so long as' the *karmic* residua which have already begun to bear fruit have not exhausted themselves by their being experienced. To quote, "Just as the arrow that has been discharged towards a certain target comes to rest only when the momentum is exhausted, so also is the case with the *karmas* which have launched themselves—they come to rest when they have exhausted themselves."[16] *Brahma Sūtra,* 4.1.15 also discusses *karmas* which have not yet begun to bear fruit (*anārabdha*).[17] Here too Śaṅkara argues that in the case of one who has attained *mukti* while still living, the *karmas* which have already brought about his body have to exhaust themselves and, consequently, the body has to live out its tenure. Here he uses the simile of the potter's wheel, rotating even after the potter has taken his hand off it, and running its course till the acquired momentum is exhausted. (This simile is also used in *Sāṁkhya-kārikā*, 67.)[18] In the light of this we can consider *waiting* for *mukti,* insofar as it is under gnosis, to be itself *mukti* but in such a way that the waiting will not be meaningless. In

15. See no. 11 above.

16. My own translation. Cf. text : *yāni pravṛttaphalāni karmāṇi yair vidvac-charīraṁ ārabdhaṁ teṣām upabhogenaiva kṣayaḥ. yathā 'rabdha-vegasya lakṣya-mukteṣvāder vegakṣayādeva sthitir na tu lakṣyavedha-samakālameva prayojanam nāstīti tadvat, Chāndogyopaniṣad Śāṁkarabhāṣyam* (Poona : Anandasram, n. d.), 380.

17. *Brahmasūtra-Śāṁkarabhāṣyam*, 849.

18. *samyag-jñānādhigamād dharmādīnām akāraṇa-prāptau tiṣṭhati saṁskāra-vaśāt cakrabhramivad dhṛtaśarīraḥ.*

"Even after attainment of perfect wisdom as a result of the seven kinds of thoughts beginning with virtue having become inoperative, the puruṣa remains attached to the body (continues to live) for a while; because of his saṁskāra which continues to function, just as a potter's wheel continues to move even after the motive power has been withdrawn," *The Sāṁkhya-Kārikā of Īśvarakṛṣṇa,* ed. and trans. by Radhanath Phukan (Calcutta : Firma K. L. Mukhopadhyay, 1960), 159.

the waiting itself, spiritually speaking, the *videha* (bodyless) state has been attained.

Nevertheless, what is described here cannot be construed as amounting to the particularized *jīvan-mukti* "ideal," although incontestably it provides a basis for it. The ideal when it was formulated by popular spirituality had these and other Upaniṣadic and Gītā texts to resort to—no doubt. The ideal originated outside the strict *Mīmāṁsā* (both *pūrva* and *uttara*) tradition of *śruti,* within which Śaṅkara himself wrote.

In Śaṅkara, the author of the *bhāṣyas,* there is no ideal of *jīvan-mukti* or any other particularized ideal of *mukti* (liberation) or of the saint's life. This statement will surprise many scholars who are accustomed to think that Śaṅkara is the supreme spokesman of the ideal, even though the *bhāṣyas* nowhere contain any terminological grounds for such accepted beliefs. I am, however, not suggesting that the notion runs counter to Śaṅkara's theology nor that it cannot be made to fit into it.

The ideal, I think, was developed outside the mainstream of Vedāntic theology. The text in which it was first consciously developed appears to be the *Yoga-vāsiṣṭha,* known also by a variety of other names such as *Ārṣa-rāmāyaṇa, Jñāna-vāsiṣṭha, Mahārāmāyaṇa,* etc.[19] S.N. Dasgupta places the composition of the text in Śaṅkara's century (eighth century A.D.) or a century earlier.[20] It is not regarded as a classical text but as a popular, didactic text like many others which arose even within the classical tradition, a few like the *Upadeśasāhasrī* being attributed to Śaṅkara himself. There are a dozen commentaries on the *Yoga-vāsiṣṭha*. It is no doubt a much revered work. It is in this work that we first come across the words *jīvan-mukta* and *jīvan-muktatā* (or its synonym *sadeha-muktatā*). There is in it a graphic description of the *jīvan-mukta* state, one in which the saint

19. Surendranath Dasgupta, *A History of Indian Philosophy,* Vol. 2 (Cambridge University Press, 1968), 231. Note : A title such as *Vāsiṣṭha-mahārāmāyaṇa* is already given by the immediate commentary of the work bearing the title *Mahārāmāyaṇa-tātparya-prakāśikā*; and the other titles and several more appear in different places, see the *Yoga-vāsiṣṭha* of Vālmīki, ed. by W. Laxman Sastri Pansikar (3rd ed.; Bombay: Pandurang Jivaji, Nirnaya Sagar Press, 1937).

20. See Dasgupta, *A History of Indian Philosophy,* vol. 2, 231.

has ceased to have any desires, and is self-contained, with eyes steadily turned inward even though perceiving all things and using his limbs. He is full of transcendental bliss, though appearing to common eyes to be just an ordinary, happy man. He has no attachment, aversion, grief, or emotion. He treats friend and foe alike. He is full of compassion and love for others, ever caring for their good. He can be happy with children and equally serious in higher discussions. His attitude towards society is not self-contained passivity but active and benevolent participation, always willing and working for the good of others. There is much similarity between the character of the saint painted here and the *sthita-prajña* (the man of settled intelligence) concept in the *Bhagavadgītā*, which Śrī Kṛṣṇa enunciates in response to Arjuna's query (2.54).[21] But the *Yogavāsiṣṭha* is much more effusive in the description of the aspect of the *jīvanmukta*'s positive and redemptive participation in the life of others and in the world. It is very likely that the Buddhist notion of the *Bodhisattva* was an influential factor in the emergence of the concept of *jīvanmukta*. However, the description of the *jīvanmukta* reflects the restraint characteristic of Vedānta. We do not notice the overpowering motive of compassion driving the saint to the point of postponing his own final *nirvāṇa* for the sake of helping others. One of the reasons, no doubt, is that in Vedānta there is no division between one's own liberation and others' liberation.

Finally, I must turn to a fourteenth-century-A.D. treatise which completed the thematization of *jīvan-mukti*. It is the *Jīvan-mukti-viveka* by Vidyāraṇya.[22] (Whether this Vidyāraṇya is the same person as the reputed author of the *Pañcadaśī* is a moot question.) The book is clearly a manual for ascetics

21. *sthitaprajñasya kā bhāṣā*
samādhisthasya keśava
sthitadhīḥ kiṁ prabhāṣeta
kim āsīta vrajeta kim.

"What is the description of the man who has this firmly founded wisdom, whose belng is steadfast in spirit, O Keśava (Kṛṣṇa)? How should the man of settled intelligence speak, how should he sit, how should he walk?", Radhakrishnan (ed.), *Bhagavadgītā* (see n. 8 above), 122.

22. *Jīvanmukti-viveka*, ed. by Pandit S. Subramanya Sastri and T.K. Srinivasa Ayyangar (Madras : The Adyar Library, 1978), 10.

(*sannyāsins*). It is not a work of great originality even as a text-book of popular spirituality for, for the most part, it draws from previous works, primarily the *Yoga-vāsiṣṭha,* but also the *Gītā* and other scriptures. The appeal to the scriptures is significant in the sense that it reflects the effort to put earlier free-lance ideas of popular spirituality into the mould of classical theological authority.

Written in five chapters it expressly states its purpose as a discussion of two kinds of renunciants' estate (*sannyāsa*)—that of the seeker after gnosis (*vividiṣā-sannyāsa*) and that of the one who has already attained gnosis (*vidvat-sannyāsa*). The former leads to *videha-mukti* and the latter to *jīvan-mukti.*

In this text the two estates as well as the two ideals of *mukti* (i.e.,*videha-mukti* and *jīvan-mukti*) are treated as complementary to, rather than separate from, one another. The concept of *videha* is employed not in the primary sense in which it appears in the classical texts but in the secondary (symbolic) sense, in which it is also found in the classical texts, especially in Śaṅkara's writings.

However, it takes on the precise psychological meaning of 'destruction of ego-mind' (*mano-nāśa*) and 'attrition of further body-constituting dispositions' (*vāsanā-kṣaya*). The seeker's effort brings about gnosis and hence spiritual freedom from the body and also assurance that after the natural cessation of the body no further body will be created. The classical texts, particularly of Śaṅkara, describe a kind of behaviour which accords with the freed state of the soul during the interval of waiting for the acquired momentum to dissipate itself. It is this waiting that is transformed into a kind of 'effort' in the thematized "ideal" of *jīvan-mukti.* The *vidvat-sannyāsa* is the *supportive effort* for the constant maintenance of the *jīvan-mukta*'s state. This is very clearly expressed in the following statement: "Insofar as with the attainment of gnosis resulting from the renunciation of the seeker future birth is prevented and insofar as in any case, the present body has to be brought to an end only by experiencing it (that is, its already acquired *karmas*), why undertake that further troublesome effort of renunciation of the knower ?" (*nanu evaṁ sati vividiṣā-sannyāsa-phalena tattva-jñānena eva āgāmi-janmano vāritatvāt vartamāna-janma-śeṣasya bhogamanta-*

reṇa vināśayitum aśakyatvāt kim anena vidvat-sannyāsa-prayāsena iti cet). The answer is: "Because the renunciation of the knower is the cause of *jīvan-mukti*" (*vidvat-sannyāsasya jīvan-mukti-hetutvāt*). We can easily see that this 'cause' (*hetu*) is the supportive 'difficult effort' (*prayāsa*) by which the *jīvan-mukti* state is actually maintained.

The treatise is full of excellent descriptions of the behaviour patterns of the *jīvan-mukta,* no doubt mostly derived from the *Yoga-vāsiṣṭha.* There is, accordingly, a special emphasis on the *jīvan-mukta* as "one who redemptively involves himself in the world's affairs in a cool spirit" (*samastārtheṣu vyavahāryapi śītalaḥ*), "attending to things that matter to others while being completely the Self" (*parātheṣu pūrṇātma*). The text ends with a call to "yogī-like performance of all duties while remaining satisfied with the nectar of gnosis" (*jñānāmṛtena tṛptasya kṛta-kṛtasya yoginaḥ*). The ideal of the *jīvan-mukta*, the *paramahaṁsa*, the saint, as an ascetic worker for the welfare of the world is elaborately set forth, but is based largely on the *Yoga-vāsiṣṭha*, with frequent (interpretive) appeals to the *Bhagavadgītā,* the latter again being seen through the eyes of the former. Like that of the *bodhisattva* the ideal is no doubt sublime, but like other pictures of perfection (human or divine) there is nothing in it which a mind so disposed cannot think up by itself. That, however, does not make such pictures of perfection meaningless although they are meaningful only in the sense of a testament to human spiritual longings. It is normal also for these pictures to be attached to classical theological systems—in the present case, to Vedānta. Nevertheless, they remain what they are, that is, expressions of (legitimate) popular spiritual longings, and without a doubt they are universal in their appeal.

At the end, therefore, it may be stated that in view of the above remarks, the historical note that has been furnished will, far from causing the ideal of *jīvan-mukti* to be viewed as being in any way outside Vedānta or as merely tangential to it, help to put it in perspective. It is rather Vedānta's response, in its extended tradition, to a great, universal spiritual longing, no doubt first appearing—as should be the case—in popular spirituality.

APPENDIX :

ON LANGUAGE

ON LANGUAGE

Introduction

Inasmuch as we have so far been discussing some Vedāntic topics in a hermeneutical-comparative way, and with attention focussed on the logos (*vāk*) it behoves us to turn our interest to language but strictly within our present framework, which although comparative, is essentially one of Vedāntic hermeneutics. The path from "logos" to "language" is a historical one, although the former is still the foundation of the latter. But the path has been travelled and we have, therefore, to consider whatever is of the logos from the point at which we have arrived in history, i.e., language. Gadamer observes :

> The word *logos* means not only thought and language but also concept and law. The appearance of the concept "language" presupposes consciousness of language. But that is only the result of the reflective movement in which the one thinking has reflected out of the unconscious operation of speaking and stands at a distance from himself. The real enigma of language, however, is that we can never really do this completely. Rather all thinking about language is already once again drawn back into language. We can only think in language, and just this residing of our thinking in a language is the profound enigma that language presents to thought.—"Man and language", *Philosophical Hermeneutics*, pp. 61-62.

As we have stated, the historic path from "logos" to "language" has been travelled. But it is obvious that this statement at present applies only to the West. But it can be applicable to the East—to Vedānta especially inasmuch as it is utterly under the power of the logos—more readily within the framework of the present-day, unavoidable comparativist situation than independently so that for the hermeneutics of what is essentially different from the West help can be drawn from the resources of Western experience and thought in such a way, nonetheless, to sustain the different in its difference. In that sense a proper comparative study, which involves hermeneutics and which in turn involves comparison—and both necessarily so—, must find its consummation and completion in the reflection upon the corresponding language worlds. Short of it, reflection upon topics—such as, for instance, constitute the titles of our essays—will remain incomplete. On the other hand, with it, the different meanings and associations of the very terms we use, such as "being", "world", "self ", "ignorance" "knowledge", etc., will be sharpened.

We must use these terms as surely we do, neutrally, simply as a conscious ploy—that is, without assuming the existence of an actual, corresponding realm of discourse or world of ideas—, while awaiting answers to the question "what is language qua language ?" This question like the question "what is thought ?", has come into being in the West, because the logos in the Western tradition is being grasped as language. Both are profoundly human, and existential, and would not have been asked had not Western thought been delivered to where it is. This is what underlies Heidegger's description of the "mystery of language", pertaining to which he writes, commenting on Novalis' *Monologue*, in the opening paragraph of *The Way to Language :* "The peculiar property of language, namely that language is exclusively concerned with itself—precisely that is known to no one."

In a hermeneutical-comparative enterprise we have to reckon with the fact that the one side, along with its logos, has remained at the stage of antiquity, continuing to the present itself in that way—and perhaps will do so in perpetuity—, while the other side has actually moved, its logos claiming attention today as "language". The logos on both sides in antiquity had to wrestle with one problem, i.e., its particularity of apprehension versus its universality, by definition. Are we done with it now ? Not really. It is only that philosophically something else, namely, that which comes to us as the question of the essence of language, has overshadowed it. Clearly, this development too has to be placed within the passage of Western logos to its present, though it has claimed attention from all.

However, the full impact of this is felt only within Western thought inasmuch as it is a dialectic within history, in the shape of leaving the boundaries of the Western logos and yet returning to it in new ways, both via thought. It has both vertical and horizontal dimensions, most explicitly inaugurated by Hegel, for whom the dialectical comprehension of both the historical and geographical-cultural realms were essential to that transformation. What Hegel began has found its consummate development so far in Heidegger, although the latter has set aside, either by design or by oversight, the comprehension of the geographical-cultural.

In a strange way, then, this neutral use of terms like 'self', 'self-knowledge', 'being', etc., we are concerned with in comparativist-hermeneutics, is sanctioned within the very dialectics of the West as it makes the quest for the essence of language. It catches us in its own movement to surpass the Western (Greek-Christian) logos, though certainly not in a comparativist direction—to expect that would be foolish. We benefit from this movement to the extent that a provisional, neutral use of the terms in question is sanctioned as a conscious ploy at least while waiting for the essence of language to appear. [It is a further matter to consider whether we should want to be caught in the re-bound when it moves back to itself, albeit in new ways, and be swept along. This calls for as much caution as against transporting oneself on the wings of a given Western philosophy to destinations one fancies upon the grounds of some Eastern thought.]

Concurrently—and this is the concrete and positive part of comparativist-hermeneutical work—we must enter simultaneously into the two actual language-worlds, where terms and symbols have their definite meanings and associations in their own phenomenological spheres. Here, however, while we juxtapose two antiquities we also realize that one of them continues as antiquity while the other, rooted as it is in its past, has also moved to the present and created the present, from the ground of which the very project of comparativist-hermeneutics has ultimately arisen. And yet juxtaposing them as two language-worlds is possible, without compromising the integrity of either—not only possible but necessary. The two language-worlds for us are the Indian, supremely represented by Vedānta, and the Western, which has its roots in the coincidence of the Greek thought and

Cristianity. However, our aim has been to help throw light on the world of Vedānta alone rather than push the implications of "comparative" to the extent of presumptuously claiming to illuminate both worlds even-handedly.

From the juxtaposition of the two language-worlds interesting phenomena also come to light, that is to say, under cover of dogmas and beliefs which set them most apart, on occasions profound similarities in onto-theological understandings becoming visible: one instance is given in the last essay, on Vedānta and Barth. Nothing need be made of it, though it calls our attention to the identical behaviour af the logos under certain conditions.

NINE

THE MYSTERY OF LANGUAGE

That intellectual activity which we designate as philosophical has among other things this distinguishing characteristic : it brings to light what lies hidden and along with it the hiddden self. [That the act of bringing to light may also entail an even deeper concealing is indeed but part of its dialectical character.] There is, therefore, the implication of self-knowledge in anything that marks itself off as philosophical. At this point, however, we must adhere to the neutral use of 'self' and 'self-knowledge', and it has to be shed gradually as we penetrate into the two different language-worlds and their distinct spheres we are concerned with.

Knowing the self is not merely knowing it inreference to particular situations of relation to objects sought to be discovered or known so that one may be able to critically grasp those situations for the purpose of an accurate knowledge of the objects concerned but knowing it quite apart from all such projections which come and go. Such knowledge of the self is not a by-product but rather something directly aimed at. This directing of knowledge to the self in and through the knowledge of objects is undoubtedly a central quality of philosophical thought. This is the reason why—to speak in the psychological terms of Yoga—when we are to think philosophically, our mind which of its own accord goes forward to the objects and assumes their form (*citta-vṛtti*) has also got to be stopped (*niruddha*) so that there results a retraction of the mind to itself and finally to the self, resulting in *samādhi.* Genuine thought, therefore, is a spontaneous activity of the mind culminating in a self-absorptive non-activity. However, the realm of object-reality, far from being surrendered, is fully appropriated and brought to the synthesizing centre of all apperception where alone it becomes knowledge. This is possible because all this takes place in the light of consciousness. But although everything must be brought to consciousness in order to be lighted, consciousness in its every-day operation is also shaded by dark areas so that thought too must seek ways to lighten consciousness. The function of thought is much more than delivering all things over to consciousness. Thought then is to be viewed as the grasping of consciousness by itself so that while it lightens all things it simultaneously expurgates any darkness that there is within it. Thought then must be regarded as a supreme activity and a supreme non-activity, such being the condition for consciousness to grasp itself. This aspect of apparent polarity between being both motion and the opposite of it is true of light—and thought is light.

Language is a mystery which belongs with consciousness. As a mystery it is hidden, and it also brings all things to light. The philosopher Hamann rightly describes language as a mystery and a revelation.

A mystery is something hidden but not something unknown. A mystery is that hidden thing the call to uncover which becomes irresistible. There should be no other reason for us to want to know it than its own inherent challenge. As such its very existence is not external to our consciousness. The quest to know it is really nothing other than acting in obedience to the inner command of consciousness. The habitation of all mystery is consciousness. Language inhabits consciousness like all other mysteries, no doubt, but does so even more intimately, because consciousness *becomes* language—like no other mystery.

When it is said 'consciousness becomes language' it means that in the same way language reveals the presence of consciousness, consciousness in turn conceals the essence of language. But somewhere at some unfathomable depth they are one. Our life is guided by specific—and sometimes isolated—injunctions which originate there and then float off up-to the surface, to our awareness, expressed through concrete verbal modes, and, taking the form of mental moods, remain poised also for translation into action. All our learning is a way of coming to a knowledge of this. The master under whom we learn is language. In learning, language turns our face to that unfathomable depth from which all manifested truths come floating up. Learning, however, is only activity, only motion, and also it is always under the control of specific truths which happen to have floated up to the surface awareness and to have been embodied in some concrete language. On the contrary, thought surpasses the limitations of activity, of motion, and surpasses also the accidental character of the truths grasping our minds. Further, while the learner remains outside what he learns, the thinker is never outside. In thought not only is our face turned toward the unfathomable depth but we make it our habitual dwelling-place. Learning is awakening while thinking is living in wakefulness itself.

At that unfathomable depth, indeed language and consciousness belong together, constituting a single mystery. Therefore the searching of the depth in one is the searching of the depth in the other as well.

The nature of language is the object of diverse kinds of inquiries in modern times. Apart from the science of linguistics and its several parts, philosophy, psychology, aesthetics and anthropology have delved deep into the phenomenon of language with the respective interests and assumptions of these disciplines. There is an enormous diversity of language describing language, and it is fairly accurate to say that no other topic has commanded the attention of so many disciplines. No one can speak for all of them. Indeed, no one can speak for philosophy, as philosophers speak diversely. However, it is not the case, unfortunately, that the proliferation of words about language always conduces to light and wisdom. On the contrary, much that is spoken and written seems to be inimical to the coming of light. Multiplication of quantity only produces false enlightenment, in other words a thickening of darkness, to which particularly in our modern age we have become hapless heirs. There is so much wealth around in our present day intellectual life, which nevertheless does not make us truly rich. Learning unguided by genuine thinking cannot in the long run help to turn our face in the right direction.

The Human Phenomenon of Language

Language is the most characteristically human of all phenomena. The unity of man and language is the most striking of all human facts, a unity which cannot be dissolved. The fact that man alone has language is immensely significant, and it cannot be ignored or circumvented by developing specious arguments about the way man came to possess the faculty of speech or the way imitative or non-imitative speaking can be accomplished by machines programmed to do so. Undoubtedly, there is a unique association whereby man dwells in speech and speech dwells in man. There are no third parties to which this relation can be extended except that, of course, by imagination mankind has fancied the gods and spirits, on the one hand, and the non-human animals, on the other, to have power of speech, as we read in our mythologies and our animal fables. In fact this work of imagination only reinforces the unique relation between man and language while adding an element of pathos to it. The gift of language is bestowed upon man only and he pays a heavy price for it, since as the world of man becomes lighted by speech he is shut off by silence from the heavens and from nature.

On account of this altogether unique relation Aristotle felt it necessary to define man as that being which has logos. (Logos originally meant language; the connotation of reason came afterwards, on which rested the later definitions of man as *animal rationale*.)[1] As a definition it speaks not only about the possession of language by man but also about its non-possession by the rest of the animal kingdom. Language, accordingly, provides a basis for distinction between man and the rest of the animal world.

Aristotle's definition in Greek is *zōon logon echon*, which included much more than the rationality of a particular animal species. "In the tradition of the West", writes Gadamer, "this definition became canonical in a form which stated that man is the *animal rationale*, the reasoning being distinguished from other animals by his capacity for thought. In truth, however,

1. *Note :* It is not alogether clear that the connotation of 'reason' (*ratio*), a word which also had the original meaning of 'speaking', had not harked back to something, albeit in a tendentious manner, that the word 'speaking' as literally understood could not project. It may well be that, as reflected in the eventual meaning of 'reason', the logos may have appropriated man as the animal in which it may show itself, and as such to be its very own *phenomenon*.

the primary meaning of this word [*logos*] is language...To men alone [unlike other animals] is the *logos* given so that they can make manifest to each other what is useful and harmful, and therefore also what is right and wrong. A profound thesis...the distinguishing feature of man, therefore, is his superiority over what is actually present, his sense of the future."[2] According to Heidegger, this definition goes into several important areas on account of such primary interpretations as these: "man is the animal that confronts face to face", because it can "perceive *itself*"—and say "I"; "man is the confronting animal which has the property that it can speak".[3]

However, on the basis of Aristotle's definition, Descartes pushed the distinction to the extreme. Language, he felt, pointed to the existence of mind in man. In this respect animals appeared to Descartes to be little better than automata, although—as he surely conceded—they had sensation and feeling. In a letter to Henry More he writes as follows:

> But the principal argument to my mind which may convince us that the brutes are devoid of reason, is that, although among those of the same species, some are more perfect than others, as among men, which is particularly noticeable in horses and dogs, some of which have more capacity than others to retain what is taught them, and although all of them make us clearly understand their natural movements of anger, of fear, of hunger, and others of like kind, either by the voice or by other bodily motions, it has never yet been observed that any animal has arrived at such a degree as to make use of true language; that is to say as to be able to indicate to us by the voice, or by other signs, anything which could be referred to thought alone; for the word is the sole sign and the only certain mark of the presence of thought hidden and wrapped up in the body; now all men,

2. H.-G. Gadamer, "Man and Language", *Philosophical Hermeneutics*, trans. David Linge, Berkeley, etc., University of California Press, 1977, p. 59.

3. M. Heidegger, *What is Called Thinking* ? trans. J. Glenn Gray, New York, Harper & Row, 1968, p.61. Elsewhere, Heidegger gives a more radical interpretation proposing that man is "that rising presence which can make appear what is present", *ibid.*, p. 68.

> the most stupid and the most foolish, those even who are deprived of the organs of speech, make use of signs, whereas the brutes never do anything of the kind; which may be taken for the true distinction between man and brute.[4]

J.G. Herder tried to substantiate Descartes' theory by means of some tests, and, like Descartes, argued "that human language is different in kind from exclamations of passion and that it cannot be attributed to superior organs of articulation, nor obviously, can it have its origins in imitation or in its "agreement" to form language."[5]

Man and language are bound to each other in an indissoluble way. But this binding can lead in one of two directions, viz., either towards a philosophy of man or towards a philosophy of language. In the Post-Cartesian West it led largely in the direction of a clearer and surer apprehension of man rather than language as such. In fact a quest for a rigorous definition of language itself would lead one towards a reduction of language to human language and finally and inevitably to man, as has invariably happened. The belonging together of *consciousness* and language must appear to be exclusively identical with the binding of *man* and language, as man would seem to be the measure of consciousness. The Biblical notion of the domination of man over nature would have left no alternative to equating consciousness with man—omitting from this field the Divine consciousness for the time being. The class of conscious beings and the class of human beings become one and the same. That was inevitable because both theological pre-supposition and empirical knowledge precluded the possibility of leaving the class of conscious beings unenclosed and unbounded. It was not

4. *The Descartes-More Correspondence*, the part relating to this theme translated by L. C. Rosenfield (L. Cohen) in the *Annals of Science*, Vol. I. No. 1 (1936), here quoted from Noam Chomsky, *Cartesian Linguistics*, New York and London, Harper & Row, 1966, p. 6. Descartes and Aristotle's conclusions though fundamentally unchallengeable must, nonetheless, be viewed in the light of recent experiments with apes, e.g. Robert and Ada Yerkes (1929 report); H. and B. Pasamanick (1959 report) and Francine Patterson (1978 report in *National Geographic*, Oct., 1978).

5. *Ibid.*, Chomsky, above, pp. 13-14.

only this but also that consciousness was apprehended as what takes place between an 'I' and a 'Thou', as their being revealed together in mutual encounter. Language is both the medium for the operation of the 'I-Thou' consciousness and, at the same time, its constriction to the world of human beings. Even if one were to extend the 'I-Thou' world beyond human beings, it would be necessary to extend language and therefore consciousness likewise, which could be done only by way of a hypothesizing act or mystical ecstasy, and both these were excluded. In this atmosphere consideration of language always pointed back to man.

It was within this framework that Descartes did his thinking on language and on consciousness. Thus he interpreted consciousness as self-consciousness expressed by the proposition, 'I think, therefore I am,' which became the ground of ultimate certainty, upon which all things, including language, could be considered. This gave an orientation to modern philosophy and science from which they have never been able to turn away. There have been, of course, other variations of the binding together of consciousness, language and man operating in the self-same framework. One of the most interesting of these variations, having special significance for the language quest, is the Romantic one associated with the names of Herder and Wilhelm von Humboldt, who, in the words of Professor Gadamer, "saw the original human character of language as the primordial linguisticality of man and worked out the fundamental significance of this phenomenon for man's view of the world."[6]

Gadamer repeats the same point more elaborately, stated elsewhere : "Herder and Wilhelm von Humboldt saw that language is essentially human and that man is essentially a linguistic being, and they worked out the fundamental significance of this insight for man's view of the world."[7] As is well-known, Humboldt's work has been the foundation for both modern philosophy of language and the science of linguistics. And his insight on man's linguisticality would seem to restore Aristotle's view. Yet critics have pointed out that it is far from being the case.

6. From a privately circulated seminar paper.
7. Gadamer, "Man and Language", *op. cit.*, p. 61.

Gadamer himself observes: "By making the language of peoples the object of his investigation, Humboldt pursued a path of knowledge that was able to clarify in a new and promising way the diversity of peoples and times as well as the common nature underlying them all." "But", he adds "this procedure merely equipped man with a capacity and elucidated the structural laws of this capacity—what we call the grammer, syntax and vocabulary of a language—and it restricted the horizon of man and language".[8] Heidegger makes a fundamentally similar criticism in *The Way to Language*, and concludes : "Humboldt's way to language is turned in the direction of man, and leads through language on to something else: the endeavours to get to the bottom of and to present the spiritual development of the human race."[9]

Linguistics has, no doubt, generally stuck to Humboldt's path, but (idealistic) philosophy of language—with the variations natural to it—has, by the same token returned to the Cartesian insight, if not method, for, as Gadamer observes, "the Cartesian characterization of consciousness as self-consciousness continued to provide the background for all modern thought".[10]

Now, apart from these three major departures in the Western tradition, which have bound man and language to each other —Aristotle, Descartes, Humboldt—, Heidegger himself offers a fourth. To quote a relevant passage from Heidegger :

> When we reflect on language *qua* language, we have abandoned the traditional procedure of language study...Instead of explaining language in terms of one thing or another, and thus running away from it, the way to language intends to let language be experienced as language...If we attend to language exclusively as language, however, then language requires of us that we first of all put forward everything that belongs to language as language.[11]

8. *Loc. cit.*
9. Heidegger, *On the Way to Language*, trans. Peter D. Hertz, San Francisco, etc., Harper & Row, 1971, p. 119.
10. "Man and Language", *op. cit.*, p. 61.
11. *On the Way to Language*, pp. 119-20.

In Heidegger's procedure the radical potentialities of Aristotle's definition are captured and brought to completion. There is no more any ignoring of the logos, for it is made to re-appear as "language"—the same but different. And all intervening developments are re-interpreted from this point.

Characteristics of Ancient Indian Thought on Language

In the West, the apprehension of language has, from Aristotle down, depended on the understanding of "man": in fact they have been mutually dependent, or locked with each other, we might say. In the tradition of Vedānta, on the contrary, what language was plugged into was consciousness *per se* rather than man. Man, no doubt, was somewhere in the picture but not in the Western sense of the self-referent being whose knowledge of himself governed all things and ratified all other knowledge, but in the much weaker sense of a temporary container destined to be broken so that the universal consciousness like space be no longer limited by the pot-like shell that "man" is. However, the Vedāntic understanding of the relation between language and consciousness as thus described, or of that consciousness itself, was not reached in one giant leap. It was reached rather via clarification of its own antecedents in the earlier parts of the Vedas. [This fact will make it necessary for us to discuss these antecedents soon.]

When we use the word 'language' in the Vedāntic context in a traditional manner we have in mind the unchanged continuity of the logos of Indian antiquity, which, nonetheless, even in times of yore had gathered into itself certain technical adjuncts like grammar, etymology and phonetics, permitting it to be treated as "language" in the purely conventional sense of human speech. On the contrary, when we speak of "language" in the Western ontological context, of course, we have the conventional sense in mind too, which has been elaborated in highly sophisticated ways both in Linguistics and in Analytical Philosophy. But we have something more in mind, governed ontologically by the powerful binding of language with man, namely the transition to the present from which all that is of antiquity is re-read so as to be integrated into the present—*which is, of course, the reversal of the path of the logos' own passage to "language"*. However, we come to realize that the sway of this Western standpoint is no longer confined to the West, and we become aware of this fact even when we speak of "language" in reference to Vedānta. And so within the framework of the unchanged continuity of antiquity, the Indian logos is rendered amenable to be looked at from the present.

Without moving from language to a definition of man on the one hand, and to things (and the world), on the other, the ancient Indians insisted on pondering the mystery of language as such and seem to have done so in a unique way. However, consciousness, not constricted as human consciousness, and the world, not limited to the enumerable things, did become the conceptual partner with language, illuminating each other.

One of the most interesting features of ancient Indian thought on the subject of language is that it understood language both in its phenomenal and transcendental aspects, while fully studying each on its own, scientifically and philosophically. They were also joined together into a single, homogeneous field where that was warranted. Detailed scientific study of phonetics, semantics, etymology, etc., were at appropriate points integrated with philosophical contemplation of language (and consciousness) as of Reality. The skill and penetration which went into these gigantic intellectual efforts stretching over centuries are to be marvelled at.

Because there was scrupulous concern for the phenomenal, there never was any temptation to bind language down as human language or to disregard the objects of the world to which language was bound. Grammarians like Gārgya (and later) Pāṇini and etymologist like Yāska were clearly concerned with human speech, with language in the empirical world, but they always kept an aperture in their systems open to transcendental inquiry, so that in the grammatical and Vedānta-Mīmāṁsā philosophies the two could be fully integrated without having to break holes in any enclosing walls. This feature of simultaneously developing the phenomenal and transcendental aspects of the same question with an eye to each other is characteristic of the Indian tradition.

In traditional Indian thought the effort to understand a given phenomenon and the contemplation of it as a mystery do not preclude each other. This dual character seems to have been maintained by all the sciences which have come out of the Vedas. The Vedas themselves, far from being a record of human thought, seem to furnish a ground upon which all human thinking—both the efforts to analyze and the contemplation of mysteries—can take place.

As in the case of everything else, Indian inquiry into language began with the *Ṛgveda*. The *Ṛgveda* has many things to say about *vāk*, meaning speech or language. The term *vāk* comes from *vac* (*Dhātupāṭha*, xxiv.55), which means to speak, tell, declare, mention, proclaim, describe, etc. [This root is distinct from the root *vad* which has an almost identical cluster of connotations, viz., to speak, tell, say, utter, report, etc.] And no doubt in later texts the verbal forms of *vac*, like *uvāca, ūce, avocat, avocata*, and *vakṣyati* are Vedic too.

The noun *vāk* is feminine in gender, and carries the meaning of speech, voice, talk, language, often suggesting the sense of 'logos'. Originally it included the meaning of sound produced with the aid of inanimate objects like a drum or a stone as in *vācam kṛ*, *ir*, or *is*, not to mention sound of animals, as for example in *Ṛgveda* 7.103.1, where we read that frogs produced a sound imitating the roar of clouds—*vācam parjanya-jinvitām pramaṇḍukā avadiṣuḥ*. Later it also acquired the connotation of statement, assertion, as in the *Manusmṛti* and the *Mahābhārata*. In classical literature the word was sometimes used with the import of promise (a word given), especially in combination with *satyam*, e.g. *vācā satyam kṛ* to give the solemn word of betrothal.

The references to *vāk* in the *Ṛgveda* are limited but they are very significant, being no doubt foundational; there are many more in the *Sāma* and *Atharva Vedas* and in later Saṁhitās, *Maitrāyaṇī*, *Kāṭhaka* and *Taittirīya*; Brāhmaṇas such as *Jaiminīya*, *Kauṣītaki*, *Taittirīya* and *Śatapatha*; Āraṇyakas, chiefly *Taittirīya*; and the *Āpastamba* and *Śāṅkhāyana Śrauta Sūtra*.

As far as the Vedas are concerned it is easy to commit errors by speculating on the ultimate origin of the phenomenon of *vāk* in them but it is the wiser course to avoid such speculations. It is possible that the ultimate origin of the phenomenon, like that of other phenomena, was already antecedent to the Vedas and it might not be reached through history or the study of texts. Even with respect to the chronological order of the development of *vāk* in the *Ṛgveda* the present state of our knowledge does not justify any definite view, as, for instance, the mere sequential arrangement of the ten *maṇḍalas* (books) has nothing at all to do with the considerations of what are historically earlier and what are later. However, in listing the occurrences of the word *vāk* in the *Ṛgveda* we may merely follow the existing order of the books, with no thought of development at all. Important occurrences are : 1.41.66, which has the phrase *imām vācam*—this word; 1.79.10, where Gotama is advised to carry *vāk* (composed with care) to *Agni*, as he desires bliss—*pra pūtāstigmaśocișe vāco gotamāgnaye bharasva sumnayurgiraḥ*; 1.143.1a, which has the statement *agnaye vācaḥ bhare* (to *Agni* I bear my words and thoughts).

Ṛgveda 1.164 is one of the most remarkable hymns as far as *vāk* is concerned, and no doubt it is also one of the most philosophical generally. Here the question about *vāk* is expressly raised, followed by some concrete suggestions. It is raised in conjunction with others, and the purport is to find out the ultimate abode of *vāk* : "I ask thee about the ultimate abode of speech, *pṛcchāmi vācaḥ paramaṁ vyoma*". In the next stanza there follows the answer : "The ultimate abode of speech is this *Brahman, brahmāyaṁ vācaḥ paramaṁ vyoma*". [The import of 'this'—*ayam* must not be missed.] This stanza, incidentally, typifies the context as well as mode of all philosophical inquiry in the *Ṛgveda*, i.e., centred around the altar and the sacrifice—and that is true also in respect of thought on the subject of language, and it is specifically stated elsewhere (4.21.5), "*vāk* was produced for the performance of sacrifice—*iyarti vācaṁ janayan yajadhyai.*" Here *vāk* must be clearly understood as 'logos', and its connections with Self-knowledge is a seminal thought already exhibited by this text. Further, its connection with *ṛta* is also significant, as it is called *ṛta's* first-born (*prathamajā ṛtasya*), because the latter stands for the regularity, invariability and consistency so paramountly important in the logos insofar as it is the *ratio* which goes with it. The idea that the imperishable *vāk* (logos) is the first born of *ṛta* shows up again in *Taittirīya Brāhmaṇa* 2.8.8.5*a* (*vāg akṣaram prathamajā ṛtasya*). Now, the question about *vāk* and the question about the Self are not associated with each other accidentally, for, on the contrary, that they are related at their greatest depth becomes evident in the Brāhmaṇas and the Upaniṣads.

The 45th stanza expresses a fundamental idea, which is eventually taken up as the basis of the entire Philosophy of Grammar [Patañjali uses it as the start of *Mahābhāṣya*]. The stanza reads :

> *Vāk* has been divided into four levels
> Which the knowers of *Brahman* know;
> People speak only the fourth (of these);
> While the (other) three are kept in a cave.
>
> (*catvāri vāk parimitā padāni*;
> *tāni viduḥ brāhmaṇāḥ ye manīṣiṇaḥ*;
> *guhā trīṇi nihitā na īngayanti*;
> *turīyam vācaḥ manuṣyāḥ vadanti.*)

Now, there is a straight line connecting *vāk* with the *Ātman* (Self), and that is grasped by the *Bṛhaddevatā* (ii.86) as it observes : "The Self in the aspect of becoming is really what is sung to and....and is also both the seer and the deity, "*ātmano bhāvavṛttāni jagau vargastathottamaḥ*; *uttamasya tu vargasya ya ṛṣiḥ saiva devatā.* [The Brahmaṇas and the Upaniṣads clearly lead all speculation on *Vāk* to the *Ātman*, which is shown as the ultimate ground of the logos.]

One of the most remarkable characteristics of the Vedas is, the two aspects of *vāk*, which may be distinguished as the revealing word and the word in invocation (or recitation), are at bottom the same. The integrity of these two is quite significant in the way the logos functions in the Vedas. And it is because *vāk* as the logos is the ground of the *ratio* that ratiocination has the potentiality to act as the open door to truth (*satyam*), although by itself it can never realize its own potentiality. But this frustrating incapacity of ratiocination teaches a positive lesson too, namely, that as *manana* it is always dependent upon, and follows, the hearing (*śravaṇa*) of the *vāk* and that it also leads the way to the deeper thinking called *nididhyāsana*. The primary complement to the mystery of self-revelation (or Self-revelation), indeed, the very concrete possibility of it, is the other mystery, namely, that of the releasement of truth the invoking word signifies. With both these, man's power to know encounters its own transcendence. The unfolding of all these hidden dimensions takes place in the Upaniṣads.

Now, of the six *aṅgas* or auxiliary sciences in the study of the Vedas, called *Vedāṅgas*, i.e., *Śikṣā* (Phonetics), *Vyākaraṇa* (Grammar), *Chandas* (Metre), *Nirukta* (Etymology), *Kalpa* (Rubrics about rites) and *Jyotiṣa* (Astrology), the first four are linguistic disciplines, and the other two are non-linguistic. Of the four linguistic ones, again, Phonetics, Grammar and Metre are traditionally assigned to the task of safe-guarding the sound aspect of the words of the Vedas. Phonetics serve to provide knowledge of correct pronunciation—important because place, factor, effort, etc., with respect to each syllable vary. Likewise also all the musical elements like resonance (*nāda*), length, interval, movement, etc., can be known only through phonetics.

With the aid of Grammar is to be known the divisions of natural linguistic factors (*prakṛti-pratyaya*). Grammar eventually took over all questions of meaning, while on the other hand, it produced a total logos metaphysics (in *Vākyapadīya*), which made out everything, even man and the world, to be its phenomena. Metre was used as a means to bind all Vedic hymns together. Now, as for Etymology, or *Nirukta*, it must be understood that it is much more than a science of roots and word derivation, as it is really a Vedic dictionary. Its foundational work *Nighaṇṭu* itself means dictionary. Yāska's commentary on it was written for the purpose of homologizing the words of the Vedic dictionary with the words of secular Sanskrit.

It must finally be said that the *Vedāṅgas* are confined to (1)the sound aspect of the Vedic *vāk* and (2) their semantic meaning and meaning in ritual usage (*viniyoga*), and do not in themselves directly serve as a tool for meaning in the higher sense of Ultimate Truth. That is the department of philosophy, i.e., of Vedānta, which too is, however, indirectly served by the Vedāṅgas, and as observed before it is most interesting that one of these, i.e., Grammar, should eventually find its way, through its own philosophy of *vāk*, to join Vedānta.

Now, returning to the Vedas, we are summoned by them. We are summoned to a quest after the mystery of language. Language must be discovered and brought to light. But the quest to which we are summoned ultimately is not after any phenomenon as such but after the one hidden Reality behind all phenomena, in the revelation of which language seems to have a special place because it is the medium of all knowledge. The question is, is the knowledge of language, the medium of knowledge, in some pre-eminent sense, an inseparable aspect of the knowing of Reality ? In the search for an answer to this question the obvious place to look is the Upaniṣads.

Language in the Upaniṣads

The Upaniṣads bring language to light—in some very significant ways—by explicitly linking it with consciousness, with the phenomenal world and with *Brahman.* The range of concepts about it is truly enormous.

Speech is often spoken of as being on a par with other faculties; yet as the instrument of understanding it eventually assumes a unique position, and is brought to its source, *Brahman* itself. As a faculty, along with other faculties, it is a medium of creation, or becoming. One most interesting passage is the *Aitareya Upaniṣad,* Chapter I, where we read of the creation of the Cosmic Person, which begins with the statement : *ātmā vā idam eka evāgra āsīt, nānyat kiṁ cana miṣat*; *sa aikṣata lokān nu sṛjā iti—Ātman* indeed was all this, one only, in the beginning; nothing else whatsoever winked; he desired 'let me now create the worlds'; he created the worlds, the elements and then the person (*puruṣa*) to whom he gave shape.

He brooded over him, the person (*tam abhyatapat*); thus brooding he gave him mouth and produced speech from mouth, and from speech fire (*mukhād vāg, vāco'gniḥ*). But this was followed by the creation of other faculties and senses; the distinction is that speech is the first, a position that is normally maintained through the Upaniṣads. Speech is the first faculty to be created in the person. In the creative process the order of source and product are reversible. Thus for instance, if fire (*Agni*) is said to have come from speech, it is also said in the next section that fire (*Agni*) having become speech entered the mouth (*agnir vāg bhūtvā mukhaṁ prāviśat*).[12]

12. *Aitareya Upaniṣad* 1.3.4.

Phenomenally, it is essential to polarize the indivisible *Ātman* as creator and the created person (*puruṣa*), although the word *puruṣa* in its primary sense does not admit the attribute of createdness. Here *puruṣa* represents becoming; in becoming, speech is the first of the "created" faculties essential to personhood. But speech must always lead to *Ātman*. Purely in terms of becoming, that is, insofar as a polarization is maintained, speech leads to *Ātman*, as it is itself not the final source of light. Thus we read in the *Bṛhadāraṇyaka* : *astam ita āditye....śāntāyāṁ vāci, kiṁ jyotir evāyaṁ puruṣa iti....ātmanaivāyaṁ jyotiṣāste*, etc. (When the sun has set and speech has become silent, what indeed is this person's light here ? *Ātman* indeed becomes his light, etc.)[13]

All the human faculties are the means by which *Brahman* manifests itself : *etad vai brahma dīpyate yad vācā vadati*[14] (This *Brahman* indeed shines forth, when one speaks with speech): so we read in the *Kauṣītaki Upaniṣad*. However, since here a different theme is pursued—the distinction between life and death—it is *prāṇa* (life-breath) which gets the primacy.[15] However, among the faculties through which *Brahman* (*Ātman*)shines forth, speech still remains the first.

Yet language must be understood not only in the becoming aspect of the person, but also in the being aspect of *Brahman*, or *Ātman*. Thus we are told that speech is *Brahman* (*vāgvai brahmeti*).[16] Speech is *virāṭ*.[17] Speech is also everything. It is the world (*vāgeva ayaṁ lokaḥ*),[18] it is the gods (*devāḥ*),[19] it is *Agni*,[20] and so on. It is the *Ṛgveda*,[21] it is the one source of all the Vedas.[22]

The *Māṇḍūkya Upaniṣad* gives the most complete expression of language, having worked out an identification of it with

13. See *Bṛhadāraṇyaka Upaniṣad*, 4.3.6.
14. *Kauṣītaki Upaniṣad* 2.13.
15. See also *Ibid.*, 2.14.
16. *Bṛhadāraṇyaka Upaniṣad*, 4.1.2.
17. *Chāndogya Upaniṣad*, 1.13.2.
18. *Bṛhadāraṇyaka Upaniṣad*, 1.5.4.
19. *Ibid* 1.5.6.
20. *Chāndogya Upaniṣad*, 3.13.3.
21. *Ibid.*, 1.7.1; *Bṛhadāraṇyaka Upaniṣad*, 1.5.5.
22. *Bṛhadāraṇyaka Upaniṣad*, 2.4.11.

Ātman at four levels through the symbol of AUM. The *Chāndogya Upaniṣad* had discussed the four quarters of *Brahman* in a different way where speech appears as but one, the other three being breath, the eye and the ear,[23] *Agni* (fire), air, the sun and the directions, also coordinated with them. The symbol of AUM also had been employed by several of the Upaniṣads before, chiefly by the *Chāndogya*, *Taittirīya* and *Maitrī*. But the *Māṇḍūkya*, the special AUM Upaniṣad, pulls all these diffuse ideas together and works out a thorough systematic correlation of them all by producing, so to say, the final symbolic equation whereby language, consciousness (the psyche) and the cosmos were all coordinated under the supreme word symbol. The *Māṇḍūkya Upaniṣad* begins this grand, systematic project with the introduction: *aum iti etat akṣaram idaṁ sarvaṁ tasyopavyākhyānam*, etc., (AUM, this syllable is all this; [here is] an explanation of it, etc.,). *Sarvaṁ hi etad brahma ayam ātmā brahma so'yamātmā catuṣ-pāt*. (All this is indeed *Brahman*; this *Ātman* is *Brahman*; this *Ātman* is four-quartered.) The conception of the mental states and the levels of the cosmos represented by the *vaiśvānara*, *taijasa* and *prājña* quarters and their integration with the three letters and leaving the fourth (*turīya*) in a transcendent state of purity, unity and homogeneity in all three respects, viz., the psyche, the cosmos and language, does bring the whole theme of language to an unequivocal clarity and completeness.

The Diversity of later systematic developments and the lessons we can learn from them

The lessons which the Vedic texts and the Upaniṣads teach us are several : (1) language is a mystery that must be sought; (2) language and consciousness, however, belong together, constituting a single mystery ; (3) while we seek to bring language to light we learn that language brings itself to light and brings everything else to light because it is light; (4) language is the framework in which our entire knowledge of Reality—and the self-revelation of Reality as well—is made possible, as the *Māṇḍūkya Upaniṣad* finally works it out by means of a great symbolic equation.

23. *Chāndogya Upaniṣad*, 3.18.2-6.

But the question is, can these truths be idealized and absolutized in such a way as to say that language simply is the Reality as expressed by the doctrine of *Śabdabrahman* ? To this we shall briefly advert. Is it not going too far, and perhaps in an unintended manner, contributing to the misunderstanding of the very truths lying underneath such an effort ?

Bhartṛhari's *Vākyapadīya* is undoubtedly one of the greatest land-marks in India's quest for the mystery of language and is the finest and the most comprehensive expression of the principle s we have mentioned, but the question still remains : by making the equation, Reality (*Brahman*) = Language, literal would it not encourage some kind of reductionism, not intended even by the *Māṇḍūkya Upaniṣad*, not to say the rest of the Upaniṣads and the Vedic Mantras, perhaps not intended by Bhartṛhari himself? Yes, indeed no truer words than the following have been ever spoken in respect of language :

Pratyastamitabhedāya yadvāco rūpamuttamam,
yadasminneva tamasi jyotiḥ śuddhaṁ vivartate.
vaikṛtaṁ samatikrāntā mūrtivyāpāradarśanam,
vyatītyālokatamasī prakāśaṁ yamupāsate.
yatra vāco nimittāni cihnānīvākṣarasmṛteḥ,
śabda-pūrveṇa yogena bhāsante pratibimbavat.
atharvaṇāmaṅgirasāṁ sāmnāmṛgyajuṣasya ca,
yasminnuccāvacā varṇāḥ pṛthaksthitiparigrahāḥ.[24]

(The most excellent form of speech, which being undifferentiated is light pure, that appears in this darkness as differentiated ;

Which those who have surpassed the multiform world perceive as an idol and worship [though] they have gone beyond the [opposition between] light and darkness;
Wherein the instrumentalities of speech, signs as it were of the letter-text [referring to AUM or even to the *Māṇḍūkya Upaniṣad*] put forth a reflection by union with pre-existing logos;

[This is] grasped in separate states of its existence as the

24. *Vākyapadīya*, I. 18-21, from K. A. Subramanya Iyer's text, Poona, Deccan College, 1966.

Atharva, Sāma, Yajus and *Ṛk* and as the letter-sounds which constitute them.)

This is Supreme *Brahman*, which it is said in the next *kārikā*, quite literally, is attained by the discipline of grammar (*tadvyākaraṇamāgamya paraṁ brahma adhigamyate*). It is claimed that language is the gateway to *mokṣa* (*taddvāramapavargasya*),[25] etc.

This doctrine of Bhartṛhari—and some of the Grammarians—have had its share of critics, the Advaitins included. But most of the criticism, have been directed at its theory of meaning, *sphoṭa*, rather than at the broader metaphysical implications of it.

At the root of it all is the question as to how one understands the difference between the symbolic and the literal. If one conceives language itself as being essentially symbolic in character, realism can somehow be maintained with regard to given aspects of it. On the contrary, within the literal, the symbolic has no place. Once we arrive at the literal equation, Reality = Language, no aspect of it can any longer be held as symbolic. The pursuit of, and meditation on, language becomes a literal technique for *mokṣa*.

There are ways in which Reality = Language can be regarded as real, that is insofar as the objective is understanding. Reality when understood expresses itself, so to say, by re-enacting the whole order of projection and creative manifestation. Since the means of understanding is language, it can be maintained unequivocally in that respect, as the means of re-counting, of re-enactment in understanding, as literally the medium as well as the source of projection and manifestation. At this point Language and Reality meet and merge but we must always keep in mind understanding as the reason for this. Of course understanding must itself be based on language, but other than in terms of understanding's own need to re-enact to itself through language the projective and creative order, there is no justification for literally reifying language.

Likewise also is the belonging together of consciousness and language. The *Vākyapadīya* has apparently turned it all into a literal and simple equation. Gaurinath Sastri, a modern exponent of this great text, seems to sum it up correctly: "The Ultimate

25. *Ibid.*, I.14.

Reality is the Absolute Consciousness, and consciousness and word being identical, it is the Absolute Word. In the system of Bhartṛhari consciousness and word are interchangeable terms. This makes for his difference from Vedānta, though both of them are at one with regard to the unitary character of the Absolute."[26]

Mr. Sastri also points out the reasons why the whole order of creative production of the world in the *Śābdika* system of Bhartṛhati based on the concept of the powers of th e word—dynamic as in Kashmir Śaivism—is so different from the Advaita order in the same respect based on the principle of *anirvacanīya* (the indefinable). Now, *anirvacanīya* concerns language as much as anything else, fundamentally because there are questions which cannot be answered by 'yes' or 'no', and yet by both in a way. All this reveals the paradoxical character in which language the foundation of all understanding and thought has to be seen.

The uniqueness of Śaṅkara's position is that he could legitimately say 'yes' and 'no' at the same time to some important propositions, as they must be subsumed under *anirvacanīya*, and yet say neither. In his *Bhāṣya* on the *Brahma-sūtra*[27] he rejected the *sphoṭavāda* associated with *Śabdabrahman* and took his stand with the *Pūrva-mīmāṁsakas* (whom he elsewhere opposed for other reasons concerning the Word as well). Śaṅkara rejected the *sphoṭa* because of its metaphysical implications. He saw a derivative order of entities from names leading to species names, implying the genesis of species thus as a real consequence of *sphoṭa*, according to which "it would not be contrary to say that gods, etc., are born of eternal words." The notion of actual origin of entities from words would be an error of realism pertaining to language, which must be avoided.

On the other hand, the co-ordination of language, consciousness and the world, if not to be pushed to an extreme of positive identity, is essential. On the opposite side of the ledger, then, is *Pūrva-Mīmāṁsā*. Although it would accept the belonging together of language and consciousness, to the extent it understood

26. *The Philosophy of Word and Meaning*, Calcutta, Sanskrit College, 1959, p. 24.

27. I.3.28.

language primarily in terms of *vidhi* (injunction) and *artha-vāda*, i.e., what is calculated to create a liking for *vidhi* in one's consciousness,[28] its view has a limiting effect on consciousness, it being understood as act. There is unity of consciousness and language at the very depth of both—in this Bhartṛhari is right, although not in his view of it as a simple metaphysical identity—and it must come up to the surface of our awareness and must be expressed comprehensively in language. This unity can be expressed only by the term *jñāna* and not to be conceived narrowly and limitedly as activity (*karma*)—or for that matter speaking in a different context, *bhakti*. This has been the great issue that Śaṅkara took with the *Pūrva-mīmāṁsakas*.

Language is the means by which we can plunge into the depth of our own consciousness. *Jñāna*, then as an object of philosophical pursuit has a certain reflexivity, which comes to us as Self-knowledge, attendant on the pursuit of the mystery of language.

28. See for e.g., *Śābara Bhāṣya* on *Jaimini-Sūtra*, I.2.7.

TEN

LANGUAGE AND TRANSCENDENCE

Language is a mystery that has to be brought to light. But side by side with this proposition we must state that language itself is the light. Here then we get the resultant of the two, which is the truth that language is a kind of self-concealing light. In order to uncover it we are summoned to understand its belonging together with consciousness, which is itself a self-concealing light. These two are again co-ordinated with the world, which left to itself is darkness. In their coordination these three give us a glimmer of light which beckons to us to reach out to a depth—or height—which is the source of all illumination, that is, the self-shining light.

Philosophy is the reaching out towards the light. But then such reaching out itself must be understood as nothing but the shining of the light *appearing* to put on the visage of human achievement. This only shows that the concealing cover cannot be actually removed: it is only rendered transparent. The cover remains.

We say that the mystery of language is to be discovered, but putting it that way is itself a way of veiling the Word by words. Language hides in itself, and this hiding is co-ordinated with its concealment in the structures of the world—and in the layers of consciousness. Language must, therefore, be sought primarily in its own hiding places. So discovering the mystery of language as a task of philosophy is only one of two poles in a dialectical whole of which the other one is letting language discover all that is hidden, including itself.

Language itself has a mission which must be set alongside of philosophy's mission. It is language that makes thinking itself possible. It is because of this that some of the major traditions of Indian philosophy consider language as self-shining light. The doctrine of *pratibhā*, along with some synonyms, as Mahamahopadhyaya Gopinath Kaviraj makes clear,[1] surely stands for this. Kashmir Śaivism calls it by such expressive words as *sphurattā* (self-illumination), *vimarśa* (self-manifestation), etc. Parallels of this idea run all across the board in Indian religious philosophies, being most certainly a central notion in Vedānta as well.[2] The notion of *paśyantī*, the highest level of language—subject to the debate whether *parā-vāk* may be accorded this status—must be taken to stand for the transcendence of the self-shining light.

When we say that the mission of language is to discover or to reveal, it also means that it has the mission to lead us to Being. We may call this the primary religious function of language but this in no way should be understood as standing apart from philosophy's task of bringing language to light. As philosophy must bring to light hidden things in their entirety it does not leave something so essential to language as its religious function unaccounted for, and hide in some obscurantism of its own wilful making.

Levels of Language: Signification, the Highest

Any attempt to look deeply into language will show that it exists at different levels. The *Māṇḍūkya Upaniṣad* gives four; the *Vākyapadīya* and its Grammatical Philosophy may give three or four, according as they are interpreted. Even if we look independently, from outside these systems, we can still see levels. It is possible to speak of four levels in a different way, not intended to correspond, however, to any of the classifications in the traditional systems.

We can think of our everyday talk as one level, language as a force in life and in the affairs of the world as another, and language in terms of its logical structure as a third. No doubt we

1. "The Doctrine of pratibhā in Indian Philosophy", *Aspects of Indian Thought*, The University of Burdwan, 1966.

2. Note : However, if we are looking for the word *pratibhā* itself in Vedānta, as Dr. Kaviraj points out, there is only one major instance to be adduced : in the ninth *anuvāka* of Sureśvara's *Vārtika* on the *Taittirīya Upaniṣad Bhāṣya* of Śaṅkara.

can also perceive that these are not levels in the strict sense of the word as they comprehend one another, and in fact belong together as the whole of language as we know it. They are applicable to every department of our lives, society, business, politics, art, love, religion, etc. Nothing is excluded. But these three either separately or all together do not tell us anything about the transcendent. And the transcendent would seem to be that which sustains the integrity and wholeness of language as its functions, at least ought to function, in our lives. A fourth level, then, is indicated.

If we speak of the transcendent as such we should recognize that the language in which it is expressed, functioning co-ordinately with consciousness, which level by level corresponds to it, alone gives us a clue to it. Hence transcendence of language and transcendence of consciousness become co-eval with the transcendent as such. In respect of language the identity with the transcendent may be essentially symbolic, but then symbol is that which bears the *name* and serves as the *image* of reality—according to the Indian tradition.[3]

The existence of parallel structures of language, consciousness (or the self) and the world is an insight of traditional Indian ontology. The only possibility of establishing Being is by means of their co-ordination. But then we also realize that traditional ontologies also function within a fundamentally mystical framework with an emphasis on "realization" or even *mokṣa*. Elaborate techniques of realization (*sādhana*) have become appurtenant to such an ontology. In certain systems like the Tāntric there arose cultic techniques with a highly esoteric flavour classically represented by *mantra-śāstra*. In these systems, although philosophy is not suppressed, it has become an activity of mere exposition auxiliary to the cult which by definition is secret and inaccessible to the "outsider".[4] Kashmir Śaivism also

3. With reference to the letter AUM Śaṅkara observes : "All the Upaniṣads teach that by reason of its being the name and image of the Supreme Self it is the best means for meditation", *nāmatvena pratīkatvena ca paramātmopāsana-sādhanaṁ śreṣṭham iti sarva-vedānteṣu avagatam*, The *Commentary on Chāndogya Upaniṣad*, 1.1.1.

4. Note : Sir John Woodroffe (Arthur Avalon) and Dr. Gopinath Kaviraj are among those who have done signal service to the world of

shares most of these tāntric characteristics. However, Vedānta and the Philosophy of Grammar, in spite of the fact that their doctrines encourage mysticism, still retain to a large extent the independence of their ontology, making it accessible to philosophy as such.

Gaurinath Sastri is among the scholars who are painfully aware of this predilection to mysticism particularly in the Philosophy of Grammar. He observes thus : "It may seem that the conclusion that word and consciousness are identical is inspired by the exigencies of religious mysticism, and that the arguments employed to validate it have been conceived *a priori* and the linguistic forms and phenomena have been so twisted as to fit into the architectonic plan in order to bolster up a mystical doctrine conceived independently and *a priori*." Mr. Sastri is confident that the ontology in question can be unhinged from mysticism and demonstrated on purely "logical" grounds. Hence he continues : "It is imperative that the plausibility of this impression should be examined in all its bearings in order to convince ourselves of the logical validity or otherwise of the grammarian's [Bhartṛhari's] metaphysical stand. This can be achieved by the critical scrutiny of the nature of word as it comes within our ken in ordinary experience."[5] While the legitimacy of this perception, underlying which there exists a wholly commendable concern for an open metaphysics of the transcendence of the Word, must no doubt be accepted, it may be that another way would be to envisage a more general ontology of language, without disturbing the integrity that language maintains with consciousness, allowing both mysticism and an alternative way of transcendence to be held together as equal possibilities.

The demand for such a general ontology does not come from the need to satisfy the conceptual thrust of the mind but rather from the need to take account of, and comprehend, alternatives which address themselves to the same goal, in the same respect,

learning by making available to us the product of their profoundly sympathetic and often beautiful studies of the Tantra, thus enriching our knowledge.

5. G. Sastri, *The Philosophy of Word and Meaning*.

but nevertheless differently. The general is only in that sense general. The phrases, "same goal" and "in the same respect" must be emphasized, which means here the concern for transcendence as well as for maintaining the integrity of language with consciousness. Mysticism as the highest form of self-activity/self-non-activity of the language-consciousness complex has a genuine counter-part in another kind of thinking, that is existential thinking or even sheer ontological thinking, which may very well be the result of most modern men's inability to participate any longer in traditional religion and mysticism. In this latter, then, the view of transcendence becomes different from the way mysticism understands it, yet is nevertheless an authentic approach to transcendence.

This modern alternative also recognizes the validity of distinguishing the essential, transcendent level of language (and consciousness) corresponding to the transcendence of Being, from the levels at which we ordinarily apprehend language. It is represented most impressively by that modern movement in philosophy centred around the name of Martin Heidegger.

Although this modern philosophy depicts a totally different kind of transcendence from the traditional Indian philosophies there are some interesting similarities in some respects, particularly in regard to the conception of the mission of language and the vital question of 'signification' as central to that mission. No doubt, Indian philosophies understand the 'essence of language' to be *vāk*, *śabda-brahman* (or *sphoṭa*), the *vimarśa* (or *sphurattā*) of God etc. (according to the system in question). Likewise, they understand consciousness to be eternal and non-temporal (and hence the Word too is eternal and non-temporal). The eternity and unity of the Word are co-ordinated with the eternity and unity of consciousness. But, Heideggerian philosophy does not understand the 'essence of language' in that way at all, while for it, in the place of eternal consciousness, there is Dasein, so temporal, so worldly that, from the Indian point of view, it calls for an inverted "mysticism" of the Word and Being. But it only outwardly resembles mysticism, even inverted mysticism.

Yet the two seem to be able to stand together in resisting certain misunderstandings about language and in the commitment to expurgate the inauthentic from language. The Upaniṣadic analysis of language, the Self (consciousness)—and the world—in a co-ordinated way, has its counter-part in Heidegger as, according to him, "we work out in advance the ontologico-existential whole of the structure of discourse on the basis of Dasein".[6] It is a decisive step to be taken if one has to grasp that 'essence of language'. Heidegger criticizes certain attempts to grasp that essence which have used as clues the ideas of 'expression', 'symbolic form', 'communication as assertion', of the 'making known of experiences', and of the 'patterning of life'. He remarks : "Even if one were to put these various fragmentary definitions together in syncretistic fashion, nothing would be achieved in the way of a fully adequate definition of "language".[7]

Heidegger presses forward to a doctrine of signification, which he believes will not result from a Romantic quest for an original language or from a descriptive, comparative study of languages but from finding its roots in Dasein. So he writes : "A doctrine of signification will not emerge automatically even if we make a comprehensive comparison of as many languages as possible, and those which are most exotic. To accept, let us say, the philosophical horizon within which W. von Humboldt made language a problem, would be no less inadequate. The doctrine of signification is rooted in the ontology of Dasein. Whether it prospers or decays depends on the fate of this ontology."[8]

Signification is associated with meaning ; it always carries meaning. The two are distinguished thus : meaning is what "can be articulated in interpretation, and thus even more primordially in discourse", while signification is what is derived by the breaking up of the "totality of signification [*Bedeutungsganze*)" which is what [actually] "gets articulated as such in discursive Articulation."[9]

Coupled with it is the fact (for Heidegger who speaks solely in terms of the West) that the handed-down structures of dis-

6. *Being and Time*, English translation by Macquarrie and Robinson, New York, Harper & Row, 1962, p. 206.

7. *Loc. cit.*

8. *Ibid.*, p. 209.

9. *Ibid.*, p. 204.

course primarily consist of assertions. Heidegger explains :

> The Greeks had no word for "language": they understood this phenomenon 'in the first instance' as discourse. But because the *Logos* came into their philosophical ken primarily as assertion, *this* was the kind of *logos* which they took as their clue for working out the basic structures of the forms of discourse and its components. Grammar sought its foundation in the 'logic' of this *logos*. But this logic was based upon the ontology of the present-at-hand. The basic stock of 'categories of signification', which passed over into the subsequent science of language, and which in principle is still accepted as the standard today, is oriented towards discourse as assertion. But if on the contrary we take this phenomenon to have in principle the primordiality and breadth of an *existentiale* then there emerges the necessity of re-establishing the science of language on foundations which are ontologically more primordial. The task of *liberating* grammar from logic requires *beforehand* a *positive* understanding of the basic *a priori* structure of discourse in general as an *existentiale*.[10]

Dasein is described as Being in-the-world and with respect to that it is stated : "Discoursing or talking is the way in which we articulate 'significantly' the intelligibility of Being-in-the-world".[11] Now the expressibility (and along with it understanding) of Being-in-the-world creates a further predicament for signification through language as a distinction between "Being-in" and "Being-outside" with respect to it (viz., Being-in-the-world). This shows that another kind of language than assertive (expressive of understanding, which in turn pre-supposes a Being outside position with respect to Dasein's Being-in-the-world) becomes necessary. Such a language exists. Heidegger clarifies it thus : "Being-in and its state-of-mind (mood) are made known in discourse and indicated in language by intonation, modulation, the tempo of talk, the way of speaking".[12] Continuing, he writes, "In 'poetical' discourse, the communication of the existential possibilities

10. *Ibid.*, p. 209.
11. *Ibid.*, p. 204.
12. *Ibid.*, p. 205.

of one's state of mind can become an aim in itself, and this amounts to a disclosing of existence."

In the Indian traditions of the ontology of language, although surely the self and consciousness are conceived in an almost antithetical way to what has been described as Dasein's Being-in-the-world, a framework of the logos (*vāk*) exists where assertive discourse and its logical structure—in spite of their having developed to the highest degree—have not captured monopoly over language. The most striking example comes from the *Chāndogya Upaniṣad*, which has set forth a profound philosophy of language as chant (based on meditation upon the *udgītha*, the *Sāma-veda*, etc.), and as invocation and such like, and in a way that expresses the centrality of the Self and its non-duality. This Upaniṣad begins with the statement : *aum iti etad akṣaram udgītham upāsīta, aum iti hyudgāyati*, etc. (AUM, one should meditate on the syllable, the *udgītha*, for one heartily chants it as AUM, etc.), to give an immediate explanation of this mysterious symbol which sums up language. In AUM that which is sundered in phenomenal language is reunited : the division between assertion, on the one hand, and invocation, chant, prayer, expression of wish, etc., on the other hand, is overcome. It restores the unity of language by recognizing it for what it is. Śaṅkara commenting on this passage states, as pointed out a few pages back, that this symbol is a representation of the Supreme Self like the image and such like, and that what is learnt from all the Vedānta texts is that it, being the name and form of the Supreme Self, is the best means of meditating upon it (*arcādivat parasya ātmanaḥ pratīkaṁ sampadyate*; *evam nāmatvena pratīkatvena ca paramātmopāsana-sādhanaṁ śreṣṭham iti sarva-vedānteṣu avagatam*).

AUM is the heart of all signification, the very origin of language. Obviously what it discloses is not primarily the individual human being's (Dasein's) Being-in-the-world and its state of mind but the Supreme Self while indicating a path by which the individual human being in his actual phenomenal and existential condition can reach it. This is language's primary mission.

A Misadventure in the Quest for the Essence and Origin of Language in the Indian Tradition

F. Max Müller did very great service to the cause of Vedic

and Vedāntic studies in his day and we have rightly not forgotten him. But the inadequate presuppositions, directly taken from the Romantic Linguistics and Philology, from W. von Humboldt particularly, having frozen into a dogma in later times, has contributed to a kind of misadventure in the quest for the origins of Indian religious perceptions, embodied in ancient language and literature of the land. The perusal of traditional texts themselves would call for a different approach to the question. Lessons learnt from contemporary philosophical investigations should make it possible for us to appreciate the traditional views of language as an envoy and plenipotentiary of the Supreme Reality and as a light unto our feet as we journey on to our highest goal.

True to his Romantic predilections, Max Müller entertained certain pre-suppositions. "The earliest work of art, wrought by the human mind", he wrote, "more ancient than any literary document and prior even to the first whisperings of tradition, the human language forms an uninterrupted chain from the first dawn of history down to our own times."[13] Language, as he argues, "still bears the impress of the earliest thoughts of man, obliterated, it may be, buried under new thoughts, yet here and there [are] still recoverable in their sharp, original outlines."[14] To pursue it to its origins would really be the task set for researchers on language. For Müller the essence of language is expression. To express oneself is a natural instinct and hence language is a product of instinct, and as such belongs to the realm of Nature. He believed that with the aid of comparative philology, we can go back to the original form of human consciousness, the *primum cognitum*.

This hypothesis has had consequences for the project of recovering the "original" signification of the names of deities, for one thing. Accordingly, physically perceived objects like the dawn of the spoken word itself, for instance, became divine, mythological beings due to a primeval transformation, which took place in the pilgrimage of language. Thus *EOS* (dawn), for instance, [corresponding to *UṢĀ*] becomes a goddess and

13. "Comparative Mythology", *Chips from a German Workshop*, II, p. 7.
14. *Lectures on the Science of Language*, p. 387.

eventually the wife of Tithonos; and *Fatum*, likewise, the goddess of fate.

It is well known that Müller applied this method to the study of religion in general and to Vedic religion in particular in his book, *Lectures on the Origin of Religion as Illustrated by the Vedas*. He pointed a direction in which many students of Vedic religion have since walked. It is, no doubt, to be agreed that the problem of the origin of religion must be resolved by drawing from insights into the essence of language; the essence of language likewise must be considered in conjunction with consciousness. Müller, after a study of names common in Aryan languages, claimed that these names had originally an expressive power, and that the discovery of them will alone explain the mythological language and "render intelligible that phase of the human mind which gave birth to the extra-ordinary stories of gods and heroes, or gorgons and chimeras—of things that no human eye had ever seen, and no human mind in a healthy state could have ever conceived."[15]

But the question arises, whether in our quest for the essence of language, when instead of considering the mystery of signification, we replace it with a concern for "origin" we are not moving the whole matter out of the only ground, e.g., consciousness, where certainty is possible. Can "origin" itself be traced through a presumedly straight path of convergence of all human (or even Indo-Aryan) languages upon some primeval, self-revealing splendour of physical consciousness ? Or is it not rather the case that we must pursue the problem of the power of signification, which lies in the corroborative evidence it furnishes, for the purpose of exegeting the essence of language in consciousness, as that is always at hand although conceals itself from clear view ? At least the *Chāndogya Upaniṣad* (as also others) in its own words and in the words of its interpreters like Śaṅkara, appear to think so. Accordingly, physical brilliance and all Nature-mediated sensations, being part of object-awareness, are merely a refraction of consciousness's mediation of its essence to itself.

The concept of brilliance is to be considered first. Explicating

15. *Chips from a German Workshop*, II, p. 53.

the terms *devas* and *asuras* (*Chāndogya Upaniṣad*, 1.2.1.) Śaṅkara writes :

> The term '*deva*' is derived from the root '*div*' to shine; hence the word '*devas*' stand for such functionings of the sense-organs as are illuminated (regulated) by the scriptures; —opposed to these are '*asuras*'—etymologically explained as '*asuṣu ramaṇāt*',[16] delighting in the spheres of all their own natural life, and 'inclinations' as pertaining to all objects of sense; hence the term stands for those natural functions of the sense organs which are of the nature of darkness (ignorance).[17]

If the *asuras* stand for darkness or ignorance, the *devas* stand for light and knowledge, and it is in respect of the struggle between the two mentioned in many places in the Brāhmaṇas and also in the Upaniṣads (see the *Bṛhadāraṇyaka*, 1.3.1; the *Chāndogya*, 1.2.1.) the word of words, the *udgītha*, becomes the primary symbol of meditation (being the primary weapon of the *devas*). Concerning the deities (*ādhidaivatam*) the *Chāndogya Upaniṣad* (1.3.1) states *ya evāsau tapati tam udgītham upāsītodyan vā eṣa prajābhya udgāyati* (Him who glows yonder one should mediate as the *udgītha*). The sun is the obvious physical expression of such glowing, or shining. In explanation of this passage, Śaṅkara writes :

> On rising, He [the Sun] dispels, for the sake of living beings, the darkness—of Night—and also the danger arising from that Darkness—One who knows the Sun as endowed with these qualities becomes the dispeller—destroyer of danger—i.e., the danger to the Self, of being born and dying;—as also of Darkness, in the shape of ignorance,—which is the source of that danger.[18]

16. Note : This derivation, however, is different from that of *Nirukta*, 3.7, according to which *asura* comes from *a-su-raḥ*, meaning delighting in evil places, or having been expelled from places, on account of the root *as* (to throw). The difference, nevertheless, is only formal and not material, meaning being not really affected.

17. Quoted from Ganganath Jha's translation of the *Chāndogya Upaniṣad* with Śaṅkara's commentary, Poona, Oriental Book Agency, p. 15.

18. *Ibid.*, p. 26.

The *devas* shine because they know the most secret essence (*rasaḥ*) of speech, which is the *udgītha*, the chant of chants. Man (*puruṣa*) stands located in the world as the essence of all that constitutes it; he is himself in need of an essential goal for his direction, which comes from the light of the highest form of speech.

Now it is clear that it is not the primitive experience of Nature, the brilliance and glory of the sun for instance, which suggested to man the idea of the gods but the light of speech which already constitutes his essential being. The Vedic and the Vedāntic explication on the phenomenon is different indeed from the hypothesis of Max Müller, and the former accords well with the understanding of the particular modern philosophy which we have sought to utilize to the permissible extent.

Language, Transcendence and "Religion"

When we pursue the primordial essence of language we must be led to the primordial essence of human, phenomenal consciousness. This has brought us to our final theme, namely the relation between language, transcendence and "religion". When we are searching for the close relation among them we are led to the conclusion that our interest hovers around not the problem of *religious language* but that of potentiality for religion in primordial language.

What is called religious language—usually the subject of so much analytical study, particularly in today's philosophy—would be simply incomprehensible unless we recognize an inclination towards "religion" in primordial language. This is our point of departure. The distinction between religious language and non-religious language is a derivative one, which comes into being owing to the essential character of self-forgetfulness built into the primordial language. Self-forgetfulness is a necessary protection against self-awareness, its scorching radiation and its infinite de-ontic power. No one can stand the terror of self-awareness. One's mind turns to the terror that Arjuna experienced in the *Viśvarūpa-darśana* as a fitting paradigm.

We have no warrant to call this primordial language *religious* language in the manner of religious or theological propositions. We know that that language is not at all language of assertion, for there is nothing to assert. There may be something to cry out, or turn one's face away from in terror, and hence invoke. In Heidegger's words here one expresses the uncanniness—unhomelikeness (*unheimlichkeit*) of existence (*Sein und Zeit*, section 188, *Being and Time*, p. 283) and the sense of being-not-at-home (*das nichtzuhause-sein*).

We should recognize (1) that there is a state of dislocation into which self-awareness throws the human self and (2) that there is an act of self-relocation spontaneously succeeding the knowledge of the former. As Heidegger makes it clear, being-in-the-world is not that which one flees as if by fleeing it one falls into dislocation; rather the contrary, because not-being-at-home is more primordial. Being-in-the-world is never being-at-home-in-the-world. If any one wants an argument to prove the fact of man's dislocation, then he is only resorting to sophistry in order to set aside an existential problem.

Nature is alienated from Being, the world is Being alienated from itself. History is alienated from Nature and Being. Likewise, Nature and History are alienated from themselves. The human self is the measure of all such alienations. Man has to bear all these burdens plus the burden of the question about God's existence and non-existence as well. All this because of man's self-awareness. But the involvement of the human self is such that the fact of dislocation is apprehended not only in itself but in the possibility of its overcoming. But how do we interpret this syndrome of dislocation and its overcoming ? The fact is, we don't, and we don't have to, because it has interpreted itself. That kind of self-interpretation, self-expression, of this peculiar human syndrome is what is historically called "religion". Our task is simply to understand the terms in which it has and does take place. The word "religion" is itself not at issue; and why quarrel over it ?

Names, particularly names of gods and goddesses, are linguistic entities, which arise in the context of the function of language in re-housing what is found dislocated, namely the human self. They do not necessarily stand for substantive entities and simply cannot be understood apart from the significatory function of language.

We must still pay heed to a parting of ways that history exhibits. There are two opposite orientations which arise from the potentiality for religion. One never manifests itself as religion, but rather refuses to be religion. It hovers on the brink of religion, and its self-sustaining dynamics is a form of radical existential scepticism which draws its substance from the actual religions and reverses the direction of what it draws: it becomes itself in history by its resistance to them. The modern age of anxiety and *scepsis* reveals it to us. The reconstruction of *logos* as language follows this pattern; whether the great Greek tradition of *logos* was actually such is, however, a moot problem. It does indeed entail a rejection of the main Western (Platonic and post-Platonic) tradition, as Heidegger argues, and one would think, all similar high metaphysical traditions of the world. The other manifests itself definitely as religion; there is a continuing tradition through which the significatory level of language has maintained a religio-metaphysical form. Here too the essence of language that we are looking for is truly found, although by muffling the sceptical, "modern" outlook it has provided a metaphysical version, a *gnosis* version of signification.

The most powerful and unbroken expression of the latter tradition is found in Vedānta. In this respect there is nothing anywhere more striking than the paradigm of the AUM symbol presented in the *Māṇḍūkya Upaniṣad*, that expresses the primordial role of language in this tradition, although because its approach is essentially mystical it speaks from the end of relocation (of ultimate unity with *Brahman*, or *Ātman*) altogether and allows no irremovable anxiety to persist in language and consciousness. Śaṅkara in his introduction to the *Māṇḍūkyopaniṣad-bhāṣya* writes:

> AUM is the substratum of the entire illusion of the world of the word (*vākprapañca*) having for its contents such distortions (*vikalpas*) as *prāṇa* etc., imagined in the *Ātman*. And AUM is verily of the same essential character as the *Ātman*; for it is the name for the *Ātman*. All *vikalpas* such as *prāṇa* etc., having *Ātman* for the substratum and denoted by words—which are but modification of AUM—cannot exist without

names. This is supported by such *Śruti* passages as, 'the modification being only a name arising from speech'; 'All this related to It (*Brahman*) is held together by the cord of speech and strands of names;' 'All these (are rendered possible) by names', etc.

This primordial structure of *vikalpa* (and of *māyā-avidyā*) is revealed to us through the counter-positing reality of the primary word (divine names, etc., included), symbolically represented by the all-comprehending AUM. As has become obvious, in the *Māṇḍūkya*, as in the *Vākyapadīya* as in all Vedānta, indeed as in all mystical tradition of the logos, or *vāk*, the word is identified either actually or symbolically with metaphysical Reality, which is not the case in the modern existentialist way, where there reigns an alternative, a radically different conception of Being. However, as the mystical word, AUM brings about awareness of itself as of that which it counterposits, namely the *vikalpa* structures.

Within the framework of the mystical and metaphysical tradition, however, *vāk* as AUM identifies itself with human self in its state of dislocation and not-being-at-home. It does not abandon man in the extremities of the *vikalpa* structures. Rather it grasps him there and carries him forward to the place of overcoming. Hence it is declared to be the best support (*ālambanam*), and man is summoned to meditate on it (*aumityātmānaṁ yuñjīta*). That is the mission of language, according to Vedānta.

Here then we have the greatest paradigm of the religious and mystical orientation in the potentiality for religion in primordial language. There is clearly a discourse form to it. But the discourse is not essentially assertion or system of assertions. It has a primary form of invocation or chant. It is also benediction, glorification, divine adoration. But it also incorporates assertion, without which language cannot function.

The language of AUM as analysed in *Māṇḍūkya* shows that it is essentially *directional* in mode, that it is essentially a *path for man* to follow. Its ontological essence (or Being) is itself a *direction*, a movement. It is like an arrow discharged from below; yet at the same time it is a self-launching missile that comes from beyond the highest flight of the human spirit. It is a messenger and guide. And also, it is the face of Reality turned towards man. It is a healer that heals, viz., the metaphysical breach between man and Being. Nevertheless, AUM or *vāk* is not religious language. Rather, it is that from which certain religious languages have come.

But in all cases we have to distinguish between the potentiality for religion present in the language of signification, that is, the essence of language, and actual languages with religious and theological meaning. Actual theological language has to have logical form and logical meaning. It is inevitable that in logical form and meaning there should be diversity, and what obtains in one theological language cannot be easily harmonized with what obtains in another. The meaning problem is acute here. Here signification itself has to stand in the service of meaning rather than clearly above it. For there is a chance that no actual religious language that claims to stand above logical meaning can do so without contradicting it. And all actual religions, except those that go to the fringes of occultism, will try to avoid contradicting logical meaning because they are aware of the peril of disorder. The problem of grasping what is beyond meaning is fraught with intense dangers. The irrational for its own sake must at all costs be avoided in religious language. Thus St. Paul warns the Corinthians against the practice of glossolalia (speaking in tongues as it is called): "I had rather speak five words with my understanding than ten thousand words in an *unknown* tongue", as he believes that "God is not the author of confusion but of peace".[19]

Religious language itself is derivative. It must have a normally propositional form. It could take the form of injunction and prohibition (*vidhi* and *niṣedha*) as in Pūrva Mīmāṁsā; or the form of commandments as in the Old Testament; or laws as, again, in the Old Testament and the *Dharma-śāstras*, etc.

The forms of religious language are always human, cultural, historical. Here we have the religions in the plural. The languages in which we apprehend the transcendent also vary; here there is no common meaning-essence to which we can reduce these different individualities.

But we never forget that religious languages are what they

19. *The First Epistle to the Corinthians*, 14. 19.

are because of the essential character of language (where lies signification) because it infuses itself into them and gathers itself from them. But existentially speaking, language bespeaks itself before it bespeaks God, revelation, scripture (or *Śruti*). That is the existential ground of transcendent unity, a unity which can never be translated into logical meaning structures; upon it and because of it religious languages can significantly differ; and also that which is non-religious can differ from that which is religious.

Language itself holds that unity; in its keeping is transcendence. Ultimately language must and does speak for itself. What we speak is an imitation of it. But the authenticity of what we speak is measured by how we imitate it, with understanding or without it. The statement concerning meditation on the *udgītha*, etc., is intended to direct us into authenticity, at least as a constant reminder.

ELEVEN

LANGUAGE AND KNOWLEDGE: IN THE THEOLOGY OF KARL BARTH AND VEDĀNTA

Here we will discuss the problem of language and knowledge from an essentially theological angle, based on the ideas of Karl Barth, on the one hand, and on the teachings of Vedānta, especially of Śaṅkara, on the other. This interest arises from our comparativist-hermeneutical situation, which both stipulates that we enter the domain of theology (perhaps in the sense of a no-man's land only) with the problem in question and that we select, in order to set side by side with Vedānta, a Western theological system which in almost every respect is unlike it and yet possesses such a monumental intellectual (though perhaps not philosophical) character as to wield great authority and power while also speaking from a modern existential standpoint of language: the choice of Karl Barth's theology, then, has been almost automatic.

As we proceed we may also be struck by the disclosure of strange affinities between the two systems on certain matters, in the midst of otherwise almost total dissimilarity. We may, of course, make nothing theologically of such a phenomenon of occasional, unexpected closeness between two systems that are so far apart. All that we may do is to note the fact and store it while right away taking the significance that arises from the difference itself into what still lies ahead for comparativist-hermeneutics, namely what goes beyond similarity and difference.

Among the themes intensely pondered in the Vedāntic tradition, none is more central than that of language. The Indian interest in the language problem goes back to the *Ṛgveda*, according to which *vāk* is the ultimate principle of the universe.[1]

1. *Ṛgveda*, 10.71;10. 125.

The importance of the speech principle continues through the *Brāhmaṇas* and the *Upaniṣads* in manifold ways. In some places it is even raised to the supreme status (for instance, in the *Bṛhadāraṇyaka Upaniṣad*,[2] where it is said : "*vāk* verily is *Brahman*, indeed *vāk* is the supreme *Brahman*"). The principle develops in a variety of ways, producing parallel notions in art, music, learning, liturgy, and metaphysics. The liturgically originated concept of *vāk* is transformed into the technical, metaphysico-epistemological concept of *śabda* (which also means logos or word). Grammatical philosophers like Bhartṛhari, the author of the great work, *Vākyapadīya*, as we have discussed in the previous two essays, clearly equated *śabda* with *Brahman* and articulated the theory of *Śabda-Brahman* (*Brahman* as the Logos).[3] Similarities between the position indicated in the Indian metaphysics of language and certain parts of Christian doctrine, particularly that implied in the prologue of the Fourth Gospel, cannot be missed. But that matter falls outside the rather restricted framework with which we are occupied here. We are only concerned with language and knowledge in revelation, in respect of which Barth's thought and Vedānta bear upon each other more than is imagined.

Language and Revelation

In Barth's opinion language is paramountly important in revelation, for "God reveals Himself in propositions by means of language, and human language at that, to the effect that from time to time such and such a word spoken by the prophets and apostles and proclaimed in the Church becomes His Word."[4] Also, "God's language refers to the form in which we hear the Word of God."[5] For Vedānta, too, the basis of authority, the revelation, is the Veda, of which the source is *Brahman*.[6] The

2. *Bṛhadāraṇyaka Upaniṣad*, 4.1.2.

3. Cf. Gaurinath Sastri, *The Philosophy of Word and Meaning*, pp. 1 ff. Sastri calls *śobda verbum*.

4. Karl Barth, *Church Dogmatics*, Vol. I, Part I, authorized translation by G. T. Thomson (Edinburgh : T. & T. Clark, 1936), p. 156.

5. *Ibid.*, p. 152.

6. Cf. *Bṛhadāraṇyaka Upaniṣad*, 2.4.10; Also *Brahma Sūtra*, 1.1.3. Cf. the *Vedānta Sūtras of Bādarāyaṇa*, with the commentary by Śaṅkara, translation by George Thibaut, New York : Dover, 1962. part I, pp. 19ff.

Veda is otherwise called *Śruti*, meaning that which was heard, and is composed of sentences (*vākyas*), the key ones being called "the great sentences" (*mahāvākyas*) (such as "That Thou art" [*tat tvam asi*] and "I am Brahman" [*aham brahmāsmi*]).

The big issue between these two different types of thought is the role of language in revelation, and the nature of knowledge that is borne through language. Their differences are symptomatic of some very crucial divergences pertaining to the whole understanding of Reality, an understanding which is of great consequence for theology. Language, Barth perceives, has "to be correlated to hearing, understanding."[7] This is an expression of the problem of the implication of knowledge which is a matter of so much concern to modern theologians. The new theologians of hermeneutics are also concerned with this problem : they hope that the thought of the later Heidegger could help resolve it, believing that Barth had not.[8] The way that these new theologians seek to amend Barth's view is of no intrinsic interest here. But Barth declares :

> The Word of God always tells us something new, which otherwise we could never have heard from any one. It is the boulder of a Thou which does not become an I, that is here cast on our path. It is this otherness, then, which is yet related to us, which yet makes itself known to us, but yet does so in this way, which stamps it fundamentally and comprehensively as God's Word....[9]

In a similar vein on the Indian side, it is said that the Veda is a reliable authority because it teaches us things that are highly fruitful (*phalavat*), because it gives us knowledge not obtained otherwise (*anadhigata*), knowledge that is uncontradicted (*abādhita*).[10] The similarity, however, ends here, for there arises the deeply dividing problem of knowledge. What is the charac-

7. Karl Barth, *Church Dogmatics*, Vol. I, part I, p. 153.

8. J. M. Robinson and J. B. Cobb, Jr., *The Later Heidegger and Theology* (New York : Harper and Row, 1963), p. 53.

9. Karl Barth, *Church Dogmatics*, Vol. I, Part I, p. 160.

10. Cf. Kumārila, *Ślokavārtika*, translated by Ganganath Jha (Calcutta : Bibliotheca Indica, 1917), pp. 184-5.

ter of the knowledge brought to man in revelation ? Does it reveal Reality ? How does man respond to it, through appropriation of knowledge, or through volitional act ? Can man cognitively participate in the knowledge that comes in God's Word, even though the Word is uttered in human language ? Or can he participate only through faith ? The answers to these questions in the Barthian and in the Vedāntic systems are radically different.

The Substance of Barth's Position

Barth considers the role of language in revelation and its knowledge-implication in the three-fold form of the Word of God, i.e., as preached, as written, and as revealed. The Word of God preached means, first, "man's language about God on the basis of an indication by God Himself fundamentally transcending all human causation, and so devoid of all human basis, merely as a fact requiring to be acknowledged."[11] Secondly, it means "man's language about God on the basis of God's self-objectification which is neither present nor predictable nor relatable to any design, but is real solely in the freedom of His grace, in virtue of which from time to time He wills to be the object of this language, and is so according to His own good pleasure."[12] Thirdly, it means "man's language about God, which is according to God's own judgement, which cannot be anticipated and never passes under our control, and in view of the object proclaimed as well as of the subject proclaiming is true language and therefore language to be listened to, language which rightly demands obedience."[13] Fourthly, it means "man's language about God, in which and through which God Himself speaks about Himself."[14] These four statements are arranged in a system like concentric circles, the last forming the innermost. We must make special note of the phrase "language which demands obedience," implying that the proper response to the language of revelation is volitional, rather than

11. Karl Barth, *Church Dogmatics*, Vol. I, Part I, p. 101.
12. *Ibid.*, p. 103.
13. *Ibid.*, p. 104.
14. *Ibid.*, p. 106.

cognitive. We may also make special note of the phrase "requiring to be acknowledged," which is again a kind of volitional way of participating in knowledge. The Word of God as preached, then, is the *third* form of the Word of God.

The *second* form of the Word of God, the Word as written, is the Bible. It is of special interest. The Bible is the Word of God in the event of "the recollection of God's past revelation, the discovery of the canon, faith in the promise of the word of the prophets and the apostles, or, better, the Bible's imposition of itself on the strength of its special content, and therefore, the existence of real apostolic succession."[15] However, it is added that this very fact of the language of God Himself becoming an event in the human word of the Bible is...God's business and not ours".[16] For Barth there is no question about the Bible being the essence of human language. The Bible is God's Word only "in so far as God lets it be so, so far as God speaks through it."[17] But both the Word as preached and the Word as written are dependent on the *first* and fundamental form, the Word of God as revealed, "which establishes the other two."[18] The Word of God as revealed is never to be regarded as abstract, for it is concrete and immediate. But, it "meets us only in the two-fold mediacy"[19] of proclamation and scripture, that is to say, in the two forms of *human* language.

The language of God must be distinguished in terms of content and character from the language of man, although in both cases the reality of the human person is revealed through speaking. The reality of God is made known through speaking by way of hiddenness. Therefore,

> The language of God is and remains God's mystery. When we sum up what is here to be carried out precisely in the concept of mystery, we are thinking of the sense the word *mysterium* has in the NT. *Mysterium* signifies not only the hiddenness of God, but rather His becoming manifest in a

15. *Ibid.*, p. 122.
16. *Ibid.*, p. 123.
17. *Ibid.*, p. 123.
18. *Ibid.*, p. 136.
19. *Ibid.*, p. 136.

> hidden, i.e., in a non-apparent way, which gives information not directly but indirectly.[20]

The language of man by contrast, is a revelation of "man's wretchedness, the discord between truth and reality in which he lives."[21] Therefore, it is a kind of hiding of his nakedness. The difference consists in the fact that there is unity between act and speech in God's language, but sheer discord in man's.[22] In spite of this intrinsic defect of human language, and in complete disregard of it, God reveals Himself "in propositions of language and human language at that."[23] This is the mystery of the "worldliness of the Word of God [and] we do not possess the Word of God other than in the mystery of its worldliness."[24] The mystery means that the matter of the Word of God is expressed in the form of human language. However, "its form is not a suitable but an unsuitable means for the self-presentation of God. It does not correspond to the matter, but, it contradicts it. It does not unveil it, but veils it."[25] The Word of God has no form; the only form it has is "really that of the cosmos which stands in contradiction to God."[26] And, cosmos is defined as the place "in which sin rules." It is not clear whether Barth equates "worldliness" with sinfulness, and it is not clear how he can avoid doing so. But, it would certainly be a real theological problem if the phrase, "worldliness of the language of God" is replaced by the phrase "sinfulness of the language of God." Furthermore, there is a logical problem of the Word of God expressing itself in the form of the language of man, which by definition is the language of discord and disunity between act and speech. Although the theological problem in this may be circumvented by instituting God's will, the logical one remains. This problem too could be eliminated by assuming a distinction

20. *Ibid.*, p. 188, Cf. Karl Barth, *Church Dogmatics*, Vol. II, Part I, translated by G. W. Bromiley and T. F. Torrance (Edinburgh : T. & T. Clark, 1957) Ch. V, No. 27, 1.

21. Karl Barth, *Church Dogmatics*, Vol. I, Part I, p. 162.

22. *Ibid.*, Ch. I. No. 3.

23. *Ibid.*, p. 156.

24. *Ibid.*, p. 188.

25. *Ibid.*, p. 189.

26. *Ibid.*, pp. 189-90.

between matter and form in human language, whereby God removes the matter of human language and uses only its form, filling it with the matter of His word. Such a distinction, if it is there in Barth's discussion, is there only by reason of some inadvertent and unrecognized implication. But an implication of that kind necessitates a distinction between form and matter in man and the cosmos, which Barth *ex hypothesi* disallows. For he makes no provision for attaching sinfulness to matter only in man, his existence, and the cosmos while exempting the form. Ultimately, this would govern man's language too.

It would appear that the whole of human language, its matter and form included, is the only way in which the Divine Word is uttered. This involves the three forms of the Word of God, as declared, written, and revealed. Apart from this, God's Word has no form in any metaphysical sense. "Form is obviously always the form of a content. But may we actually speak of a content of the Word of God ?"[27] Elsewhere Barth says : "It always has a perfectly definite, objective content. God always utters a *concretessimum*. But this divine *concretessimum* can neither be anticipated nor repated."[28] Hence God's Word is not a formal possibility of divine speech, but its sheer actuality. In other words, Barth insists upon the "contingent contemporaneousness" of the language of God. God's Word is an occurrence, not something to be studied through the form-metaphysics of the logos theory. [Barth rejects both form-metaphysics and the theory.] "God's Word means God Speaks."[29] Therefore, there is no permissible way of translating 'logos' "in a way different from the concept of language."[30] How the formless Word of God can be expressed in the only possible form in which it is available to man, namely his own language, is the key problem. "That 'how' is the reflected image, attainable by man, of the unattainable nature of God."[31] In the light of the brokenness of human propositions, and in the light of the fact that "there is

27. *Ibid.*, p. 149.
28. *Ibid.*, p. 155.
29. *Ibid.*, p. 155.
30. *Ibid.*, p. 151.
31. *Ibid.*, p. 150.

no human awareness corresponding to this divine utterance,"[32] the problem is a very serious one. Although a dogmatic solution can be imposed by suggesting that it is God's business and not ours, the logical part of the problem remains. Language, even God's language, is a communication of reason with reason, person with person.[33] Such communication lies in "the sphere of the *ratio*."[34] This way of communicating is even identified as "deliberate intellectualism" in God's choice.[35] Although the *ratio* is not intellect alone, it is "the intellect at least also and not last of all."[36] What character reason really retains in the light of the sinfulness and brokenness of human language and the fallenness of human understanding is the question.[37] For Barth understanding and language are human properties, and, therefore, they share the spiritual fate of man.

Is the character of reason such as to permit some link in knowledge between divine communication and human understanding ? To admit the possibility of such a link one has to admit the existence of a *ratio* that has been exempt from the condition of fallenness. Barth rules out that possibility, and he does not recognize the similar possibility of a transformed capacity of reason. In order to skirt this difficulty, Barth introduces the notion of acknowledgement, which he insists "involves the concept of knowledge."[38] But one cannot resist the conclusion that acknowledgement is really something outside the frame of knowledge. Acknowledgement, if it is knowledge, is nothing more than an echo of the divine Word produced in a background of its own choosing, a background constituted of human reason and language. If acknowledgement is outside the frame of knowledge, knowledge too is outside the frame of acknowledgement. The attributes of acknowledgement constitute its substance, which are :

[relation] to the presence of a definite power of disposal,

32. *Ibid.*, p. 149.
33. *Ibid.*, pp. 152, 234.
34. *Ibid.*, p. 153.
35. *Ibid.*, p. 150.
36. *Ibid.*, p. 234.,
37. *Ibid.*, p. 189.
38. *Ibid.*, p. 234.

> positive or negative, respecting the person who acknowledges something...respect for the character of the fact which takes place in the Word of God...decision...calling a halt to an enigma, getting satisfaction about a situation which is not open, but from the acknowledger's point of view unexplained.[39]

Particularly it means that the Word of God forces man's conscience, will, intellect, and feeling into conformity with itself.[40] Acknowledgement in essence signifies an act of man, a movement. If these are its attributes and essence, it is impossible to call acknowledgement knowledge.

The Deficiency of Language

A problem with several facets is here emerging. Because of the absence of any knowable form in God's language, its only point of contact with the form of man's language is God's will. Therefore, human language for Barth is nothing more than a shell. What it is in itself, in its inherent structure, and in its ontological genesis, has no bearing whatsoever upon what it is made to do, namely, to bear God's message. Sheer divine arbitrariness seems to be the only rule to guide us in the understanding of the nature and role of human language. For this reason and for the reason that human understanding is fallen, knowledge is not a possibility; its place has to be taken by certain acts, primarily that of acknowledgement. Knowledge of God can be spoken of legitimately as Knowledge by God of Himself.[41] Barth concedes that this does not mean "either the abrogation, abolition or alteration of human cognition as such and therefore its formal and technical characteristics as human cognition."[42] But insofar as "views are images in which we perceive objects as such [and] concepts are counter-images with which we make these images of perception our own by thinking them, that is, rearranging them,"[43] it will be wrong to say that we can know God through

39. *Ibid.*, p. 234.
40. *Ibid.*, p. 235.
41. Cf. Karl Barth, *Church Dogmatics*, Vol. II, Part I, pp. 181, 183.
42. *Ibid.*, p. 181.
43. *Ibid.*, p. I81.

the media of images or concepts. "Knowledge of God is [still] only an event enclosed in the mystery of the divine Trinity."[44] Acknowledgment, therefore, remains the only cognitive alternative for man when the equations between divine absoluteness and human nothingness have been precisely worked out. Acknowledgement as a form of knowledge is abrogation of human fallenness, created and sustained by the grace of God. "At this point, in faith itself, we know God in utter dependence, in pure discipleship and gratitude."[45] Knowledge conceived in this way amounts to "the knowledge of the hiddenness of God."[46] [To this position we may address a simple query: What is the object of revelation ? Is it knowledge of the hiddenness of God, or knowledge of the hidden God ? There is another perilous implication in Barth's position. If the knowledge of the hiddenness of God intersects with concept-thinking, this situation could give rise to a cancer of conceptual knowledge which could spread through the body of faith. That would be a strange rider to a Barthian theorem.] The knowledge of the hiddenness of God is simply abstract, faith being its prop, whereas the knowledge of the hidden God is concrete. This assertion reverses the Barthian idea about the abstract and the concrete —and possibly it can be demonstrated.

Clearly, Barth's view of language is dependent on a general principle of opposition, or polarity, between God and man. He expresses it himself in the following words : "In the question of the content of the Word of God we find ourselves faced with the same difficulty...as in the question of the nature of God in general."[47] Barth observes the law of polarity scrupulously in his theology, and there is no doubt that this principle undergirds his whole thought. Reasoning from this principle of polarity, Barth castigates our "failure to realize the nature of the opposition between God and man."[48] In view of this infinite qualitative distinction "we must seriously recognize that the

44. *Ibid.*, p. 181.
45. *Ibid.*, p. 183.
46. *Ibid.* p. 183.
47. Karl Barth, *Church Dogmatics*, Vol. I, Part I, p. 149.
48. *Ibid.*, p. 228.

togetherness of God and man in man's experience of the Word of God is not a togetherness on the same level, to be surveyed like the coincidence of any other pair of ordinary entities, and therefore to be contemplated as a possible togetherness."[49] It is the logic of this polarity that ultimately leads Barth to assert that the image of God "is not only as we say with the exception of some remnants ruined, but annihilated."[50]

This polarity falls short of a genuine dualism (such as there may be between God and the devil). In Barthian terms man can no more be even a sinner in the serious sense, as the image of God in him has been totally annihilated. On the contrary, if man had been treated as a creature of devilish tendencies and demonic capacities under the framework of a dualism, his condition would have been understood differently. In Barthian terms man cannot even be described as being in revolt; we can only say that he revolted primordially and is now reaping the consequences of that revolt by having been turned into a mere shell. [The creative possibilities of genuine dualism are quite outside this framework.]

Although the awareness of this polarity is founded on manifestation of the Word of God, or revelation, yet without a doubt some very obvious tautological processes of deduction have been employed to support that awareness. [This is natural, for, once certain axioms have been set up, rigorous tautology must lead to some forseeable conclusions. Here the concept of revelation, defined in a certain way, is the primary axiom. These observations only hint at the possibility of internal criticism.]

The Vedāntic Tradition of Language

Three important facets of the problem posed by the Barthian position may now be taken up for consideration in the light of Vedānta. These are : (1) the question of form, (2) the question of language, and (3) the question of knowledge.

1. *Form*. This will be taken up first, for the other two depend on it. Barth's opposition to form is obviously due to a suspicion of form-metaphysics based on his concern to estab-

49. *Ibid.*, p. 229.
50. Cf. *Brahma Sūtra*, 1.3.28.

lish the unconditional transcendence and freedom of God. He asserts that reason, the action of revelation, and the adoption of human language for the utterance of God's Word are determined by nothing other than God's own indeterminable will, which replaces forms. Forms are rejected because they bind God. Therefore, since there are no forms to mediate, what takes the place of knowledge—namely, acknowledegment—is interpreted as the response of man's divinely rekindled will to Divine Will.

While Vedānta is equally concerned with the freedom and transcendence of God (according to which God's being is what it is in itself and hence without any reference to anything outside), it nevertheless sees the need for the mediatorial reality of the forms, which it does not fear can bind God. This mediatorial reality is the basis of both creation and revelation, but it is nothing of itself. It is something only when viewed from a phenomenal perspective. The forms are not Being, but are rather the very dynamics of Becoming. However, Becoming by necessity is grounded in Being and must return to it.

In Vedānta the forms converge on the Veda. The world and all levels of contingent being (including men as phenomenal *jīvas*) originate in conformity to the Veda.[51] Here too, however, there is no form-metaphysics, because God as *Brahman* is above the forms. Language (which for Vedānta is the logos) is the expression of the forms, and hence the Veda is composed in language. But insofar as language is rooted in the forms, it is not defined as human or other. Language is not an attribute of man or vice-versa; it is simply the case that they coalesce dynamically in the forms. Hence there is no problem of relating divine revelation to human language through the interrelation of two kinds of will and two kinds of act. Only the Veda is true language. For incorporeal being like the gods, revelation is manifest of itself,[52] but for man it is knowable only through human language. Here Vedānta escapes the necessity of dychotomizing God and man and splitting language into divine and human, in the manner of Barth, while escaping also the necessity

51. Cf. Thibaut, *op. cit.*, Part I, pp. 201 ff.
52. Cf. Thibaut, I, pp. 198-9.

of absolutizing the forms. As we acquire a new approach to the forms, we also acquire a new approach to language. Likewise, there emerges a new possibility for knowledge. The forms are themselves an object of knowledge, but the Veda does not treat them as ultimate object of knowledge. (Only *Brahman* is that,[53] though *Brahman* is always a non-object [*aviṣaya*].[54]) Knowledge is not only possible, it is the true door of release. There is no other way to release (*mukti, mokṣa, nirvāṇa*). [55] The Veda leads men to release: release does not mean reaching the forms, but rather *Brahman* who is beyond them.

The whole position seems to be a counter-point to the structure of polarity and the attendant tautological method of reasoning which are essential aspects of Barth's thought. In place of tautology Vedānta uses a method unique in Indian philosophy: namely, the method known as non-contradictoriness (*abādhitatva*). Specifically, Vedānta emphasizes truth as the absence of contradiction (*satyatvaṁ bādharāhityam*).[56]

Now we move to something which shows that in the difference between these two positions there is also some remarkable (but unacknowledged, and perhaps unacknowledgeable) closeness. [However, difference will again ooze out through the very accord.] As does Barth, Vedānta finds an *Archimedean* point outside reason from which to move, criticize, control, or even reject reason. Barth finds it in the Word of God and Vedānta finds it in the Veda (*Śruti*). Reasoning independent of scripture, says Vedānta, depends upon the theoretical speculations of individuals, and speculations are unrestricted and devoid of proper foundation.[57] Vedānta feels called upon to give an epistemological account of this *Archimedean* point. It sees the Veda or *Śruti* as the foremost *pramāṇa* (knowledge by the very act of assumption which governs

53. Cf. Thibaut, I, pp. 22 ff.

54. *Ibid.*, 1.1.4. Cf. Thibaut, I, p. 31.

55. *Ibid.*, 4.3.14. Cf. Thibaut, II, pp. 399-400.

56. Cf. *Pañcadaśī*, translation by Hari Prasad Sastri (London : Santi Sadan, 1954), III, 29.

57. *yasmān nirāgamāḥ puruṣotprekṣā-mātranibandhanāstarkā apratiṣṭhitā bhavanti utprekṣāyā niraṁkuśatvāt*, Śaṇkara's *Commentary on Brahma Sūtra* 2.1.11. Cf., Thibaut, I, p. 314.

the character of reason). The only role of *pramāṇa* is to argue itself out of the context of knowledge and let truth remain. On the other hand, Barth sees the Word of God as the foundation upon which there arises—along with the act of acknowledgement—a series of movements in tautological deduction, of which the first fruits are the structure of polarity. According to Vedānta, the *Archimedean* point is implicit in reason, which makes it unnecessary for reason to take one step away from itself in a serial, deductive movement. And one cannot say that the assumption of that point is a work of reason, because by saying so the absoluteness of that point will be destroyed. Also, saying that the assumption of the point is a work of reason involves contravention of the very nature of reason. It makes reason assume something contrary to it in design. This intrinsic necessity of reason to yield to truth in order to render that *Archimedean* point meaningful is what is meant by non-contradictoriness. The work of reason is to provide a logic and a methodology by which to remove itself from the scene of truth. Although the role of reason may sound negative here, it is of paramount importance in the phenomenal world. Non-contradictoriness, therefore, makes possible a new and different method of reasoning. In non-contradictoriness, reason turns itself upside down, with the eventual consequence that it eliminates itself, leaving the self-established truth unaffected. This procedure has the beneficial effect of giving reason a status under revelation[58] without involving it in judgmental propositions and will-oriented injunctions as is the case with Barth.

Speaking for Vedānta, we can suggest that in the presence of revelation reason recognizes its *truth-emptiness*; it interiorizes revelation while resisting every one of its own immanent possibilities that go counter to the truth. *Truth-emptiness* is a very positive thing: *it is the phenomenal receptacle for the transcendentally originated truth*. When reason envelops the truth there arises understanding (*vijñāna*), which is a precondition for the disappearance of reason and the emergence of knowledge (*jñāna*). In this way, reason finds itself internally related to revelation, while the latter is neither internally nor externally related to the

58. Cf. Thibaut (trans.), *The Vedānta Sūtras*, I, p. 307.

former. This gives reason a new freedom, a new strength, and brings out its genuine *telos*. On the surface, the position here outlined might appear to be not very different from Tillich's view of the "depth of reason." "The depth of reason," Tillich states, "is the expression of something that is not reason but which precedes reason and is manifest through it."[59] According to Vedānta, reason's depth is irrelevant; what is relevant is its truth-emptiness, which it discovers only in the presence of revelation (*Śruti*). Therefore, it turns out that revelation is not the manifestation of the depth of reason, and there is no such thing as a "quest" of reason "for revelation" (see Tillich's chapter on "Reason and Revelation" in *Systematic Theology*, Vol. I, Part I). For one thing, Vedānta does not have Tillich's framework of the distinction between ontological and technical reasons.

2. *Language*. The polarity affects language, especially as the gulf between the Divine Word and human language is a particular subject of emphasis for Barth. It can be said that the polarity scheme is maintained by adhering to the "human" in the divine-human opposition. It is maintained in perpetuity by always seeing things divine from the perspective of the "human". On the contrary, Vedānta believes that in revelation the divine word can overcome the opposition that is implied in the "human". When the Upaniṣadic texts testify to Reality in utterances like: "Whence words return along with the mind, not attaining it,"[60] it is the inadequacy of independent human language that is really meant. But they also attest to the possibility of another language which is adequate to the self-expression of God (*Brahman*) phenomenally. Śaṅkara in his commentary on *Taittirīya Upaniṣad* says that the import of sentences like the above is that *Brahman* is unspeakable (*avācya*) and cannot be the meaning of a sentence, because it is implied to be the substratum of the negation of all duality[61] (which means polarity is overcome). Divine language is not different from the human

59. Cf. Paul Tillich, *Systematic Theology*, Vol. I (Chicago : University of Chicago Press, 1951), pp. 79 ff.

60. *Taittirīya Upaniṣad*, 2.4.1 (From S. Radhakrishnan, p. 545).

61. Cf. *Taittirīya Upaniṣad with commentary by Śaṅkara*, edited by Pandit Vamana Sastri Islampurkar (Poona: Anandasram, 1929), Sanskrit Original, p. 52.

formally or materially, but only in intent, and therefore in origin. Divine language is simply that human language which intends *Brahman* (God, Reality) and salvation (*mukti*), and this indicates its spiritual origin. But for Barth, the moral origin of language is the real ground for polarizing, which is not an independent problem for Vedānta. In Vedānta moral origin is absorbed into the spiritual (metaphysical). It is true, however, that even language that intends *Brahman* cannot express *Brahman* positively, but only negatively, the algebra of which is *neti*, *neti* (not this, not this).[62]

Vedānta believes that language can be a transpersonal entity which, instead of being a product of man, can condition him. It is transpersonal because it is revelation. As revelation, instead of hovering over man without contact with him, it becomes the center from which man's recovery through thought and act is made possible. This assumes that there are transpersonal instruments of thought and action, of which language as revelation (*Śruti*) is supreme.

Language somehow binds the human and the divine rather than polarize them. Revelation is language as seen from the divine end, and what is purely human is somehow inseparable from it. The purely human, personal, and empirical can and must be purged. Language purifies, as it is said: "Verily, that which purifies here [i.e., the wind] is the sacrifice, for he moving along purifies all this. And because moving along, he purifies all this, he is the sacrifice. Of that mind and speech are the ways."[63] In purifying, language purifies itself, as revelation implies the *purgation* of language. The *Chāndogya Upaniṣad*, the Upaniṣad of the chant, is unique in this respect; language is shown to purify itself through ritual chant.[64] The essence of all speech is AUM. AUM, especially in the *Māṇḍūkya Upaniṣad* recasts all phenomenal reality into sound (speech) symbols, leading it to its noumenal origin. There is achieved in Vedānta a combination of high precision and extreme fluidity of symbolic modes of language in which language is not only purged, but made to utter truths beyond its inherent capability.

62. Cf. *Bṛhadāraṇyaka Upaniṣad* 4.4.22.
63. *Chāndogya Upaniṣad*, 4.16.1.
64. *Chāndogya*, Ch. 2 is of particular interest in this respect.

The original ritual purgation of language in the Upaniṣads has subsequently yielded several (notably three) ways of conditioning language and fitting it for the expression of transcendent Reality. *First,* we may note the psycho-metaphysical way or meditation. Transpersonal thinking is very characteristic of Vedānta, and this is used to effectuate the purgation of language, to remove the accretions of person and ego images which are believed to distort the truth. In an individual sense transpersonal thinking may even be described as *de-thinking*, implying an unconditional disengagement from categories, in itself a vital act of purgation. Yoga philosophy has perfected the purely psychological techniques of transpersonal thinking. Vedānta argues, however, that Yoga must be understood essentially as a technique of thinking, not a substitute system of knowledge.[65] It could be asserted that Vedānta has gone more deeply into the problem of this kind of thinking and its relation of transcendent revelation than any other system within India or outside.

One may certainly question the value of it all and question also its actual ontological basis but the fact that it has been perpetuated from generation to generation and has established its vogue over much of the Indian religious landscape, supported by meticulously written manuals and text-books, must in itself warrant serious consideration of its claims. The Vedāntic tradition, however, is insistent on subordinating this psycho-metaphysical transformation activity or meditation rigidly to that which has been revealed by the logos (*vāk*, *śabda*) and objectively communicated as the Vedic texts (*Śruti*). In this, again, it is in deep accord with Barthian dogmatism although on the opposite side of the fence.

Secondly, there is this thing which we may call grammatical purgation of language of *śabda-saṁskāra*, in a genuine sense another arm of Yoga, and hence called *language-yoga*, or *śabda-pūrva-yoga*. The fundamental work of this tradition is Bhartṛhari's *Vākyapadīya*, claiming its authority from previous texts, chiefly the great grammatical work of Patañjali, the *Mahābhāṣya*. The

65. Śaṅkara denies the self-sufficiency of Yoga techniques for attaining saving knowledge : only the Veda (revelation) can provide that. Cf. Śaṅkara's *Commentary on Brahma Sūtra,* 2.1.3. Also, Thibaut, I, pp. 296-7.

whole programme of this tradition is a kind of discipline akin to the Yogic psycho-metaphysical discipline, but in a way more directly based on the essence of the logos and of human speech. Gaurinath Sastri writes :

> The discipline which leads to this consummation consists in meditation upon the essence of the Word (vāk)—the Eternal Verbum disentangled from impurities. The grammatical errors are symptomatic of spiritual back-slidings and the purge of solipsism eventuates in the emergence of spiritual competency and moral power. The repeated course of meditation upon this pure form conducts the spiritual aspirant to a stage in which the intuition of the Supreme Reality dawns.[66]

Clearly, purification does not apply to the logos but to the actuality of human speech (and thought/understanding). It simply means clearing human language of its numerous accretions and making it conform to the logos, so that logos speaks when man speaks—and thinks. The *Vākyapadīya* speaks about it in these ways: "It is the straight path" (*mārgo'yam āñjasaḥ*), 1.12; "it is the gateway to liberation" (*taddvāramapavargasya*), 1.14; "it is the royal road for those who strive for liberation" (*iyam sā mokṣamāṇānām ajihmā rājapaddhatiḥ*), 1.16.

This grammatical yoga tradition, like other systems which look up to the logos (ordinarily, expressed in some concrete religious scripture) faces the task of putting human language in front of it and of adjusting the two—and by implication, of evaluating human reason as well. And it seeks to reconcile them by purifying the latter, which, of course, is the substance of language-yoga. But reconciliation will be unavoidably metaphysical and will involve the "forms". On the contrary, a non-metaphysical approach is also possible, which might be either just existentialist or positivist or both, and it means leaving the Divine and human languages as they are and facing the consequences of it under faith perhaps—as sheer acknowledgement or as something more—or under some other bold resolution. Barth, of course, is the paradigm in modern theology for that particular

66. Gaurinath Sastri, *The Philosophy of Word and Meaning*, p. 16.

non-metaphysical approach under an existentialist-positivist resolution—of faith, in the form of sheer acknowledgement. Clearly, Barth speaks from the modernity of the human linguistic situation, but like all that is positivist and unlike all that is still at least vaguely idealist his standpoint does not hark back to the Western logos, albeit for overcoming and surpassing it, but rejects it. It is clear that this existentialist-positivism of Barth is reflected in his view as we showed above, of "the sphere of the *ratio*", which residing in God's language, is a communication of reason with reason, and person with person, described as "deliberate intellectualism" in God's choice. [Note, the word 'intellectualism' itself is very positivistic.]

Thirdly, we make note of the logical purgation of language. Vedānta (like other Indian systems) has been much concerned with the science of logic, or *pramāṇa-śāstra*, and that primarily for the sake of purification of language. Logic is not able to lead to truth independently, but it is accessory to the clearing and conditioning of the vehicle of truth. In spite of the immensely elaborate and highly complicated logical system it has forged the role assigned to it is a very humble and self-obliterating one. In fact, logic is conceived as an instrument of self-obliteration. It is the highly precise and elaborate technique by which the negative is negated.

3. *Knowledge.* Vedānta is built upon the doctrine that knowledge of *Brahman* is real and possible through the Word of the Veda (revealed Word). How is knowledge possible through the Word ? According to Śaṅkara, the *mahāvākyas* (the great sentences like : "That Thou art" and "All this is *Brahman*") produce knowledge which removes the awareness of all entities other than *Brahman*. The main purpose of the *Upaniṣads* is to impart this knowledge. Vedānta always insists that *Brahman* alone is real, and even the Veda which gives knowledge of *Brahman* is itself part of the illusory (*mithyā*) world. Nevertheless, Vedānta teachers argue that these sentences are able to give knowledge of *Brahman*. Śaṅkara's argument is that real effect can arise from unreal causes as a person can sometimes die from imaginary venom.[67] But knowledge here is not new knowledge, it is coeval with Reality it-

67. *Commentary on Brahma Sūtra*, 2.1.14. Cf. Thibaut, I, pp. 322 f.

self. Over against this view we can place the Barthian insistence on acknowledgement as the only legitimate knowledge possible in the light of the Word of God.

Concluding Remarks

In the immediately preceding paragraph we observed that Barth speaks from the modernity of human linguistic situation. We might reiterate that point as we move to the conclusion of this essay, which although on comparative theology, is within the farmework of our understanding of language as such and within comparativist-hermeneutics. Modern questions on language raised from the standpoint of where we have been brought by the logos in its own passage are quite different from those that occur within a still lively antiquity such as represented by the great Eastern tradition of Vedānta. Now it bears mentioning that among those who raise such modern questions some attend to the logos in its passage within the numerous epochs of Western philosophy (and theology), while others prefer to break with it. In theology, Barth is important because in him the intention and the effort to break —though not the break itself—are complete. And partly because the break itself is not actually as thorough-going as might be and partly due to other reasons, we notice spots of strange similarities with an absolutely self-consistent system like Vedānta especially as regards an *Archimedean* point, which is undoubtedly *a priori* and logos-based. [This, of course, compels us to ask, when revelation is really subjected to thought, even under the resolution of faith, can the logos be avoided ?]

Now the big question to which this matter, in fact the whole of Barthian theology itself, finally leads is that pertaining to knowledge of the Divine. Now from Barth's standpoint it would be quite absurd to construe the knowledge of the Divine as either direct knowledge of God as he is in himself or as participation in God's own knowledge (of all things and of himself —and of us). All that we can legitimately hope for is acknowledgement of God's revealing Word and act. In this again we can not but see the great importance of the modernity of the human situation. The three tenses of time are contained in the one tense, the present. That is the basis of acknowledgement, which is existential—sheer temporality of Time. And language has to be keyed in to the present. [It is well-known that Heidegger revolutionizes many concepts including the "present" by "presence", and theology has not quite caught up with this revolution yet.]

On the contrary, in the Vedāntic view, language belongs to a process-eternity (*pariṇāma-nityatā*)—to be, no doubt, distinguished from pure eternity (*kūṭastha-nityatā*). And here Time is one and the divisions—and qualifications—are merely attributed to it.[68] [The process of purifying language also has a bearing on "thought-activity", entailing the dissolution of temporal sequence in it.[69]] In this sense the knowledge that language brings is really part of the process-eternity. [And the question of how it stands with knowledge (*jñāna*), which is Ultimate Reality (*Brahman, Ātman*) itself is a very intricate matter, and it is not relevant here to consider it, but let us say that the logos is, nevertheless, the connecting concept.]

Finally, everything that we have discussed so far boils down to two kinds of knowledge, i.e., knowledge of God and self-knowledge (with, no doubt, knowledge of the World as a strong contender, which however, has not been part of our present interest). These two kinds of knowledge have been inquired into under language. Theology traditionally, and by definition, is concerned with the knowledge of God; and at least that tradition in philosophy which has steadfastly stood by the questions of Being, the Dialectics of Being as well as of thought, and the internal constitution of Reason, bringing even matters concerning knowledge of the world, under them, has always been predisposed to the problem of self-knowledge.

In human civilization everywhere there has existed a pattern of man finding his place in the world through naming things. George Gusdorf observes: "Naming establishes a right to existence. It is words that make things and beings, that define relation according to which the order of the world is constituted: to situate oneself in the world, for each of us, is to be at peace with the network of words that puts everything in its place in

68. See the essay "Time Within Logos and Without".
69. Cf. G. Sastri, *op. cit.*, p. 17.

the environment."[70] But the Greeks directed it in a special way through philology tending towards self-knowledge. Socrates thought that through the understanding of words one could move from the illusion of commonsense and opinion to good sense, and hence to truth and self-knowledge. Socrates knew that words originate in the mutual engagement of man and the world but also that words tend to get detached and go off on their own. So Socratic wisdom pertaining to self-knowledge entailed the re-call of the original situation of that engagement and the pursuit of words to their origin. This paramount concern with self-knowledge, so paradigmatic in Socrates, quite powerful in St. Augustine (no doubt, mixed with the question of the knowledge of God) surfaced again in Kant, but now as the inquiry into the very internal constitution of reason. Envisaging his new, revolutionary project, Kant states: "It is a call of reason to undertake anew the most difficult of all its tasks, namely that of self-knowledge...."[71]

Kierkegaard, who had entered a Kantian world by a side-door, so to say, and strove to re-live the Socratic thought in a peculiar, Protestant-Christian manner sought after a tragic kind of self-knowledge, which re-appeared in Barth in an unusual blend with a positivism of the Word of God and of human language. Further, in Barth's understanding of the Word of God it permits its "self-interpretation of its form as a human word".[72] With this goes a kind of existential self-knowledge on the part of man, as Barth writes: "For it is precisely the man who is placed in the real knowledge of the Word of God who recognizes himself as completely existing in his self-determination."[73]

To conclude this discussion, it can be truly said that these two interests, knowledge of God and self-knowledge, have moved what is deepest in human thought. They involve the mission of

70. George Gusdorf, *Speaking* (*La Parole*), Part I, trans. Brockelman, Evanston, Illinois, North-Western University Press, 1965, p. 39.

71. Kant, Preface to First edition of the *Critique of Pure Reason*, trans. N. K. Smith, Toronto, Macmillan, 1965, p. 9.

72. Cf. Karl Barth, *Church Dogmatics*, Vol. I, part II, trans. G. W. Bromiley and T. F. Torrance, Edinburgh, T. & T. Clark, 1956, pp. 712 ff.

73. *Church Dogmatics*, Vol. I, part I, p. 228.

language too. Does the project of clearing language play a part in correcting the illusions and errors that language itself constantly brings to us ? Do they help to correct each other ? Again, is it the case that the quest for the knowledge of God comes to us wearing the guise of self-knowledge, and, vice-versa, the quest for self-knowledge comes to us wearing the guise of knowledge of God ? Can language be helpful in deguising them ? Is that the clearing of language that we are awaiting ?

It can be truthfully said that Vedānta in its own tradition of purification of language, plugged to Self-knowledge (capital 'S') would not be alien to the spirit of these questions, and perhaps would serve as a foil to them in the way modern man may be impelled to ask them in his situation of language. The Vedāntic alternative to the problems posed by the knowledge of God and self-knowledge, i.e., that of Self-knowledge (*Brahman*-knowledge), may not be, it could be objected, either the one or the other. But its power to suggest new paths to both will not be truly known untill the foil, i.e., the claim—ungrounded as it may turn out to be—that Self-knowledge is both at once, is put to philosophical test and examined from the inside, but without losing sight of one's own ground. The last question is, can such Self-knowledge (capital 'S') be approached as a projection of the quest for self-knowledge (small 's') so vital a need not only for those within the Western tradition but for all ? Does it indicate a further mission for language and perhaps the possibility of a new partnership for thought ?

INDEX

(A name like Śaṅkara and a system like Vedānta because of their frequent occurrence are not listed. Also, words which appear throughout such as *Brahman* and *Ātman* are not listed.)

ERRATA

	Incorrect	*Correct*
p. 7, para 2, line 4.	retionale	rationale
p. 11, line 11 from top.	canceling	cancelling
p. 13, fn. 8, line 2.	*taṭasthalaksaṇa-tvamiti*	*taṭasthalakṣaṇa-tvamiti*
p. 19, para 3, line 7.	guaged	gauged
p. 30, fn. 12.	*Upaniṣād*	*Upaniṣad*
p. 49, para 2, line 3.	pharse	phrase
p. 81, line 2 from top.	shoutd	should
p. 81, line 7 from bottom.	cosmos is also not...	cosmos is also......
p. 86, fn. 3, line 2.	Śridhara	Śrīdhara
p. 117, line 6 from top.	*aham mam*	*aham mama*
p. 132, fn. 21, line 6.	whose belng	whose being
p. 140, line 1.	Cristianity	Christianity
p. 164, line 9 from top.	its functions	it functions
p. 180, fn. 3, line 2.	*śobda*	*śabda*